The Evangelical Mind and Heart

The Evangelical Mind and Heart

Perspectives on Theological and Practical Issues

Millard J. Erickson

BAKER BOOK HOUSE
Grand Rapids, Michigan 49516

Published by Baker Book House Company
P. O. Box 6287, Grand Rapids, Michigan 49516-6287

Printed in the United States of America

Library of Congress Cataloging-in-Publication Data

Erickson, Millard J.
    The evangelical mind and heart : perspectives on theological and practical issues / Millard J. Erickson.
      p. cm.
    Includes index.
    ISBN 0–8010–3219–9
    1. Evangelicalism. I. Title.
    BR1640.E69 1993
    277.3′.082—dc20   92–42723

To my students
at Bethel Theological Seminary
1969–92

It is with their generation that
the future of evangelicalism lies.

Contents

Preface

Evangelical Christianity has become a significant force within American society in the past fifty years. Rising from the ashes of a fundamentalism which had fallen into disrepute and had been pushed to the fringes of the social, intellectual, and political life of the nation, it has come to a place of recognition and influence. In a very real sense, the dreams of those who founded the National Association of Evangelicals, Fuller Theological Seminary, the Billy Graham Evangelistic Association, and *Christianity Today* have been realized.

This new vitality has stimulated a great deal of study and literature. Organizations for the study of evangelicalism have been formed. Political pollsters regularly take note of developments within evangelicalism. The movement has been treated historically, sociologically, and thematically. This volume seeks to contribute to that literature by examining various theological and practical issues within evangelicalism, some of which are topics of controversy at the moment.

The ideas developed here have been tested in a number of different settings. Chapters 1 and 2 are based upon the Theological Lectures given at Moody Bible Institute on April 14–15, 1988, and the Staley Lectures at Southeastern College (Lakeland, Fla.) on November 7–8, 1990. Chapters 3 and 4 are based upon two messages given at a seminar on ecology sponsored by the Christian Life Commission of the Southern Baptist Convention. Delivered in Fort Worth on April 25, 1991, they subsequently appeared as chapters in *The Earth Is the Lord's: Christians and the Environment*, published by Broadman Press. Chapter 5 appeared in the Fall 1991 issue of *Review and Expositor*, and chapter 6 in the Spring 1991 issue of the *Southwestern Journal of Theology*. Chapters 7–10 consist of lectures given at Western Conservative Baptist Seminary on January 21–24, 1992.

I appreciate all who, on the occasions mentioned above and at other times, have interacted with me over the issues explored in this volume. They have helped me sharpen my thinking, and have encouraged me to share these thoughts in wider circles. Pat Krohn typed portions of some of the chapters. Allan Fisher and Jim Weaver of Baker Book House have encouraged me to publish the manuscript, and Ray Wiersma has once again applied his masterful editorial skills to the material.

Part 1

Evangelicalism and Its Influence on Society

1

The Record
of Evangelical Influence
on Society

The subject we are addressing in this chapter is a large one on which many volumes have been written. To attempt to deal with it in a brief chapter must necessarily result in considerable selectivity and what some might regard as superficiality. Yet if we scratch the surface of the subject and in so doing stir the interest and curiosity of some readers to go on to study it more deeply, we will have accomplished our purpose.

Definitional Matters

Let us begin with some definitional matters. We are here referring to as evangelicals those who believe that all humans are in need of salvation and that this salvation involves regeneration by a supernatural work of God. Based upon his grace, this divine act is received solely by repentance and faith in the atoning work of Jesus Christ. Further, evangelicals urgently and actively seek the conversion of all persons worldwide to this faith. They regard the canonical Scriptures as the supreme authority in matters of faith and practice.

Note that this definition does not go as far as some might wish in specifying the particulars of belief and practice. It does not include a statement about the deity of Christ or the full trustworthiness of the Bible, for example. Its primary emphases are its particular understanding of salvation and the necessity of proclaiming the gospel. In all likelihood, those who fit our definition would also hold to high views of the person of Christ and of Scripture. Those views, however, as a rule are marks of sophisticated evangelicals, theologically reflective evangelicals. There are many, on the other hand, who have had an evangelical experience of salvation but do not self-consciously think through their faith this completely. So we need to distinguish between how much one must believe in order to be saved and how much one can, upon careful study and reflection, deny. Is it necessary to believe in the inerrancy of Scripture in order to be saved? Before answering, think about the large number of children who come to saving faith. Do they understand and believe the doctrine of biblical inerrancy? If not, must we conclude that they are not evangelical believers? By omitting some of the more specific doctrines from our definition of "evangelical," we are not condoning denial of them, but simply acknowledging that understanding them may not be essential to identification as an evangelical Christian. In so doing, we are seeking to include within our definition the evangelical denominations as well as evangelicals in independent, mainline Protestant, and Roman Catholic churches. We are also including the large number of Pentecostals.

Note also that our definition does not distinguish between evangelicals and fundamentalists, as some have done. Rather, fundamentalists are here included within evangelicalism, so that nonfundamentalist evangelicals would have to be further specified in some other way. We are attempting to include Christians both to the left and to the right of certain groups who sometimes claim the designation *evangelical* in some special fashion. In so doing, we are aware that there are some who would wish to debate at some length the exact application of the term. That is a topic for another time, for we must hasten on to the topic that is our responsibility in our first two chapters.

Evangelicalism's Historical Record

Nineteenth-Century Involvement in Societal Problems

When we look back into the nineteenth century (as far back as I intend to go in a brief historical survey), we find that evangelicals exercised a considerable amount of influence upon American society. This has been adequately documented several times, but I venture to add a brief summary here. The Calvinistic ethic of industry and frugality tended to hold persons responsible for their own economic condition. Thus, some Christians regarded almsgiving as an interference in the natural workings of divine justice. Rather, the poor should suffer the consequences of their laziness.[1] As the conditions of what we today call urbanization grew, however, there came to be an increasing realization that the church must grapple anew with these issues. During the revival in Boston in 1842, the evangelist Edward Norris Kirk criticized the opposition to charity, noting that the same type of objection could be applied to the preaching of the gospel.[2] Such concern for the poor spread rapidly among evangelicals.

There arose a consciousness that it was not sufficient to deal merely with the symptoms of social problems; the cause would also have to be removed. One of the most energetic efforts by evangelicals in this regard was the temperance movement. There was a widespread conviction that drunkenness was the leading cause of poverty. Thus the way to destroy poverty was to banish alcohol. Although a Puritan personal ethic frequently lay behind the endeavors of the leaders of the temperance movement, the reform of society was just as much their aim as was the regulation of personal behavior.[3] The Women's Christian Temperance Union was the major expression of these endeavors, but it was actively supported by a number of evangelical denominations and organizations, including the Salvation Army and the Christian and Missionary Alliance, as well as by publications such as the *Christian Herald*. This movement resulted in the passing in 1919 of the Eighteenth Amendment and the Volstead Act, prohibiting the manufacture and sale of alcoholic beverages. Here was a major element of political change in which evangelicals had played a significant role.

Another area in which evangelicals were active was the antislavery movement. We should note immediately that the record is a mixed one, for many Southern slave-owners were by belief and experience what we would refer to as evangelicals. By contrast, Northern evangelicals played a significant role in the cause of emancipation. To be sure, one of the most vociferous of the early abolitionists was William Lloyd Garrison, a Unitarian and an opponent of anything that resembled evangelical Protestantism. Yet equally outspoken in the abolitionist cause was the evangelist Charles Finney.[4]

1. Timothy L. Smith, *Revivalism and Social Reform: American Protestantism on the Eve of the Civil War* (Baltimore: Johns Hopkins University Press, 1980), p. 163.
2. Edward Norris Kirk, *A Plea for the Poor* (Boston: Saxton and Pierce, 1843), p. 40.
3. Charles C. Cole, Jr., *The Social Ideas of the Northern Evangelists, 1826–1860* (New York: Octagon, 1954), pp. 116–24.
4. Smith, *Revivalism*, pp. 180–87.

The cause of abolition became a source of great tension within many denominations. In the Presbyterian Church in the U.S.A., some of the most outspoken advocates of abolition also challenged highly prized Presbyterian doctrines by espousing such ideas as free will and human ability. The church responded by excising both Arminianism and abolitionism in a single act. Thus the Princeton theologians were found arguing for slavery on much the same grounds that were utilized in arguing for predestination: the Creator intended some people to be slaves and others to be masters, just as he has elected some to salvation and reprobated others to damnation. In large part to neutralize this defense of slavery by Princeton, McCormick Seminary was founded in the Midwest.[5]

This situation posed a profound dilemma for evangelical abolitionists, who found themselves, as one of them put it, "between the upper and nether millstone of a *pro-slavery* Christianity, and an *anti-Christian* abolitionism."[6] The desire to avoid schism within denominations which spanned both North and South prevented unequivocal declarations. On the other hand, most of those groups which were in a position to make such statements without the risk of schism lacked a strong central authority, and hence such statements tended to be merely local in nature and extent. This might have led to a state of moral paralysis. As Timothy Smith put it, "Had not morality been larger in human hearts than movements to support it and liberty a braver force than those who sang of it at Fourth-of-July celebrations, the slave might yet have languished in his bonds."[7] Evangelical Christianity might have failed in what was potentially its period of greatest opportunity. Yet better days were ahead.

It was to a large extent the new revival movement associated with persons like Finney that produced an evangelical effort toward abolition. This effort branched into several channels. One was the large number of religious newspapers which were speaking out vigorously against slavery. A change in editorial leadership at the Methodist *Zion's Herald* resulted in an unequivocal voice. The new editor, Daniel Wise, in his very first editorial said, "Toward slavery, especially, we cannot show aught but undisguised abhorrence."[8] The *Congregationalist,* the Baptist *Watchman and Reflector*, and the *Northern Christian Advocate*, which was published by Methodists in Upper New York State, all spoke out clearly against the ill of slavery, as did the *Independent*, founded by in-

5. William S. Jenkins, *Pro-Slavery Thought in the Old South* (Chapel Hill: University of North Carolina Press, 1935), pp. 215–16.
6. "The Vital Forces of the Age," *Christian Review* 26 (1861): 566.
7. Smith, *Revivalism*, p. 187.
8. Ibid., p. 205.

fluential Congregational pastors such as Henry Ward Beecher and George B. Cheever.

Even hymnals took up the cause. When the Wesleyan Methodist denomination separated from the larger Methodist body, it published a hymnal, *Miriam's Timbrel*, which had the unusual subtitle, *Sacred Songs, Suited to Revival Occasions; and also for Antislavery, Peace, Temperance, and Reform Meetings.* It included songs like "Ye Who in Bondage Pine," which was sung to the tune of "America":

> Ye who in bondage pine,
> Shut out from light divine,
> Bereft of hope;
> Whose limbs are worn with chains,
> Whose tears bedew our plains,
> Whose blood our glory stains,
> In gloom who grope.
>
> Shout! for the hour draws nigh,
> That gives you liberty!
> And from the dust,
> So long your vile embrace,
> Uprising take your place
> Among earth's noblest race,
> By right the first!

Preaching was another significant means of countering the evil. The revival preaching of Finney and Elder Jacob Knapp emphasized the union of personal holiness with concern for societal problems. William Arthur and Gilbert Haven delivered especially pointed and influential messages. There also was considerable writing demonstrating the incompatibility of the Bible with slavery. Among those who published treatises along this line were Cheever, Albert Barnes, Joseph P. Thompson, and Charles Elliott.

Nor was the influence of evangelicals absent from the political realm. The crucial role played by Abraham Lincoln in the abolition of slavery is of course widely known. What is not so widely known is the influence of evangelicals on the president. Timothy Smith has argued that their role was not inconsiderable: "Both before and during the war . . . the citizens who by ethical conviction were best able to share Lincoln's ends and by painful experience most qualified to understand his conservative means were the evangelical ministers of the North. Many of them considered themselves his friends and advisors, none more so than Bishop Matthew Simpson, who gave the address at the president's burial in Springfield."[9]

Political influence was not limited to the United States, however. There were individuals in England who sought to bring that country into the American Civil War on the side of the South. A number of well-known American evangelicals were in England during the early stages of the war, seeking to convince the British people that preserving the Union would also have the effect of eliminating slavery. Among them were Finney and Beecher. Although their efforts supported the cause of the Lincoln administration, in most cases they went at their own initiative.

One other area where evangelicals were active was in assisting escaped slaves who were fleeing to the North. A number of evangelicals took some personal risk in working with the Underground Railroad.

In this case, the cause with which many evangelicals had aligned themselves soon proved successful. While it is difficult to measure the extent of the influence which they exerted, it is gratifying to note that they spoke out and thus helped to bring about a permanent change for the good in American society.

Rise of the Social-Gospel Movement

Evangelicals not only offered support to the cause of social justice and reform, but were in many cases at the forefront of it. They united the messages of personal regeneration and societal reformation. Gradually, however, the situation changed. To a considerable extent, the evangelicals' burden for social problems was proportional to their personal contact with such problems. As the American population became more urbanized, as social problems consequently grew, and as the church became more heavily involved in urban areas where these problems abounded, pastors and laypersons became increasingly conscious of the needs and began to speak out and work against unacceptable conditions more vigorously. For some, this became a preoccupation, so that the proclamation of the gospel of personal regeneration came to be heard less often. One of the foremost spokespersons of this development was Walter Rauschenbusch, a German Baptist pastor in a deprived area of New York City. His preaching came gradually to emphasize transforming the structures of society in order to change the individual persons who make it up. This "social gospel" increasingly was associated with a liberal theology. Belief in the radically sinful and evil nature of individual humans was exchanged for an understanding of sin as primarily societal or collective in nature.

9. Ibid., pp. 201–2.

The liberals or modernists also held convictions that differed from the evangelical position on various other doctrines, such as Scripture and the deity and virgin birth of Christ. As liberals emphasized the social gospel increasingly, evangelicals, by way of countering or balancing the liberal emphasis, gave more and more attention to individual regeneration. Thus evangelicalism began to neglect the social application of the gospel, which became almost the exclusive domain of the liberals. For them, the social application of the gospel was the gospel.

The New Learning

Another area to which evangelicalism reacted was the new learning of contemporary culture. The nineteenth century had seen a growing tension between conservative theology and a number of developments occurring in several other disciplines. One was the realm of historical criticism, where the same methods used to determine the authenticity and accuracy of secular documents were being applied to the Bible; the critical conclusions contradicted many of the traditional views of authorship, dating, and accuracy. Similarly, in the realm of philosophy Immanuel Kant's critical treatises undercut the usual arguments for the existence of God and even for the possibility of cognitive knowledge of a transcendent god. These two developments did not have the far-reaching effects of some others, however, for in both cases many lay-persons either did not understand the arguments or did not recognize their implications. It was in the natural sciences that the real threat appeared.

In many ways natural science was just beginning to come of age. Some centuries earlier, astronomy and church doctrine had collided head-on when Copernicus claimed that the sun, not the earth, is the center of the solar system. Although some leaders of the church continued to contend that the Bible teaches the centrality of the earth, the struggle had resulted in the surrender (or at least the accommodation) of the church, and in the conclusion that the Bible does not really teach the geocentric view. That, it was concluded, came from Aristotle, not from Paul (Eph. 4:26) or James (1:11). With the passing of several centuries, the issue was laid to rest.

Geology as a science basically rose in the nineteenth century. Prior to that time there had been some suspicion that the earth might be much older than popularly believed, but there was no basis for precisely ascertaining its age. Relatively accurate means of dating, however, began to come into use. Here there was an immediate conflict with the prevailing popular opinion. A number of biblical scholars had attempted to establish a chronology of the Bible, using especially the genealogies found in the opening books of the Old Testament. While various schemes were developed, the most widely accepted was that of Archbishop James Ussher. According to his calculations, the earth had been created in six days in the year 4004 B.C. This meant that the entire creation was less than six thousand years old. The newly developing geology seemed to offer quite solid evidence that the earth was much more ancient than that.

To deal with this serious problem for the orthodox understanding of the Bible, a number of theories rather quickly arose, many of which involved revised interpretations of the pertinent biblical passages. One explanation posited a gap between Genesis 1:1 and 1:2, during which a catastrophe of some sort befell the original creation; then, after a long period of time, God proceeded to restore or re-create the fallen and damaged creation. Another theory held that during the flood of Genesis 7, which covered the entire globe, unusual conditions involving great pressures prevailed; during those forty days geologic processes which ordinarily would require much longer periods of time took place. One ingenious explanation was that God created the earth in six days in 4004 B.C., but he created it to appear as if it were already millions or even billions of years old. Yet another view posited that the "days" of Genesis 1 were not literal twenty-four-hour calendar days, but long periods of time. Whatever technique was employed for reconciling the Bible with the geological data, there seemed to many to be relative relief from the tension.

The real test for the orthodox view came with the theory of biological evolution, especially signaled by the publication of Charles Darwin's *Origin of Species* in 1859. Orthodox Christianity had accepted largely at face value the account in the first three chapters of Genesis of the creation of the human race in the image of God and of the fall of Adam and Eve into sin. The ascendancy of the evolutionary theory had rather serious effects upon this traditional belief. Sin was no longer taken so seriously, for in substantiating his argument that all humans are sinners, Paul had contended that the entire human race descended from one primal pair, Adam and Eve. If no such pair had been created by God, then there was no fall, and sin was perhaps neither so intense, so universal, nor so inevitable.

The conservative church soon saw this theory as a serious threat. The teaching of evolution must be resisted in any way possible and effective. First, the church sought to oppose evolutionism by intellectual refutation. This it attempted to do largely through religious publications, since most scientific and general publications were controlled by persons favoring the evolutionist view. A second major means employed was the legal system. Influence was brought to bear upon several legislatures, especially in the Southern states. The result was the passage of laws outlawing the teaching of biological evolution, that is, the view that the human race descended from other forms of life by a process of natural selection.

It appeared that the conservative forces, or fundamentalists as they were known, had succeeded. While some public-school teachers continued to teach evolutionary views, no issue was made of their action. This situation changed, however, in 1925 in the small mining town of Dayton, Tennessee. There a high-school biology teacher, John Scopes, and a mine manager named George Rappelyea colluded to provoke a test case: Scopes lectured from a text that expounded evolution, and Rappelyea filed a complaint against him. The upshot would eventually come to be known as the "Monkey Trial."

The trial attracted much more attention than would have been expected for a minor violation of a statute in a small and obscure town. Notable attorneys entered the contest. Clarence Darrow, a famous defense lawyer and opponent of orthodox Christianity, volunteered to serve as attorney for the defense; and William Jennings Bryan, three-time Democratic nominee for the presidency of the United States and an eloquent orator, came to assist the prosecution. The guilt of Scopes was quickly established. Darrow, however, placed Bryan on the witness stand and succeeded in demonstrating that Bryan was not competent to argue against biological evolution. The press portrayed Bryan as an ignorant, bigoted, and dogmatic defender of an archaic view.

What had happened here was repeated in some other circles. In many cases, the persons who spoke in defense of orthodox, evangelical theology were not competent to speak to the issue. For example, one of the arguments against the descent of humans from higher primates was that similarity does not prove common origin: one can get milk from a cow, from a coconut, and from a milkweed, but they are not related.[10] An equally unimpressive argument was made by one of the editors of the *Bible Champion,* who observed after a day at the zoo that monkeys were still behaving exactly as they had behaved when he was a child. If they had made no progress in that period of time, certainly evolution could not be at work.[11] Such arguments served neither to refute evolution nor to change the general public's perception of the intellectual quality of fundamentalism. This is not to say that there were no capable conservative scholars; indeed, men such as J. Gresham Machen were highly regarded even by secular thinkers. Machen and his peers did not rush out to fight the most conspicuous battles, however; and conse-

10. Norman F. Furniss, *The Fundamentalist Controversy, 1918–1931* (New Haven: Yale University Press, 1954), p. 21.
11. *Bible Champion* 32 (1926): 503–4.

quently the general public did not form its estimation of conservative Christian scholarship on the basis of their excellent work.

Evangelical Losses

In many areas, then, evangelicalism during the first third of the twentieth century was losing the influence which it had once possessed and withdrawing from engagement with American culture in the broader sense. This was both ironic and tragic. Many of the private institutions of higher education in this nation, for example, Harvard and Yale, had been founded by evangelical Christianity for the express purpose of providing biblically based education, and particularly the education of ministers. Now, however, those who kept that purpose in view were being forced out of control of such schools, which had become liberal and secular. Evangelicals were being forced to found their own schools, giving up the resources which had been accumulated. A particularly notable case was at Princeton Theological Seminary, from which a group of conservatives including Machen, Oswald T. Allis, and Robert Dick Wilson withdrew to found Westminster Seminary in Philadelphia.

Evangelicals were experiencing losses in other areas as well. In the major denominations they were losing political control. In the Presbyterian Church in the U.S.A., for example, the election of the moderator of the general assembly was a major issue. Each year a conservative and a liberal would vie for this important position. And each year in the early 1920s the conservative candidate was elected, but the margin of victory was steadily declining. Finally, in the year 1925 the conservatives did not have enough votes to elect their candidate.[12] Just as in the case of the schools, so in the control of the denominational machinery the conservatives were again and again losing that which formerly they had possessed. It appeared that they would have no ecclesiastical base from which to conduct their ministry, and would fade into obscurity. In the legal, denominational, and academic realms, they were losing ground. Even the prohibition law for which they had so vigorously contended was widely violated and in 1933 was repealed by another amendment to the Constitution.

At the same time that evangelicalism was falling into disrepute and minority status, the ecumenical movement was rising. Growing out of what had initially been a missionary endeavor, the ecumenical movement emphasized the social gospel and advocated either a conciliar arrangement of denominations working together or even a merger into one giant ecclesiastical organization. The Federal Council of Churches (later the National Council of the Churches of Christ) and its counterpart, the

12. "General Assembly Elects Erdman," *Christian Century* 42.22 (28 May 1925): 707.

World Council of Churches, were regarded as the official representatives of Protestantism in this country. The future looked dim for evangelicalism, which presumably would continue, but in reduced form and without any true influence on society. Although the funeral of evangelicalism had not yet taken place, many were already writing its obituary.

Resurgence of Evangelical Vitality

Just like sports and the stock market, however, the American religious realm did not develop. according to expectations. During the 1930s there were some developments which were surprising and, to liberals, disturbing as well. With the evangelicals' having separated from many major denominations, it was possible to compare the two groups statistically. Although rather discredited on the academic scene, the evangelical groups were growing more rapidly, making more converts on a relative basis than were the liberals. Although drawn as a rule from the lower socioeconomic classes, the evangelicals greatly outstripped the more liberal Christians in per capita giving. Even in the number of candidates for the ministry, evangelicals were doing much better.[13]

Yet there was dissatisfaction even within evangelicalism. Independently at first and then collaboratively, several young evangelical scholars were assessing American evangelical Protestantism and concluding that it must change if it was to have any real impact on society. Harold John Ockenga, pastor of the Park Street Church in Boston, Carl F. H. Henry, a professor at Northern Baptist Theological Seminary in Chicago, and Edward John Carnell, a professor at Gordon College in Boston, all saw flaws in evangelicalism which they believed needed to be rectified. Their concerns focused upon two points: the need for a more adequate rationale for evangelical Christianity, and the need for a renewed social application of the gospel. Their writings both issued a clarion call for and made a start toward fulfilling these needs. Another goal was a more positive and cooperative approach to other Christians and Christian groups.

Several developments marked this newfound zeal. One was the establishment of the National Association of Evangelicals (1942). Intended to be evangelical and yet not ultraseparatist, this group adopted the slogan "Cooperation without Compromise."

A second development was the founding of Fuller Theological Seminary in Pasadena, California (1947). Established by the radio evangelist Charles E. Fuller in memoriam to his parents, the school was intended

---

13. William Hordern, *New Directions in Theology Today*, vol. 1, *Introduction* (Philadelphia: Westminster, 1966), p. 75.

to combine excellent scholarship with evangelistic fervor. In addition to Ockenga, who was to serve as president in absentia for the first three years, the faculty consisted of Henry, Wilbur Smith, Everett Harrison, and Harold Lindsell. Soon other scholars of comparable caliber joined the faculty, such as Gleason Archer, George Ladd, and Carnell.

A third development was the rise of the Billy Graham Evangelistic Association. Beginning with a very successful tent crusade in Los Angeles in 1949, Graham's evangelistic ministry spread rapidly. Crusades were held in cities throughout the United States and around the world. In addition to the large numbers who attended the crusades and went forward in response to the gospel invitation, many millions listened on radio and later watched on television and made decisions for Christ. A film ministry soon followed. Billy Graham became a household name, but more significantly, large numbers of people who would not otherwise have heard the essential message of salvation were exposed to and even became familiar with it. What was unique about Graham's ministry, as compared with that of other mass evangelists, was his deliberate attempt to involve all the churches and pastors of the host city regardless of their theological position. Although he was criticized from both the left and the right for this tactic and his message, he thereby succeeded in reducing evangelicalism's abrasive image. Graham himself, carefully avoiding the flamboyance and excesses sometimes associated with mass evangelism, came to be held in very high regard by American society.

One additional development was the establishment of the fortnightly periodical *Christianity Today*. Begun in part as an evangelical alternative to the *Christian Century*, it was at first sent free of charge to large numbers of clergy through a subsidy from a wealthy layman. In its initial format, it consisted especially of scholarly articles advocating various dimensions of evangelical Christian faith. Later it took on a more popular character, but even then it continued to give visibility to the new quality of evangelical thought.

The influence of evangelicalism began to grow in several other ways. One was a twofold impact, small at first, upon academics. On the one hand, evangelical scholars such as Henry and Carnell were beginning to write in liberal and secular journals. Soon the number of evangelicals participating in professional societies had grown greatly, and they were actively reading papers and holding office. The catalogs of nonevangelical publishing houses began to carry titles by evangelical scholars. In addition, competent evangelicals were being appointed to the faculties of major universities, at first primarily in the natural sciences, but later in social sciences and humanities as well.

The other method of fighting the intellectual battle was through campus evangelism at secular colleges and universities. Inter-Varsity Christian Fellowship, which had begun in the early 1940s, helped to prevent the erosion of the faith of evangelical students and also was successful in reaching unbelieving students. This was followed in 1951 by Campus Crusade for Christ, a more aggressive evangelistic program. Some leaders of the future came to faith in Christ through these endeavors.

The superior rate of numerical growth which evangelicalism had displayed in an earlier period continued and even accelerated. In his book *Why Conservative Churches Are Growing*, Dean M. Kelley points out that whereas the ecumenical churches had plateaued and even begun to decline in membership and attendance, the conservative churches had continued to grow and at an accelerating pace.[14] Actually, a more accurate title might have been *Why Strict Churches Are Strong*, for the churches that were prospering were those that demanded much of their members and set high standards for belief and living.[15] Part of the problem, as Kelley describes it, was that the liberal clergy's view of what the laity wanted did not accord well with what the laity had to say when allowed to speak for themselves. Whereas the clergy made social action a top priority, the laity accorded the supreme place to evangelism. Those churches which emphasized winning others to Christ were growing. To be specific, while virtually all denominations showed growth between 1955 and 1965, only the evangelical groups continued that trend after 1965. Since 1965, membership in liberal denominations has declined at an average five-year rate of 4.6 percent. Evangelical denominations, on the other hand, have increased at an average five-year rate of 8 percent.[16]

More impressive yet are the financial statistics. Not only has the number of members in the liberal churches declined, but the giving of those who are members has also declined. Since 1965, liberal Protestants have decreased their per capita giving (measured in constant 1970 dollars) at an average five-year rate of 1.6 percent. By contrast, evangelicals during the same period have increased their giving at an average five-year rate of 3 percent. A very striking fact is that on a per capita basis evangelicals outgive their liberal counterparts by 77 percent! In 1983, evangelicals donated an average of $535, compared with $301 given by liberals.[17]

14. Dean M. Kelley, *Why Conservative Churches Are Growing*, rev. ed. (New York: Harper and Row, 1977), pp. ix–x.
15. Ibid., pp. vii–viii.
16. James Davison Hunter, *Evangelicalism: The Coming Generation* (Chicago: University of Chicago Press, 1987), p. 6.
17. Ibid.

The disparity between the two groups is particularly impressive when foreign missionary activity is examined. From 1958 to 1971, for example, six denominations that are members of the National Council of the Churches of Christ and the World Council of Churches all showed declines in the number of foreign missionaries under appointment: the American Baptist Convention, 407 to 290; the Episcopal Church, 395 to 138; the Presbyterian Church in the United States, 504 to 391; the United Church of Christ, 496 to 356; the United Methodist Church (including the Evangelical United Brethren), 1,453 to 1,175; and the United Presbyterian Church in the U.S.A., 1,293 to 810. On the other hand, during the same period the number of missionaries related to the Evangelical Foreign Missions Association showed an increase from 4,688 to 7,479; those related to the Interdenominational Foreign Mission Association increased from 5,902 to 6,164; the Wycliffe Bible Translators, from 705 to 1,762; and the Foreign Mission Board of the Southern Baptist Convention, from 1,186 to 2,494.[18]

It is rather widely recognized that evangelicals exert more effort and expend more funds on evangelism than do nonevangelicals. This would be expected given the platforms of the two groups. We would, of course, expect the liberals to do much more by way of social action and social ministry. Upon closer examination, however, this is seen not to be the case. Not only do evangelicals give more to spreading the gospel than do liberals, but they give more to benevolences or social welfare. James Davison Hunter comments, "Though liberals emphasize social concerns rhetorically, it is the conservatives who are, in actual dollars, far more generous along the lines of social welfare."[19]

In other respects as well, evangelicals have been expanding their influence and quite rapidly. This is particularly true of the use of mass media. One has only to turn on the television on Sunday morning, or to tune the radio band any evening, to discover that the religious broadcasts are dominated by evangelicals. As of 1985, the 1,180 members of the National Religious Broadcasters (an affiliate of the National Association of Evangelicals) accounted for 85 percent of all Protestant religious broadcasts in the United States and 75 percent of all Protestant religious broadcasts in the world. This is surely an impressive figure.[20]

Two other areas of strong influence are education and publishing, where evangelicals have shown marked growth in recent years. Private evangelical primary and secondary schools increased in number from

18. James Leo Garrett, Jr., "'Evangelicals' and Baptists—Is There a Difference?" in James Leo Garrett, Jr., E. Glenn Hinson, and James E. Tull, *Are Southern Baptists "Evangelicals"?* (Macon, Ga.: Mercer University Press, 1983), p. 81.

19. Hunter, *Evangelicalism*, p. 256 n. 30.

20. Ibid., p. 7.

1971 to 1978 by 47 percent, with a 95 percent increase in enrolment. As of 1985, the number of such schools was estimated at between 17,000 and 18,000, with the number of students totaling about 2,500,000. This growth, it should be remembered, took place during a period in which there was a sharp decline in enrolment in most elementary and secondary schools (13.6 percent between 1970 and 1980).[21]

Publishing has also been a burgeoning area for evangelicals during the post–World War II years. The number of periodicals affiliated with the Evangelical Press Association has increased to 310. The number of specifically evangelical publishing houses grew to more than 70 during a period in which mergers of publishing houses were common occurrences. In addition, a number of secular publishing houses, such as Harper and Row, Macmillan, and Westminster, have considerably increased the number of evangelical titles they publish. There are approximately 6,000 independent religious bookstores in the United States, of which almost 3,500 belong to the Christian Booksellers Association. In 1984 these stores had $1.25 billion in gross sales.[22]

In recent years evangelicalism in American society has experienced a surge in influence (or at least in celebrity). In 1976, George Gallup published a poll indicating that approximately a third of Americans were evangelicals, that is, they thought of themselves as born-again Christians. On the basis of this finding, which was considerably higher than had been expected. Gallup proclaimed 1976 the "year of the evangelical."[23] In that year, Jimmy Carter, a Southern Baptist and self-proclaimed born-again Christian, was elected president of the United States. Many recent presidents have in one way or another given the impression that they were born-again Christians, but have not been this open about it. In some cases, actions seemed to belie this identification. The language used by Richard Nixon on the White House tapes, for example, shocked many Christians who had thought of him as a fellow believer. Ronald Reagan's less than exemplary record of worship and giving nullified his claim to being an evangelical. It seems that a conservative political stance may sometimes be confused with a conservative theological position, and that the courting of evangelicals may sometimes be a political ploy. In the case of Carter, however, there was every indication of genuineness. Faithfully attending church and even teaching a Sunday-school class on occasion, he did not explicitly relate his beliefs to his political actions, but did make his testimony clear. With the exception of some ill-advised comments in an interview with

21. Ibid., pp. 6–7.
22. Ibid., p. 7.
23. "Half of U. S. Protestants Are 'Born Again' Christians," *Gallup Poll*, 26 Sept. 1976, pp. 1–7.

Playboy magazine, his personal conduct, including his obvious faithfulness and devotion to his wife, was above reproach or even rumor. Evangelicalism seemed to have achieved success, reaching even to the highest elective post in the land.

This celebrity status for evangelicalism was by no means restricted to politics. Noted athletes and entertainers identified themselves as evangelicals. Although the designation was sometimes used rather loosely and applied somewhat prematurely, a certain credence was given to the movement. When the reputation of the person before conversion was somewhat questionable, the testimony seemed even more impressive. Thus the conversion of Charles Colson, one of the convicted Watergate criminals, gathered considerable attention for the movement.

It now became difficult for non-Christians to avoid hearing the Christian message, even when they took steps to escape it. Consider, for instance, what happened in a small town in Colorado, where an evangelical preacher was asked to give the high-school commencement address one year and used the occasion to deliver an evangelistic message. Secularists in the community were incensed, and the board of education resolved that there would be no recurrence in the future. The next year a member of the Denver Broncos was asked to speak, a seemingly safe choice. He spoke on the topic of success. All seemed to go very well until, near the end of his address, he said, "Now all of what we have been talking about really does not mean anything unless you know Jesus Christ as your personal Savior. That is what success is all about."

Evangelicals have acquired a growing ease and boldness in giving witness to their faith. In times past this was sometimes a rather awkward and difficult matter. A testimony or an evangelistic presentation was considered an intrusion upon the privacy of the non-Christian. The sharing of one's faith was fairly uncommon. That has changed, however. Some of us who are Christians find that we are witnessed to periodically. On a flight from Seattle to Minneapolis I struck up a conversation about spiritual matters with the woman seated next to me. Everything seemed to be going extremely well, when suddenly each of us recognized, with a laugh, that we were attempting to witness to one another. Notice the number of persons who publicly pray before eating. The stigma attached to being a Christian seems to have diminished. The willingness to pray publicly and the diminution of the stigma feed each other in a circular cause-and-effect relationship.

There has also been an increase in political awareness and involvement by evangelical Christians. In the past, politics was frequently considered dirty, as somehow being the possession of the devil. Consequently, evangelicals seldom engaged in political activity other than voting. While this is still true of many evangelicals, many others have become involved in the political process. Much of this activity takes place through organized groups. The Moral Majority included non-evangelicals and even non-Christians, but a large portion of the core consisted of born-again believers. And then there are the political action committees (PACs), which seek to bring about the nomination and election of persons holding their views on a particular issue. There has also been increased participation in political parties, especially through local caucuses. In some cases, Republican-party regulars of long standing have found themselves elbowed aside by hordes of evangelicals, who are mere newcomers. Coupled with their rising influence in other areas—the broadcast media, education, publishing—the increasing political involvement by evangelicals has made them a powerful force in today's society.

2

The Challenge

In the preceding chapter we looked at evangelicalism's relationship to and influence upon society. We noted that there has been a mixed history, with the record at times being very encouraging, and at other times something of which we are less proud. There are some indications today that evangelicalism needs to take a hard look at what it is doing and even at how it is constituted if it is to continue to have a desirable influence upon society.

Indications of Difficulties for Evangelicalism

Disrepute

The first indication of difficulties for evangelicalism is the disrepute that has resulted from the exposure of improprieties by some of its most visible spokespersons. We are referring to the now painfully familiar revelations regarding Jim and Tammy Bakker and Jimmy Swaggart. It will not be our purpose here to evaluate the actions of those people. Rather, we will note the public perception of them, and how that has colored the view of evangelicalism and affected its influence upon society and culture. Especially vivid was the conversation on "Washington Week in Review" one Friday evening when the details of the Bakkers' lifestyle were beginning to appear. As Haynes Johnson of the *Washington Post* described the homes, the automobiles, the gold-plated bathroom fixtures, Gloria Borger of *Newsweek* could be seen shaking her head in disbelief. Then he said, "It's not what you usually think of as piety." The spectacle of Swaggart's public confession of sexual misconduct, especially in view of his having severely condemned Bakker and perhaps even being responsible for the revelation of Bakker's tryst with Jessica Hahn, simply contributed to the growing perception that television evangelists are charlatans, using their ministries to their own benefit. Not only the sexual exploits and the affluent lifestyle, but the fact that these people were exposing one another and then retaliating, suggested that the temptations of sex, money, and power were mastering these Christian leaders, rather than vice versa. A friend of mine referred to 1987 as the year of the evangelical debacle, and the stream of bad news may not be over yet.

Disrepute has also been one of the offshoots of the fact that evangelicals of various types have become active in the political realm in recent years. Inspired in part by the presidential candidacy of Pat Robertson, evangelicals have appeared in much larger numbers than in the past at local political caucuses, particularly in the Republican party. There they have often distinguished themselves as interested in a single issue, such as abortion or prayer in the public schools. The press, perhaps unjustifiably, has depicted these political newcomers as relatively uninformed and even irresponsible. This perception was reinforced with the public by candidate Robertson's sometimes rash statements, such as that there are missiles in Cuba pointed at the United States and that George Bush was responsible for leaking the information about Swaggart as a way of embarrassing Robertson.

Conformity to Culture

While these isolated incidents have been widely observed, there are some more pervasive indications that the strength of evangelicalism is being sapped. In fact, there have been warnings for some time that not all is well within evangelicalism. The first to appear in print was Richard Quebedeaux's *Worldly Evangelicals*.[1] An earlier treatise, *The Young*

---

1. Richard Quebedeaux, *The Worldly Evangelicals* (San Francisco: Harper and Row, 1978).

Evangelicals, had looked with apparent favor upon the developments taking place within evangelicalism, and had seemingly identified with the movement it described.[2] In 1978, however, Quebedeaux viewed with some alarm the developments which he observed. Indeed, the question on the dust jacket of the book, "Has success spoiled America's born-again Christians?" indicated the magnitude of his concern. Quebedeaux described continuing trends which seemed to pull evangelicalism closer to liberalism and threatened its vitality.

For the most part, however, Quebedeaux did not cause a great deal of alarm within what he termed "Establishment Evangelicalism." This was due in part to the lack of precise documentation, which gave the book at times an almost gossiplike quality. Surely, thought most evangelicals, the failings Quebedeaux targets must be isolated or be taking place somewhere else. There also was a certain lack of analytical precision despite some rather carefully categorized statements. Finally, Quebedeaux's own involvement in the evangelical dialogues with the Unification Church raised questions as to whether he really was a sympathetic evangelical critic or an outsider.

More impressive is James Davison Hunter's *Evangelicalism: The Coming Generation.*[3] Hunter had done an earlier study with the avowed purpose of giving evangelicalism a sympathetic and open-minded treatment, which he felt had too long been lacking.[4] Indeed, evangelicalism was usually stereotyped or caricatured. The earlier book was a study of evangelicalism's reaction to modernity and was notably sympathetic in tone. The follow-up volume added some empirical data, a survey of nine evangelical colleges and seven evangelical seminaries. There are some obvious weaknesses to the survey. The selection of seminaries was probably not as representative of current evangelicalism as it might have been. Dallas Theological Seminary and Trinity Evangelical Divinity School were not part of the study, but Wheaton College Graduate School, really not a seminary, was. This may be simply a reflection of willingness to participate in the study. There also is some lack of theological precision. For example, Hunter infers that a positive response to the statement, "The Bible is the inspired Word of God, is not mistaken in its teachings, but is not always to be taken literally in its statements concerning matters of science and historical reporting, etc.," would automatically entail a positive response to the statement,

2. Richard Quebedeaux, *The Young Evangelicals: Revolution in Orthodoxy* (New York: Harper and Row, 1974).
3. James Davison Hunter, *Evangelicalism: The Coming Generation* (Chicago: University of Chicago Press, 1987).
4. James Davison Hunter, *American Evangelicalism: Conservative Religion and the Quandary of Modernity* (New Brunswick, N.J.: Rutgers University Press, 1983), p. 3.

"Some, if only a few, statements in the biblical literature that were intended by the author to be historical or scientific in nature may in fact be mistaken or contradictory." This seems to reflect a lack of consciousness or understanding on Hunter's part of the extensive hermeneutical discussion regarding authorial intent. Despite these shortcomings, however, Hunter's study is a helpful presentation of the problems facing evangelicalism.

A basic contention of both Quebedeaux and Hunter is that evangelicalism, in its desire to relate to and influence general culture, has instead become more like that culture, and has adopted many of the ways of thinking and acting that characterize the rest of society. The younger generation of evangelicals, for instance, has advocated some changes in the area of theology. Perhaps the first doctrine to provoke some degree of controversy was biblical inerrancy. This issue has stirred discussion even within the Evangelical Theological Society, whose lone doctrinal article pertains to Scripture and particularly to scriptural inerrancy. A number of developments indicate a departure from the traditional position of American evangelicals. One is the promulgation of the view known as "limited inerrancy," which is taught especially by Daniel Fuller. This draws a distinction between, on one hand, doctrinal or salvific matters pertaining to faith and practice and, on the other, historical and scientific references. The former have been revealed by God, and therefore are fully truthful and trustworthy. The latter, however, may contain errors, since the subjects they deal with do not "make us wise unto salvation." Even this distinction, however, did not suffice for Paul K. Jewett, who has found in Paul's teaching about men and women a mixture of the thoughts of the new Paul, which were divinely revealed to him, and those of Paul the rabbi, which reflected his early training.[5] The thoughts of Paul the rabbi are, in some instances, simply mistaken. A commentary on Matthew by Robert Gundry, a professor at Westmont College, also caused considerable controversy. He maintained, for example, that the account of the wise men was Matthew's transformation of the account of the shepherds to emphasize the theme of Christ's mission to the Gentiles. This was Gundry's attempt to preserve the concept of inerrancy, which he continued to insist he affirmed.[6] There was considerable controversy in the Evangelical Theological Society over Gundry's views, with one group attempting to expel him on the grounds that he did not really hold to inerrancy. The controversy was resolved when Gundry resigned from the society.

5. Paul K. Jewett, *Man as Male and Female* (Grand Rapids: Eerdmans, 1975), pp. 111–19.
6. Robert H. Gundry, *Matthew: A Commentary on His Literary and Theological Art* (Grand Rapids: Eerdmans, 1982), pp. 26–32.

Problems have surfaced in other doctrinal areas as well. One of these problems concerns salvation, or at least its exclusiveness. In Hunter's survey, 32 percent of the college students and 31 percent of the seminarians agreed with the statement, "The only hope for Heaven is through personal faith in Jesus Christ except for those who have not had the opportunity to hear of Jesus Christ." Here is one of those places where Hunter's theological analysis is not sufficiently sophisticated. The affirmative responses may simply indicate that the students were uncertain about deciding who believes and who does not, or they may have been allowing for the salvation of Old Testament believers, who certainly did not hear of Jesus Christ, at least not by name. On the other hand, there do appear to be a growing number who actually hold that there is some sort of chance after death for those who have not heard. Clark Pinnock, for example, advocates such a position: "Of one thing we can be certain: God will not abandon in hell those who have not known and therefore have not declined his offer of grace."[7]

There also seems to be some growing openness to neoorthodoxy, at least in some circles.[8] This is in contrast to an earlier period when evangelical theologians such as Edward John Carnell and even Bernard Ramm engaged in extended criticism of neoorthodoxy.[9] Later, however, Ramm advocated that evangelicals adopt Karl Barth's methodology in doing theology,[10] and numerous younger evangelical theologians desire to be involved in the Karl Barth Society.[11] Both Quebedeaux and Hunter see Fuller Seminary as either being or becoming the leading center of neoorthodox theology in the world, and this at a time when most theologians have tended to move beyond neoorthodoxy.[12]

It is with respect to lifestyle, however, that the most dramatic changes have taken place. For example, the percentage of evangelical students who feel that certain activities are wrong all the time has declined markedly: in 1951, 93 percent disapproved of smoking cigarettes—that figure declined to 70 percent in 1961 and 51 percent in 1982; in 1951, 98 percent disapproved of drinking alcohol—that figure declined to 78 percent in 1961 and 17 percent in 1982; casual petting on dates was frowned upon by 48 percent in 1961 and by only 23 per-

7. Clark Pinnock, "Why Is Jesus the Only Way?" *Eternity* 27.12 (Dec. 1976): 13–34.
8. Note, e.g., that the book *How Karl Barth Changed My Mind* (Grand Rapids: Eerdmans, 1986), edited by an evangelical, Donald K. McKim, includes essays by self-proclaimed evangelicals Bernard Ramm, Donald Bloesch, and Clark Pinnock.
9. Edward John Carnell, *Christian Commitment: An Apologetic* (New York: Macmillan, 1957), pp. 268–69; Bernard L. Ramm, *The Pattern of Authority* (Grand Rapids: Eerdmans, 1957), pp. 91–101.
10. Bernard L. Ramm, *After Fundamentalism: The Future of Evangelical Theology* (San Francisco: Harper and Row, 1983).
11. Quebedeaux, *Worldly Evangelicals*, p. 100.
12. Ibid.

cent in 1982; heavy petting by 81 percent in 1963 and 45 percent in 1982; and premarital sexual intercourse by 94 percent in 1963 and 89 percent in 1982.[13]

The attitude toward oneself is another area of dramatic change. Here Hunter finds a decline of what he calls "inner-worldly asceticism." For example, 68 percent of evangelical-college students and 52 percent of evangelical-seminary students agreed with the statement, "I feel a strong need for new experiences," as compared with 78 percent of public-university students. More telling, however, was the response to the statement, "For the Christian, realizing your full potential as a human being is just as important as putting others before you." In this case, 62 percent of the evangelical-college students and 46 percent of the seminary students indicated agreement, as compared with 44 percent of public-university students.[14] Much more detail could be given. Hunter's summary statement, however, is particularly telling:

> In a word, the Protestant legacy of austerity and ascetic self-denial is virtually obsolete in the larger Evangelical culture and is nearly extinct for a large percentage of the coming generation of Evangelicals. The caricatures of Evangelicalism as the last bastion of the traditional norms of discipline and hard work for their own sake, self-sacrifice, and moral asceticism are largely inaccurate. Far from being untouched by the cultural trends of the post–World War II decades, the coming generation of Evangelicals, in their own distinct way, have come to participate fully in them.[15]

In order to understand these trends, we need to ask about the underlying factors. Hunter has proposed two.[16] First, there has been a tendency to dissolve the boundaries between Protestant orthodoxy and the general culture. In the heyday of evangelicalism, there were clear statements about both doctrine and behavior. *The Fundamentals* and other doctrinal statements served to distinguish Christians who believed in the inerrancy of the Bible from those who held that the Bible might be mistaken in some of its teachings. Similarly, subscription to the virgin birth distinguished evangelicals from those who did not hold that Jesus was divine and thus qualitatively different from the rest of us humans.

What was true in terms of belief also was true with respect to lifestyle. Certain actions considered worldly or taboo were codified in lists. Students in evangelical colleges were required to live by certain standards (to take the pledge, as students in one school put it). These stan-

13. Hunter, *Evangelicalism: The Coming Generation,* p. 59.
14. Ibid., p. 61.
15. Ibid., pp. 73–74.
16. Ibid., p. 161.

dards served to distinguish evangelicals from general society. Although the codes were sometimes trivial, negative, and contributory to both hypocrisy and externalism or formalism, the point is that there was a clear consciousness that there was to be a difference between the values and actions of a person who professed to be a committed Christian and a person who made no such claim.

By contrast, there is wide disagreement among younger evangelicals today about what is right and what is wrong. As Hunter puts it, issues which were once clear are now opaque. What is of more concern than the rejection of the old standards and prohibitions, however, is the fact that they are not being replaced by any new ones. Living in accordance with specific values simply does not seem to be as important as was once considered to be the case. Hunter says, "The cultural infrastructure of orthodox Protestantism for many who claim to be orthodox is visibly weakening, eroding from the inside out."[17]

Some of this change has resulted from the evangelistic efforts of the younger evangelicals. Whereas evangelicals in the past did not want to spoil their testimony to the unsaved by engaging in worldly practices, some evangelicals today feel that such separation is actually a hindrance to witness. So they engage in some of the practices of non-Christians in order to build bridges to them, fearing that failure to do so will be construed as judgmental. Quebedeaux talks about left-wing evangelicals in whose conversation four-letter and other once-proscribed words are common. He explains this in terms of the desire of members of the Jesus movement to communicate with hippies and street people in their own language. Unfortunately, however, accommodation to the lifestyle of others often leads to acceptance of it as one's own.[18]

The second factor underlying the change in trends is that the doctrinal and behavioral criteria of orthodoxy are being redefined. In many cases, the formal term is still the same, yet the referent is changing. What usually happens is that the application of the term is broadened. Take, for example, the concept of biblical inerrancy, which has taken on considerably wider meaning than it had a generation ago. Carnell, for all of the negative reaction his ideas elicited from fundamentalists, remained to his death quite conservative in his definition of inerrancy. It was he who contributed to Fuller Seminary's original statement of faith the article on Scripture, which characterized the Bible as free from all error, "in the whole and in the part." Harold Lindsell, author of *The Battle for the Bible*, once remarked to me regarding that wording, "I

17. Ibid., p. 162.
18. Quebedeaux, *Worldly Evangelicals*, pp. 118–19.

must say, that is one of the tightest statements I have ever seen!" On one occasion, when asked the meaning of inerrancy, Carnell said simply, "Inerrant means inerrant." Contrast with this what my doctoral mentor, William Hordern, had to say about the position of the new conservatives: "They say, 'The Bible is inerrant, but of course this does not mean that it is without errors.'"[19] We seem to have here what another of my graduate-school professors, Eliseo Vivas, used to term "the infinite coefficient of elasticity of words," or what *1984* would term "newspeak" and others would label "doublespeak." Other doctrines are being similarly redefined.

As we examine what is happening within evangelicalism, one question keeps reoccurring: Are we reliving history? Are we witnessing what happened in the modernist-fundamentalist controversy sixty to eighty years ago, when liberals continued to use the traditional terms, but poured new meaning into them? One observer evaluated the situation in the following way:

> In these contentions the Fundamentalists are correct: it is precisely the abandonment of such doctrines which the Modernists desire to effect in the Protestant churches; and to an impartial observer there does seem, in the liberal positions, much confusion and lack of precise thinking, as well as the appearance at least of a lack of frankness and a fondness for esoteric "reinterpretation" that may approach in its effects actual hypocrisy.

I have frequently read that quotation to my classes and asked them who they think authored it. Most students guess someone like Carl Henry or Harold Lindsell. Yet those words were actually written in 1926 by John Herman Randall, Jr., professor of philosophy at Columbia University, whose own religious views and practices were at most humanistic.[20]

It appears that one of the major institutions created by evangelicalism to preserve its distinctives, Christian higher education, has to some extent failed it. Hunter shows that the orthodoxy and moral and vocational asceticism of evangelical students are least maintained in those schools which provide the greatest amount of insularity against the encroachments of secularism, and best maintained in those schools that provide the least insularity, namely, the secular colleges and universities. He attributes this to the vigilance with which students at secular schools must guard against threats to their evangelical faith, and the sense of security that students at Christian institutions have in their environment.[21]

19. William Hordern, *New Directions in Theology Today*, vol. 1, *Introduction* (Philadelphia: Westminster, 1966), p. 83.
20. John Herman Randall, Jr., *The Making of the Modern Mind* (Boston: Houghton-Mifflin, 1926), p. 527.
21. Hunter, *Evangelicalism: The Coming Generation*, pp. 176–77.

This sense of security, however, seems not to be entirely well placed. Hunter observes that the educational process even in Christian institutions tends to secularize individuals and to undermine rather than reinforce the traditions of orthodoxy.[22] This is so, at least in part, because, according to Hunter's survey, the faculty in evangelical colleges are even less committed than are the students to the theological and cultural traditions of the evangelical heritage. The lack of commitment is particularly prevalent among the faculty in the social sciences and the humanities, less so in the arts, natural sciences, and business curricula.[23]

This leads us to another observation. Earlier in this century evangelicals perceived the intellectual threat to orthodoxy to be from natural science, and particularly biological evolution. The social and behavioral sciences had not really come to maturity at that time. In the present era, however, it is the social sciences which seem to compete for the ideological loyalty of evangelicals. Perhaps this is because evangelicalism has been very concerned with the experiential aspects of life and has emphasized personal relationships. Out of a desire to find fulfilment in these areas, evangelicals have not been as critical of the social sciences as they were earlier of the natural sciences. As a result, some issues that are genuinely theological in nature are now being settled at least as much by the social sciences as by the Bible. Evidence of this is the fact that many evangelicals accept relational theology, which stresses such ideas as being true to oneself (do not try to imitate anyone, not even Jesus), and accepting others as they are (pressing for any change would suggest that they are unacceptable as they are).[24] Whether cause or effect, these ideas are intimately connected with a decline in belief in human depravity.

Steps to Be Taken

Given that evangelicalism is in danger of losing its vitality and ability to influence society, and is instead being influenced by society, what steps ought we to take? Because I write from within the context of Christian academe, my suggestions will relate primarily to the cognitive dimensions of human experience. There are, it seems to me, a number of emphases that we need to recapture within evangelicalism, and others that we ought to initiate.

22. Ibid., pp. 173–75.
23. Ibid., p. 175.
24. Bruce Larson, *Ask Me to Dance* (Waco: Word, 1972), pp. 55–69.

Reemphasize the Antithesis
Between Christianity and Secularism

First, there needs to be a reemphasis upon the antithesis between the Christian world-and-life view and what seems most plausible to persons who do not proceed from Christian theistic presuppositions. When I was growing up, there was a strong emphasis upon this disjunction. To be sure, it frequently was expressed in terms of certain behavioral prohibitions, but at least there was a clear sense that the church and the world were different. On the basis of Paul's statements in 1 Corinthians 1:18–2:16; 2 Corinthians 4:3–4; and Romans 1:18–32, I entered college with the sense that there would be some conflict between Christian teaching and the secular world's conceptions. I expected to have my faith challenged, and in turn to challenge the secular world-and-life view. Attending a state university where I majored in philosophy and minored in psychology, I did considerable reading in apologetics in order to get a balanced understanding of some of the issues where there was evident conflict between the faith in which I had been raised and what I was hearing from the logical positivists and the behaviorists. Even their use of the classic statements of unbelievers proved not to be straw men. On the first day of abnormal-psychology class I heard, "If you think you have a soul, hang it on the hook over there when you come in, because we don't believe in souls here." And the conundrum "Can God make a rock so large he can't lift it?" was posed seriously in a philosophy course covering "Puritanism to Pragmatism." The antithesis was real, and so I was skeptical of what I heard at the university.

A number of evangelical scholars have called our attention to the importance of challenging the non-Christian presuppositions of competing ideologies. Perhaps the most consistent and persistent of these scholars was the late Francis Schaeffer. In writing after writing, he pointed out the fundamental differences between Christianity and popular non-Christian worldviews, and called for a linking of reason and hope, which he felt only Christian theism could do adequately. I was teaching at a well-known Christian liberal-arts college when Schaeffer came to give a series of lectures which later became *The God Who Is There*. A number of faculty, particularly in the humanities, objected to his fundamental thesis, but the students vigorously maintained that he was accurately describing what they were experiencing.

Carl F. H. Henry is another scholar who has sought to emphasize the antithesis. His *God, Revelation, and Authority*, as well as many of his other writings, underscores the difference between, on the one hand, biblical theism and, on the other, contrasting secular worldviews and inconsistent versions of Christianity. Somewhat earlier, Cornelius

Van Til had, perhaps to an extreme, pressed the issue of contrasting presuppositions.

It is not only with respect to doctrines that we must be prepared to accentuate orthodox Christianity's differences from its competitors. The issues of lifestyle come into play here as well. At times the church has taken the objective of a distinctive lifestyle to extreme, unnecessary, and perhaps inappropriate lengths, as in the case of the Amish. Nonetheless, there is to be a difference. Inasmuch as the major meaning of the word *holy* is "separate or set apart," we ought to ask whether we are living by the values espoused in Scripture, or whether the world has squeezed us into its mold, as J. B. Phillips rendered Romans 12:2. We have sometimes treated 2 Corinthians 6:14, "Do not be yoked together with unbelievers," in a formal fashion, as if it refers essentially to marriage, business partnerships, and the like. I believe that the intent is broader, however. We are not to be linked with those who represent the ethos of secular culture. Paul's frequent entreaties to his readers not to walk as the Gentiles, not to fulfil the lusts of the flesh, but to walk worthy of their calling as new creatures, support this interpretation.

We must, then, challenge the set of values that the world lives by, for example, its pursuit of material things and power. Jesus on more than one occasion contrasted what his disciples were to do, how they were to live, with the standards of the Gentiles. Apropos here is a technique used by a Christian professor in a church-related but rather secular and liberal university. In her introductory course to the New Testament she asks the students why they are in college, and writes their reasons on one side of the board. Typical answers include to get a good job and to make a lot of money. She then puts down Jesus' teachings in the Beatitudes on the other side. The contrast between the two is striking.

We need a renewed emphasis upon the reality of the world. One does not hear much about that these days in evangelical circles. Consequently, the fact that there is a system of reality which is in conflict with Christian values is not a very vivid idea to many Christians. Reemphasizing the antithesis will not involve a return to defining the world in terms of drinking, smoking, moviegoing, and the like. Rather, we must pay more attention to certain overlooked areas: the notion that material prosperity is a direct indication of God's will and his blessing, the emphasis upon fashionability, the quest for power.

Scrutinize Cherished Ideas to Determine Which Are Biblical

Very closely related to the preceding step is the need for carefully scrutinizing our ideas to determine what is really biblical. This will be hard and possibly painful work, but it clearly needs to be done. We must identify precisely what the Bible says concerning how we are to conduct our lives. Scripture and tradition must be separated. Tradition is frequently thought of as beliefs that have been held for a long time, but it may involve new ideas as well; it is in essence human judgment about basic matters, ideas that we acquire elsewhere and then bring to Scripture and to the conduct of our lives. Scrutinizing our ideas might produce some interesting surprises. We may find that some of our most cherished notions do not really have biblical grounding.

One example comes to mind. We have heard a great deal in recent years about the importance of being positive, of not inducing guilt. To be sure, we have all experienced appeals to action which utilized feelings of guilt in a manipulative way. This does not mean, however, that all guilt feelings are illegitimate. When we look at the preaching of the prophets, John the Baptist, and even Jesus, we discover that their message frequently was anything but positive in nature. Indeed, when judged by the modern conception of spirituality as a positive mentality, Jesus was not very Christlike. I recall a student who objected to the "negative language" which I was using. I quoted several of Jesus' statements, then asked the student whether his quarrel was with me or with Jesus. He concluded, rather reluctantly, that it was with Jesus. We may find that some of our ideas about human nature and motivation derive more from Sigmund Freud or John Dewey than from Jesus.

We must be sure that our scrutiny of ideas is consistent. In this connection I remember a discussion with a group of pastors about the role of women in the church and in ministry. One of the pastors was especially concerned that we base our views upon the Bible, not merely upon societal movements and values, a concern which I share. He questioned whether the increasing role for women had really arisen out of new insights derived from exegesis, or whether this was a succumbing to the winds of opinion in our society, and especially feminism. A majority of the pastors seemed to be of the same persuasion. I was tempted to ask them whether their churches' stand on divorce and remarriage had changed in the past ten to fifteen years, and if so, whether this change had resulted from new exegetical insights into the text.

Develop a Complete Hermeneutic

Determining which of our ideas are truly biblical will require the development of an appropriate hermeneutic, in the broad sense of that term. That is to say, we must develop not merely the techniques or rules for determining the meaning of the biblical text, but also the science and art of getting from the biblical situation to the situation in which we are living here and now.

There are two types of cases where a complete hermeneutic is especially needed. One is where the Bible speaks to a situation for which a literal equivalent can be found today, but it is questionable whether the Bible should still be followed literally. It is not too difficult, for example, to find situations to which the prohibition in Leviticus 11:9–12 and Deuteronomy 14:9–10 against eating fish without scales would apply. Catfish is widely eaten in our country, especially in the South; and in the part of the country where I live, bullheads are a common, if unwelcome, fish. Indeed, we may be violating the biblical prohibition when we consume a fishburger at McDonald's. But are we to be governed by that prohibition today? That is a significant question, not for its effect on our diet, but for its implications regarding interpretation of similarly clear statements in Scripture.

The other type of situation where a complete hermeneutic is especially needed is where the Bible does not seem to address the issue we are facing. Given the complexity of modern society, it is not surprising that many vital issues are not explicitly dealt with in the Bible. Nuclear generators were not even conceived of, nor were AIDS, organ transplants, subliminal advertising, and many other problems which we face today. We must not, however, assume that lack of an explicit reference means that the Bible has nothing to say about an issue. Such an assumption would lead us to turn for guidance to secular sources exclusively. One Old Testament scholar has said, "The Bible does not say anything about abortion," a statement which in one sense is true, since the word *abortion* does not occur in the Bible. What he failed to realize was that he was thereby declaring the Bible to be irrelevant to one of the most significant ethical issues facing the church today. Here careful work will need to be done; the Bible will have to be searched not for legal regulations, but for ethical principles, and that requires a thoroughgoing hermeneutic. It requires close inquiry into what biblical situations resemble in significant ways those which we face today, and then an attempt to derive some guidance for ourselves. For example, the Bible's teaching about lepers and their treatment may help the church develop an appropriate attitude and ministry to AIDS sufferers.

Return to a True Theocentrism

Another important goal should be a return to a true theocentrism. There needs to be something of a Copernican revolution theologically if evangelicalism is to retain the vitality to influence our society. Over the years there has been a shift of emphasis from theology proper toward a theological anthropology. The Bible, by contrast, stresses the fact that God is God, which means that he is the highest object, the highest value, the one self-existent being who from all eternity has existed and who will always be. He is the source of all things, the one who has brought into being all that is and who governs it. He is the one whose will is to be honored. He is to be the center of our lives, in fulfilment of the first great command, "Love the Lord your God with all your heart and with all your soul and with all your strength and with all your mind." Humans and the rest of the creation exist for his sake and his glory, not vice versa. The first half of the Decalogue deals with the human responsibility and response to God. The first portion of the Lord's Prayer petitions that God's name be glorified, his kingdom come, and his will be done.

When, however, Christianity comes to be stated primarily in terms of meeting human needs rather than glorifying God, we have an unacceptable situation. This does not mean we cannot begin our presentation of the gospel with something in the listener's experience. That is both good psychology and good evangelism. What we must guard against is never progressing beyond that point. If the basic purpose of our ministry is to satisfy those needs which individual humans perceive, we will have inverted our theology. Then God becomes the servant who is loved for what he can do for us, and we are little concerned about what we can do for him. Instead of emulating the prayer of Samuel, "Speak, LORD, for your servant is listening" (1 Sam. 3:9–10), we will in effect be saying, "Listen, Lord, for your master is speaking."

One of the documentable trends in evangelicalism is a shift toward understanding Christianity as the solution to human needs. The huge number of evangelical how-to books relating to success in one's occupation, marriage, child rearing, attainment of peace of mind, and similar topics, bears witness to this trend. If God is simply the one who meets our needs and solves our problems, he is little more than a *deus ex machina.*

One problem with understanding Christianity as the solution to human needs is that such an approach makes us the judges of what is right and true. We decide what God is to do. God is faulted for not providing for us, or for not sparing us from some of the difficulties of life. And what do we do when our ideas and values conflict with those of others? Then we usually invoke God as the source of our ideas, so that he is on our side. In practice, such situations tend to degenerate into shouting matches.

A second problem with treating Christianity as a way to fulfil human needs is that it is self-defeating. In making human satisfaction the chief goal, it ignores the fact that happiness is a by-product of something else. Jesus, it should be remembered, cautioned his disciples, who were concerned about what they would eat and wear, that they should not be anxious about such things. Rather, they were to seek first God's kingdom and his righteousness, and these things would be theirs as well (Matt. 6:33). In a similar vein Jesus also said, "Whoever wants to save his life will lose it, but whoever loses his life for me and for the gospel will save it" (Mark 8:35). The attempt to make God the satisfier of our needs proves frustrating in the long run. When, instead, we seek to do his will above all else, satisfaction results.

Take Sin Seriously

We must again begin to take sin seriously. As Hunter has demonstrated, there has been a softpedaling of the idea of sin and the need for repentance. One reason for this is that evangelicalism, in his judgment, has become civil.[25] It does not want to offend people in a way which would drive them away from the kingdom. That was a fear that Jesus apparently did not have. He told the rich young man to sell all that he had, give it to the poor, and come and follow him, whereupon the young man went away sorrowful. Jesus was in effect asking him to turn away from his reliance upon, and satisfaction with, his personal wealth.

When we minimize sin, urging people to believe and follow Jesus, but failing to place a concomitant emphasis upon repentance, we are in danger of proclaiming the sort of cheap grace that Dietrich Bonhoeffer wrote about in *The Cost of Discipleship*. Grace is cheap when we are not required to negate our sinfulness. Discipleship is easy when sin and consequently repentance are minimized. It becomes popular to follow Jesus under such conditions. And with the popularity of Christianity comes a danger which I have observed more than once in the life of new congregations. When a church is first planted, it is made up of a highly dedicated group of people. This is necessarily the case, for in a small new church there is nowhere to hide. Everyone is put to work. When, however, the church becomes larger, erects an attractive building, and demonstrates its stability, people begin coming in larger numbers. Herein lies danger. For there is no winnowing process. Now people come for what they can get from the church, rather than what they can contribute to it, and they tend to drag the spiritual level of the congregation down to their own. (Some more recent methods of church planting, which begin with a larger group of people, experience this effect earlier.)

Accept Unpopularity

Taking sin seriously means that the evangelical church today must be willing to be unpopular if need be. Hunter has mentioned civility. In

25. Hunter, *Evangelicalism: The Coming Generation*, pp. 183–84.

fact, this often becomes virtually an avoidance of any disagreement with anyone. In so doing, however, while not offending anyone, we also are no longer capable of influencing others either. For if there appears to be no real difference between the non-Christian and us, why should the non-Christian desire to change? And conversely, why should we wish to remain Christians?

Part of the problem here seems to be a practical collapsing of the law of contradiction. It now seems to be possible to say something like this: "I believe A. You believe not-A. My view is correct. Your view is also correct." If this is what evangelical Christians hold, then they are really no different from the college students whom Allan Bloom describes in *The Closing of the American Mind*. But if no view is untrue, even a view that contradicts another view which is true, then, by implication, no view is really true either. To be sure, those who are of the mentality we are describing would not be concerned about logical implications. If, however, truth and logic are objective, as I believe they are, then the existential effects will sooner or later be felt. That means that eventually a belief in the relativity of truth will lead to a diminished conviction regarding one's other beliefs and to a reduced commitment as well. Perhaps that is what evangelicalism is already experiencing.[26]

Reemphasize Integrity of Belief and Profession

Further, there needs to be a renewed emphasis upon integrity in belief and profession. Quebedeaux has suggested that there are some who no longer hold the traditional tenets of orthodoxy, but who continue to claim to be evangelicals.[27] They may do so for any one of several reasons, not the least of which is an emotional or sentimental attachment to a group of which they have been a part. So they continue to use the same terminology but give it different content. Here, however, we have a misrepresentation, whether intentional or inadvertent. We also have a problem here with integrity, which is a value more broadly espoused than is theological orthodoxy.

What we need to insist upon is that those who want to bear the name of evangelical make a direct and clear statement of what they believe on major issues. It will not do to keep the name *evangelical*, while changing the beliefs. At the very least one could say something like, "I am an evangelical, but I do not believe what evangelicals have usually been thought of as believing." There have been category shifts in recent years, so that what was called neoorthodoxy when I was in graduate school is

26. Leith Anderson, *Dying for Change* (Minneapolis: Bethany, 1990), pp. 107–8; George Barna, *What Americans Believe: An Annual Survey of Values and Religious Views in the United States* (Ventura, Calif.: Regal, 1991), pp. 83–85.
27. Quebedeaux, *Worldly Evangelicals,* p. 166.

now labeled evangelicalism by some, and what was known as evangelicalism then is now called fundamentalism. This seems, however, to be less than forthright. Nonevangelicals will not likely be impressed. Bear in mind the comments of Hordern, Vivas, and Randall (p. 38). And such tactics will probably not win the admiration of society, as illustrated by the furor which arose some time ago when Coca-Cola changed its formula without changing the name.

Conform Personal Lifestyle to Social Values

We will also need to press for a conformity or agreement between social values and personal lifestyle. It is difficult to understand how some people can simultaneously express great concern for the plight of the poor and pursue the lifestyle of the rich and famous. I am reminded of a politician who was elected to office on a platform advocating policies designed to aid the poor, but whose wife, while he held office, spent several hundred thousand dollars per year on her personal wardrobe. It finally dawned on me that his concern for the poor was politics, and that public policy was something different from private practice. There must be agreement between what we evangelical Christians say and what we personally do, lest we fail to obey the biblical injunction of 1 John 3:18. I recall being flabbergasted upon discovering that one of the signers of the Chicago Declaration (a 1973 call for evangelical social concern) not only owned a very nice second home at a popular Christian vacation spot, but also had the largest and most powerful speedboat in the area. In the long run, this simply will not do. Evangelicals have erred by failing to emphasize social ethics sufficiently and to become involved in influencing politics. They can equally err by neglecting the personal implications of their social beliefs.

Work to Preserve the Commitment of Young People

We also need to rethink our strategy of preserving the evangelical commitments of our post–high school young people. It may be that a Christian college or Bible-school education is not the best choice for all young people, as I learned while serving as the interim pastor of a small group which had not yet become an organized congregation. We met on Sunday mornings in the chapel of an exclusive girls' school, a number of whose students fulfilled the requirement of weekly church attendance by coming to our services. After one of those services, seven of the young women accepted Jesus Christ as personal Savior. I remember also a Wednesday meeting of our home Bible study at which a student from a secular liberal-arts college in the area became quite excited. She had found great insight in a biblical teaching that probably is very familiar to most Christians, but was new and fresh to her. The next morning, I faced my class of seniors taking a required Bible course at the evangelical liberal-arts college where I was a faculty member. Some of them were bored with topics that they had at least superficially been exposed to all their lives; few of them had ever had to test their beliefs and practices in the outside world. Counseling some of our young people to attend a secular institution for part or all of their college careers, together with providing a good campus ministry, might well be the best stimulus to their faith.

We should also take a hard look at what is happening in evangelical institutions of higher education. Perhaps we have placed too strong an emphasis upon academic prestige, to the point where we have emulated not only the good, but also the bad qualities of higher education in general. Keenness of intellect and warmth of spiritual commitment clearly belong together—we should never have to choose between the two. "With Heart and Mind" was the title of my address when I was installed into an administrative position at an academic institution; it later became the name of an official publication of that institution. But if in voting on a faculty appointment I ever have to choose between a brilliant but spiritually naive scholar, and one who meets only the minimum requirements academically but has a warm, mature commitment to Christ, I will unhesitatingly choose the latter.

Emphasize Evangelicalism's Positive Heritage and Tradition

Finally, we need to emphasize the positive heritage and tradition of evangelicalism. I think it to be no accident that the decline of evangelical convictions has taken place at a time when evangelical young people, like other young people, have a diminished sense of history. We need to make clear to them that evangelicalism is not, as one evangelical young woman once put it, "middle-aged men in horn-rimmed glasses and double-knit suits." Evangelicalism is a vital faith with an exciting history including some great heroes and heroines. We need to unashamedly challenge young people with that heritage.

There are many flaws in evangelicalism, and we need to expose them. Indeed, there are individuals and publications that specialize in satirizing evangelical weaknesses. Yet by their failure to present positive alternatives, they show that they know little about discipleship to the Lord, who of course spoke words of criticism, sometimes quite satirical, of the Pharisees, but whose ministry was predominantly one of constructive instruction and encouragement. Accordingly, evangelicals should concentrate attention not on their weaknesses, but on loving service rendered to God and our fellow humans.

Part 2

Evangelicalism and the Environment

3

An Evangelical Theology of Ecology

We begin our discussion of concern regarding the environment by seeking to ascertain what God says about the world, about us, and about the relationship between himself, his creation, and us. For our treatment of the environment will follow from our understanding of these particular areas. Our aim in this chapter is to formulate a theology of ecology, an objective basis for a biblical stance vis-à-vis the rest of creation. In the following chapter we will attempt to draw from that understanding an ethic of ecology, a proper course of action.

The Indictment of Christianity

As Christians we have a special stake in establishing clearly the biblical teaching that bears upon ecology. Among the reasons for this concern is that, whether we acknowledge it or not, there is an ecological crisis in our world today. The limitations of space will not permit us to describe this crisis in anything but the most cursory of fashions, but it could be documented at great length.

As blame is sought for the present condition of the creation, one frequently heard charge is that Christianity, and especially conservative or evangelical Christianity, is the major culprit. Indictment is directed at both the behavior of Christians and the ideology of Christianity, which is deemed to justify or even imply such behavior.[1] Actually, the indictment is not a single charge, but a whole series of them. Four in particular can be noted:

1. The call to have dominion (Gen. 1:28) entails treating the earth as intended solely for the good of the human; the result has been the rape of creation.[2]
2. Modern science and technology's exploitation of the earth has been condoned by Christianity.[3]
3. Christianity has promoted a dualism that regards the natural, the physical, and the secular as of less value than the spiritual and the otherworldly.[4]
4. Belief in the second coming, which will usher in the complete and perfect reign of Christ, has in effect removed any sense of need for ecological concern.[5]

These charges have led to the contention that Christianity must be supplanted by the Eastern religions, with their pantheistically based appreciation and even virtual reverence for nature.[6]

In responding to these charges, Christians must keep two concerns in view as they investigate the biblical teachings bearing upon ecology. The first is evangelistic in nature. If Christianity is to be of positive influence in a world increasingly concerned about ecology, if it is to win and retain the commitment of sensitive persons, it must demonstrate that its ideology does not contribute to the ecological crisis. Beyond that, however, as a matter of discipleship we Christians must ascertain

1. Arnold Toynbee, "The Religious Background of the Present Environmental Crisis," in *Ecology and Religion in History,* ed. David Spring and Eileen Spring (New York: Harper and Row, 1974), pp. 145–46.

2. Ian L. McHarg, *Design with Nature* (Garden City, N.Y.: Natural History, 1969), p. 26.

3. Lynn White, Jr., "The Historical Roots of Our Ecological Crisis," in *Western Man and Environmental Ethics,* ed. Ian G. Barbour (Reading, Mass.: Addison-Wesley, 1973), pp. 43–54.

4. Wendell Berry, "A Secular Pilgrimage," in *Western Man and Environmental Ethics,* ed. Barbour, p. 135.

5. Wesley Granberg-Michaelson, *A Worldly Spirituality: The Call to Redeem Life on Earth* (San Francisco: Harper and Row, 1984), pp. 33–34.

6. Toynbee, "Religious Background," p. 149.

the true teaching of Scripture on these matters, so that our practice may correctly fulfil God's intention for us. The aim of the following presentation, then, will be to draw out and in some sense synthesize or systematize major biblical and theological themes.

Biblical and Theological Themes Pertinent to Ecology

God as the Creator and Source of All That Is

In the biblical understanding, God has created whatever exists. Everything finds its source in him. Though this belief is well known and widely accepted in Christian circles, it is nonetheless in need of some documentation and elucidation. The importance of this doctrine for all aspects of Christian understanding is seen in the fact that it stands at the very opening of the Bible: "In the beginning God created the heavens and the earth" (Gen. 1:1). The all-inclusiveness of this action is portrayed through the expression "the heavens and the earth," which is simply a Hebrew idiom for "all that exists."

Genesis is not the only place this doctrine appears. It is even found in the New Testament, where creative activity is attributed to the Word, Christ himself. John 1:3 says, "Through him all things were made; without him nothing was made that has been made." Paul clearly says twice in Colossians 1:16, "By him all things were created." It is apparent that to the Scripture writers the universe and all within it was not simply something that was there; it had come from God and owed its existence to him.

This understanding also permeates the religious practice of the Hebrew believers, especially as expressed in the Psalms (e.g., Ps. 19). Here God is glorified, praised, and thanked for having brought the entire universe into being. The worshipers acknowledge God's greatness in creating and watching over the universe. They also give God credit and thanks for their own existence.

We also need to note the variety and complexity of God's creating work. He made many different kinds of creatures, each on its own day, and each after its kind. Each was a creation of God, and evidently each was an important part of his creating work, for it was not until the completion of the entire process that God looked upon his creation and pronounced it very good.

Nor was this the end of God's originating work. If we believe, as the Bible teaches, that God is in control of all that happens in his creation, causing it to fulfil his intended purposes, then its continued growth in variety and complexity is also God's work, even if he does not act directly. The continued growth is part of the ongoing work of the Holy Spirit making the entire creation fruitful (Isa. 32:15). Thus it is good that the creation has this fullness and richness.[7] And thus each part of the creation, each type, each "kind," to use the biblical terminology, is important to making the creation all that it is. The elimination of any one of these kinds is consequently a loss that causes God regret and grief.

On a continuing basis, numerous species are becoming extinct. It may seem a small matter to us when one of several similar obscure species, such as the snail darter, passes out of existence. Yet in God's sight the creation has, at least to some degree, become poorer. An additional indication of this principle is seen in the account of the flood. Noah was commanded to take seven of every kind of clean animal, two of every kind of unclean animal, and seven of every kind of bird. The reason given was "to keep their various kinds alive throughout the earth" (Gen. 7:2–3). It was evidently important that all of the creation God had brought into being be preserved.

Another point to bear in mind is that by virtue of having given everything existence, which it would not otherwise have had, God is the owner of everything. While he has lent or entrusted his creation to the human race to watch over, develop, and maximize, this is a case of lending, not giving. He is still the rightful owner, which is another way of saying that he is truly the Lord of all of creation. It is to obey him, to carry out his will. This obedience takes several different forms. The physical creation obeys God mechanically. It functions according to the natural laws with which it has been structured. The animals obey God instinctively. Their actions are manifestations of impulses divinely implanted within them. Humans, however, have the capacity to obey God voluntarily. They can choose to obey or disobey.

Each type of creature glorifies God by obeying him. That obedience is an evidence of the greatness and wisdom of God, his superiority over all that is. The degree of glory thus ascribed to God increases with elevation in the scale of creation, so that humans bring greater glory to their Maker by honoring him than does the rock or the plant. Yet it is still true, as the psalmist wrote, "that the heavens declare the glory of God" (Ps. 19:1).

It is important for our purposes to note that the ability of the creation to carry out the divine intent depends to a large extent upon its being in the state of perfection in which God created it. To the extent that it has lost the pristine purity which he gave, it will imperfectly manifest the power, wisdom, and splendor of its Maker.[8] And indeed there are some indications that the creation is not all that it was intended to be, that it

7. G. K. Chesterton, *The Everlasting Man* (London: Hodder and Stoughton, n.d.), p. 282.
8. Robert P. Meye, "Invitation to Wonder: Toward a Theology of Nature," in *Tending the Garden: Essays on the Gospel and the Earth,* ed. Wesley Granberg-Michaelson (Grand Rapids: Eerdmans, 1987), p. 48.

is in some sense fallen. In Romans 8:18–25, a difficult passage, Paul speaks of the creation as being in bondage, as groaning and travailing. It appears from verse 20 that this is in some sense tied to the sin of humans. There seem to be two possible meanings here, both of which probably bear upon the matter at hand.

First, as a result of human sin God pronounced a curse that has inhibited creation's witness to his glory and greatness. The farmer encountering thorns and thistles as he carries on his burdensome toil, and the mother giving birth in anguish, are experiencing the effects of the fall. They do not necessarily experience the creation as very good, and thus as the product of the good Creator.

The second possible meaning of Paul's statement is that humans, through their sinful activity, bring the creation into bondage. Nature is frequently the victim of human greed and selfishness, as they seek to obtain the maximum of material good at a minimum of cost. Their plundering and polluting of the environment enslave and bind it, affecting its ability to bear adequate witness to its Maker.

We can do relatively little to alter the first set of effects of human sin, since they were largely onetime, major, and permanent (although medicine, agriculture, and other forms of technology have helped at some points). With respect to the second group of effects, however, which we inflict upon the world in more direct fashion, we have both a responsibility and an opportunity to exercise our stewardship by preserving and optimizing the creation.

The Entire Creation Valued and Loved by God

We also need to observe that according to the biblical teaching, every part of the creation is valuable to God and loved by him. We are, of course, familiar with the many statements about God's love for humans. One of the best known is Jesus' statement in Matthew 10:29–31, which compares the Father's care for humans with his watch over the birds of the air, and points out that not even a sparrow, trivial though its value may be, can fall to the earth without the knowledge and permission of the Father. The main emphasis of the passage is, of course, that God loves and cares for human beings, but the logic of the argument depends upon the fact of God's love and care for other creatures:

Because of their value to him, God watches over the birds of the air.
You are more valuable to God than are many sparrows.
Therefore God will watch over you to an even greater extent.

While the argument is not explicitly stated in this way, the first premise must be true if the conclusion is to follow.

55

A comparable passage occurs at the very end of the Book of Jonah. Jonah had been called upon to go preach to Nineveh, but had refused. God then used some forcible persuasion to overcome this reluctance, so that Jonah went to Nineveh, where he preached the message of impending divine wrath, the people repented, and judgment was averted. Instead of being pleased, however, Jonah was unhappy that God had not destroyed the city. God replied, "But Nineveh has more than a hundred and twenty thousand people who cannot tell their right hand from their left, and many cattle as well. Should I not be concerned about that great city?" (Jon. 4:11). "*And many cattle as well*"—that is an amazing statement, inasmuch as it is offered as a partial explanation for God's not destroying the city. The cattle were of value to him; he did not want them to perish.

It is important for our theology to maintain a proper balance between God's transcendence and immanence. Where the transcendence is emphasized excessively, his care and concern for his creation are overlooked.[9] We must ever bear in mind that Scripture pictures God as intimately involved with the creation. As Odil Steck writes, "The one God Yahweh is now, as creator, related to the whole of the natural world in general and to everything that lives in it."[10]

The Creation Partly for Human Use and Enjoyment

Another theme of our theology of ecology is that the rest of the creation has at least *in part* been provided for the use and enjoyment of the human race.[11] God provided as food for Adam every seed-bearing plant and every tree that has fruit with seed in it (Gen. 1:29). These plants were also intended to be food for the animals. Then, following the flood, God declared every moving animal to be food as well (Gen. 9:2–3). These various creatures existed then and exist now to sustain and nurture the human, although that is not the sole reason for their existence. There is nothing wrong, therefore, when humans utilize the rest of the creation to sustain their own lives and meet their legitimate needs. They must, of course, be certain that in the process they do not violate or compromise any other command or principle of God.

Note to whom it was that the whole creation was given. It was to Adam, which is both a proper and a common noun. Adam was a definite historical individual. Let us make no mistake about that. He is not simply or merely a symbol of the human race. Nevertheless, he (together with Eve) was the entire human race at that point. Every human who will ever live was contained within him germinally. Thus the rest of the

9. Granberg-Michaelson, *A Worldly Spirituality,* pp. 81–82.
10. Odil H. Steck, *World and Environment* (Nashville: Abingdon, 1980), p. 110.
11. Ibid., p. 46.

creation was not promised and provided merely to him, nor were its benefits to be enjoyed only by him. They were to accrue to all members of the human race.

How do we know that this promise was to Adam as the human race rather than to Adam the individual? Evidence for the more generalized understanding is that the promise was repeated and even broadened to Noah after the flood. Indeed, the very wording is significant. God said, "Just as I gave you the green plants, I now give you everything" (Gen. 9:3). We are not told of any previous statement giving the green plants to Noah. Having given them to Adam meant that God had given them to Noah, as a descendant of Adam.

In addition, the context of the statement to Noah is a universal setting. For when God promised that he would never again send a flood that would wipe out all life, he told Noah and his sons, "I now establish my covenant with you and with your descendants after you" (v. 9). And when he gave the rainbow as a sign, he indicated that the covenant was "for all generations to come" (v. 12). God's commitment was not to a single generation, but to all generations that would ever be.

The Noahic covenant is yet another evidence of God's care for the nonhuman creation. The promise never again to send a flood to destroy all life was made not merely with Noah and his sons, but also with the entire supporting cast, so to speak: "I now establish my covenant with you and with your descendants after you and with every living creature that was with you—the birds, the livestock and all the wild animals, all those that came out of the ark with you—every living creature on earth" (Gen. 9:9–10). This dimension of the covenant is repeated five more times in the ensuing verses: "every living creature" (v. 12); "the earth" (v. 13); "all living creatures of every kind" (v. 15); "all living creatures of every kind on the earth" (v. 16); "all life on the earth" (v. 17). The intent of God, and the extent of his covenant, seems to be quite clear in this passage.[12]

It should be noted, however, that the covenant appears to apply only to living creatures, that is, animals. "All those that came out of the ark with you" (v. 10), for example, quite definitely refers to the animals. Does this mean that God's covenant and concern do not extend to plants and the inanimate members of the creation? It should be observed that the specific promise of the covenant is that the world would never again be destroyed by such a flood. Note also that the biblical account nowhere mentions any destruction of plants by the flood. Although many of the existing plants would have been destroyed by the flood, their seeds may well have continued to germinate, grow, and pro-

12. Granberg-Michaelson, *A Worldly Spirituality,* pp. 78–79.

vide new members of their species. In addition, the flood may not have been of sufficiently great duration to kill certain existing plants. Note that the dove Noah sent forth returned with a freshly plucked leaf in its beak (Gen. 8:11). Moreover, the rest of the physical universe could not be destroyed by such an event, although problems like erosion might occur. We conclude that the fact that only the animals are mentioned in the covenant does not indicate a lack of concern for the other members of the creation. The reason they are not mentioned is that a flood would not subject them to obliteration. Thus the omission is not significant. In this case, we may not argue from silence. Note, however, that we also are not given any positive evidence here of God's love for the rest of creation. Proof of that love will have to come from another source.

There are other considerations bearing upon this issue. Although there is no direct evidence, there may well be indirect evidence that the rest of creation is of value to God. Even if plants and minerals are not valuable in and of themselves, they are valuable to the extent that they are necessary or at least contribute to the existence, survival, and welfare of humans and of animals. Further, there are definite indications of divine pleasure (which may or may not be identifiable as love) with the creation below animals. At the end of the third day, after gathering the waters and the land, and creating plants, and at the end of the fourth day, after making the sun and the moon, God saw that it was good. This expression is identical to what is said in reference to the end of the fifth day, and in reference to the sixth day prior to the creation of the human. It is only when the humans are introduced that we read that God saw that it was very good (Gen. 1:31). This statement refers to God's seeing *all* that he had made. The completeness of the creation is the stimulus to extra pleasure.

Humans as Part of the Created World

As we move from discussing the creation to human responsibility for it, we should take special note of the fact that humans are part of the created world, and that there is therefore a linkage between humans and the rest of the creation. This linkage is seen in the fact that the account of the creation of the man occurs in the same passage as the account of the creation of the other beings. There is, of course, a distinction in the circumstances: the other creatures are all said to be created "after their kind," whereas the human is made by God in his own image. Further, a second account elaborates upon the method God used in creating humankind (Gen. 2:4–25). Thus it is evident that there are some points of similarity between the human and the other creatures, but also some points of difference. Significantly, the creation of the human did not even involve a separate day of creation; it occurred on the sixth day, the day on which the animals were created.

We are, then, in some sense kin with the rest of the creation. This is not to say that we evolved from them, but that like them we are creatures; we have been brought into being by the same Creator. Thus, like them, we are finite and dependent upon God for our existence. Kinship with them also means that our purpose in life is like theirs, namely, to obey and glorify God. Further, the empathy we feel (or should feel) for other human beings will to a lesser degree be extended to the rest of the creation as well. The physical side of this spiritual kinship is that we are made of the same ingredients, so to speak, as are the other parts of the creation. Chemically, our bodies are made up of the same elements as are the animals, the plants, and the inanimate members of the universe.

We need to be aware here of what I would call anthropological docetism. We are all familiar with christological Docetism, the view that Jesus' humanity was not genuine. It was only apparent humanity, or partial humanity. The implication is that Jesus does not (indeed, cannot) participate fully in the human race, and therefore is not able to represent it completely, nor to redeem it by his death. Anthropological docetism holds that humans do not participate fully in the realm of nature; they are not really part of it. The separation between humanity and the rest of the creation is great, and perhaps even qualitative in character. Such a position implies that humans are not limited by a created nature and are not interdependent with the rest of the creation.

What we have sought to elucidate from Scripture, however, is also supported by the general revelation. The natural laws governing the rest of the creation govern human beings as well. This is most noticeable in those creatures closest to humans—the higher animals. Conditions that lead to the death of a mammal will lead to the death of a human as well. Thus general revelation confirms that humans are in a sense kin to the rest of creation.

The Interconnectedness and Interdependency of the Creation

A related point in need of amplification is the interconnectedness and thus interdependency of the various parts of the creation. This is seen, for example, in the creation account, where the plants are given for food not only to the human, but also to the animals (Gen. 1:29–30). Then, at a later point, the animals are also given to humankind for consumption (Gen. 9:3). The lesson, by way of inference, is quite clear: humans are ultimately dependent, either directly or indirectly, upon the welfare of the plants and animals. What is good for them is also good for us.

The interconnectedness of creation is empirically confirmed in a number of ways. Most of them, unfortunately, have a negative impact. The type of consumption which requires maximum productivity results in an earth-encircling envelope of pollution, which holds in the heat and also turns reflected sunlight back to earth. This appears to lead to global warming. Discernible increases in the earth's temperature will in turn gradually melt the polar ice caps and produce flooding of coastal cities such as Los Angeles. This will necessitate the building of massive seawalls or the evacuation of low-lying areas, either option exacting great cost.

A more concrete example can be found in central Africa, where the numbers of hippopotamuses had been increasing to the point where they were becoming a considerable nuisance (as well as being unattractive, of course). The government modified the law to permit and even encourage hunting of these great creatures. Soon an outbreak of schistosomiasis occurred. It was discovered that the disease is spread by a particular type of snail which lives in rivers. With the reduction of the hippopotamus population, the snail population had multiplied unrestrained. The consequent epidemic of schistosomiasis illustrates that when humans attempt, even out of the best of motivations, to alter the balance of nature, they frequently upset the system, with unfortunate results which they had not anticipated. The fortunes of one part of the universe are tied up with the other parts. It is worth noting that the term *ecology* derives from the Greek word *oikos,* meaning "house." The creation is a household; what happens in one part of the system affects the other parts as well.

Perhaps nowhere is the interconnectedness of the human and the rest of creation seen more clearly than in the second creation account. God is said to have made Adam by taking the dust of the earth and breathing into it the breath of life (Gen. 2:7). We are not told precisely what this dust of the earth was. It may have been literal dust or earth, or it may have been some basic raw material that underlies all of reality, such as hydrocarbon molecules. We do know, however, that this dust was not an already living being, for we are told that at this point "man became a living being," which reflects the terminology used in Genesis 1:20, 21, 24, and 28. Whatever the exact designation of the term, the dust of the earth appears to represent the common stuff of reality; it ties the human closely to the rest of creation and combats any tendency toward anthropological docetism. It thus fulfils a role similar to that performed for Christology by the birth narratives.

Humans as Stewards of the Created Universe

A most significant motif from our perspective is that God has commissioned humans to be stewards of the created universe. That is to say, we are to rule over, tend, and maximize the creation. This principle is conveyed in several passages. Foundational is Genesis 1:26–28, where God first purposes and then acts to create humans in his own image and to give them dominion over the rest of the creation. This dominion is first implemented when Adam names the various animals (Gen. 2:19–20). It is also seen when Noah brings the various animals into the ark. Dominion is exercised as well by those who till the ground and those who herd animals.

Note, however, that human management of the creation does not mean that the creation exists solely for human benefit and use. For this dominion is to be understood in light of the role of the kings of Israel relative to the nation. The purpose of dominion was not to benefit those exercising it, but those who were being ruled. Thus the kings of Israel were expected to show concern for the people over whom they ruled, but whom they actually served.[13] This means that animals, plants, and minerals are not merely means to human ends. They are ends in themselves. They are not merely to be utilized and exploited, but cared for. Their welfare is the responsibility of the human, the caretaker of God's kingdom, who must see to it that they fulfil God's highest and best intention for them.

This command and authorization are given in the same universal context as the granting of the plants to Adam for food, where Adam is not merely a historical individual, but the first human as well and thus, at this point, the whole of humankind. Clearly the responsibility and authority for exercising dominion and ruling over the creation are for all humans at all times.[14] This means that all persons, in proportion to their abilities, should participate in this process. Some, of course, will have particular gifts which will especially enable them to direct certain parts of the creation to their appointed ends. Others will have more limited scope for this stewardship, but are equally responsible for what has been given to them. This is the thrust of Jesus' stewardship parables. The man who had two talents was held as responsible for them as was the first man for his five, and the man with only one talent was rebuked for his failure to make good use of it.

13. William Dyrness, "Stewardship of the Earth in the Old Testament," in *Tending the Garden,* ed. Granberg-Michaelson, pp. 53–54.

14. Leonard Verduin, *Somewhat Less than God: The Biblical View of Man* (Grand Rapids: Eerdmans, 1970), pp. 34–45.

The original commission is very concrete: humans are given actual control of the plants and animals. In reality, this involves anything pertaining to the organization, direction, and development of the whole world system, including politics and communications. In effect, all human culture derives from and depends upon the responsibility to exercise dominion.

One of the most difficult tasks of Christian social ethics is to determine the legitimate limits of the exercise of dominion. That is to say, where is the borderline between, on one hand, legitimate cultivation and fulfilment of the potential of creation and, on the other, encroachment upon creation? Are zoological parks, for example, a harnessing and cultivating of creation as God intended, or are they improper limitations of the freedom and activity of some of God's creatures? This will require some careful theological definition.

Or when does regulation become slavery? Slavery is clearly wrong, since it greatly restricts the freedom of human beings, but what about government laws that restrict various human activities? Should we enact and enforce laws which, while facilitating realization and development of what humans ought to be, at the same time restrict their free choices? In practice, we seem to show considerable variation, depending upon the issue. Most of us, for example, would probably argue, even theologically, that compulsory public-school education is a good thing, at least up to a certain point. It does develop one's rational capacities. But what about a compulsory religious practice, such as mandatory worship, or mandatory prayer in public schools? Here we would probably tend to disagree. It is apparent that what is really needed is a teleological definition both of humanity and of nature.

One need not be an Aristotelian to see the value of defining an entity in terms of its end. Aristotle insisted that something is not really what it is unless it is fulfilling its end or purpose.[15] Thus, a telephone being used as a paperweight or a hammer is not really a telephone. And creation must be understood not only in terms of what it is in its natural, undisturbed, or undeveloped condition, but also in terms of what it could become. This is true of the human as well.

Some aspects of what humans are intended to be can be fulfilled involuntarily, while others must, by their very nature, be voluntary if they are to be genuine. Requiring persons to eat (or feeding them intravenously), for instance, so that they can realize their human telos is not improper, even though they might have chosen not to eat. On the other hand, some human functions cannot be commanded or coerced. One cannot be forced to love another, although one can be forced to do things

15. Aristotle *Metaphysics* 2.2.

that would be deemed loving if the correct motivation were present. Thus, religious devotion cannot be coerced. One cannot be made to love and glorify God, although one can be compelled to go through the motions of love.

The Purpose of Human Life

One other very important issue concerns the nature, purpose, and destiny of human life. True fulfilment does not consist in the accumulation of wealth or, for that matter, of fame, comfort, ease, or any other kind of pleasure. This may appear at first to contradict a major set of biblical passages, found especially in the Old Testament, where wealth seems to be an indication of God's blessing. Some of the people most favored by God were persons of substance. Abraham, of course, immediately comes to mind, a man with large flocks and herds. Another is Job (although his situation changed rather radically). Even the first psalm seems to say that whatever the man of God does prospers; presumably his economic situation is part of what is in view.

Yet alongside these passages we must range the New Testament testimony. Here several texts stress that life is not primarily a matter of wealth and possessions. Jesus himself was not a well-to-do person. His family did not even have the means to offer the usual purification sacrifice for a newborn infant. Instead of the usual lamb, they brought doves or pigeons (Luke 2:24; cf. Lev. 12:8). And although the birds of the air have their nests, and the foxes their holes, Jesus during his ministry did not have anywhere to lay his head (Matt. 8:20). In this he seemed to contrast his status with what he promised his disciples (Matt. 6:32–33). On one occasion when he needed to pay the temple tax, he instructed Peter to pay it with a coin he would find in the mouth of the first fish he caught. If we hold that the life God intends for us is the "good life," doing well rather than doing good, then Jesus somehow missed God's intention for his children.

What Jesus taught by example he taught directly as well. He urged his hearers not to lay up for themselves treasures on earth, where moth and rust corrupt and thieves steal, but to lay up for themselves treasures in heaven, where no such dangers threaten (Matt. 6:20). He urged them not to be anxious about such matters as food and clothing. He even instructed one man to sell all that he had and give the proceeds to the poor, so that he might come and follow Jesus (Matt. 19:21). Jesus also stated that one's life does not consist in the abundance of things (Luke 12:15). This theme runs through the remainder of the New Testament. The author of Hebrews urges us to be content with such things as we have (Heb. 13:5). Similarly, Paul urges us to be content with food and clothing (1 Tim. 6:8).

The Old Testament statements linking wealth and God's blessing must be understood in the light of other statements about the means employed in acquiring wealth and the responsibility for using it properly. The Old Testament prophets, especially Amos, condemned persons who acquired wealth through exploitation and oppression of the poor (e.g., Amos 5:11). This theme is reiterated in the Book of James (2:6–7), where the author depicts the rich as oppressors. While possession of wealth may not in itself be wrong, the acquisition of wealth by taking advantage of others is wrong, and failure to share one's wealth with deserving needy persons is wrong. Wealth possessed is not one's own to be used exclusively on oneself.

To summarize the biblical teaching: Quality of life is not directly related to quantity of possessions. To make wealth a major goal of one's life is wrong; and, in particular, to acquire wealth by disregarding the needs and welfare of the rest of the creation, especially of other humans, is wrong. The possession of wealth imposes a special responsibility to use it to care for those less fortunate.

The Purpose of Human Multiplication

The final major motif of our theology of ecology concerns human reproduction and multiplication. This is a factor in various other issues, for the number of persons which the environment must support has great impact upon the earth. Is there a biblical theology of human multiplication?

On the surface, it appears that the Bible gives no basis for limiting human reproduction. On the contrary, maximum reproduction seems to be justified, for the creation account includes the command to be fruitful and multiply and fill the earth. Moreover, children, like wealth, seem to be a sign of God's blessing. While barrenness is thought to signify that God is withholding his blessing (Sarah, Rachel, Hannah), a large number of children is taken to indicate God's special favor (Ps. 127:3–5).

How are we to understand this? We have seen that wealth, though seemingly commended in Scripture, takes on a different hue when the whole sweep of Scripture is examined. Perhaps, in like manner, the apparent testimony to the desirability of fecundity is not normative either. What we must do is determine whether the command to be fruitful and multiply and fill the earth is absolute, universal, and permanent, or temporary, local, and limited. To answer this question, we must look very closely at the original setting and then compare it with the current situation.

It is highly significant that the command to be fruitful was given in the immediate context of the command to have dominion and subdue the earth. At that time, Adam was the entire human race. It would have been impossible for him to subdue the earth. Not only was he alone, but he had no mechanization, automation, or robotization. Consider also that agriculture in the generations immediately following Adam was labor-intensive, and would remain so for many millennia. Further, the very survival of the human race depended upon their multiplying and doing so rapidly. In comparison with the size of the human race at that time, the natural resources of the universe were virtually unlimited. Given the primitive state of technology, the potential for polluting the universe was infinitesimal. That basic situation continued throughout biblical times. The population was relatively small in proportion to the size of the earth and the task of subduing it. In addition, it was imperative to produce children, for they were both the work force in a largely agrarian society and the social security system that cared for their parents in old age.

Today, however, it appears that the command to fill the earth has been fulfilled. Indeed, overpopulation is now a great problem. There is a sufficient population to direct and guide the creation, to have dominion over it. In addition, exercising dominion is presumably a much less labor-intensive endeavor now than it was when the command was originally given. The mechanization of agriculture, for example, has greatly reduced the ratio of workers to acres under cultivation. These are among the considerations to be kept in mind as we proceed to formulate an ethic of ecology.

4

An Evangelical Ethic of Ecology

We are inclined to think of the ecological problem as something relatively recent in origin. In actuality, it has been with us for a long time. In A.D. 61 the Roman author Seneca wrote, "As soon as I had gotten out of the heavy air of Rome and from the stink of the smoky chimneys thereof, which, being stirred, poured forth whatever pestilent vapors and soot they held enclosed in them, I felt an alteration of my disposition." In the twelfth century Eleanor of Aquitaine, the queen of Henry II, moved from Nottingham to Tutbury Castle to get away from what she termed "the undesirable smoke," and in 1661 the diarist John Evelyn described the unhealthful effects that the "hellist and dismal cloud of sea coal" had upon the residents of London.[1] In recent years, with the rapid growth in population and industrialization, these problems have been greatly exacerbated. As Christians we have a responsibility to help alleviate this situation.

Having developed a brief theology of ecology, we now turn to its implementation in terms of an ethic of ecology. This requires first that we state something about our understanding of the nature of belief and its relationship to Christian ethics, and then a bit about our ethical methodology.

In our understanding of the Christian faith, belief is very closely connected with action. Consider, for example, Jesus' metaphor of the tree and its fruit, culminating in his question, "Why do you call me, 'Lord, Lord,' and do not do what I say?" (Luke 6:46). Paul repeatedly applies to ethical living the theological truth which he has been expounding. Thus his ethical statement that "we are God's workmanship, created in Christ Jesus to do good works," follows upon his theological statement about salvation by grace through faith (Eph. 2:8–10). Sometimes the application precedes the statement of doctrine, so that the doctrine is introduced as the justification for the command, as in Philippians 2:1–11, where humility is commanded on the basis of Christ's attitude and conduct. The crux of the argument is found in verse 5, "Your attitude should be the same as that of Christ Jesus." Even the Old Testament law tied doctrinal tenet to ethical living: "I am the LORD your God; consecrate yourselves and be holy, because I am holy" (Lev. 11:44).

Note that the action implied by the theology is not restricted to one's relationship to God, that is, to religious behavior. To be sure, the first and great commandment, given us in the Old Testament and reaffirmed by Jesus, is to love the Lord with all of one's being (Mark 12:30). But the second, which Jesus said is like it (Matt. 22:39), is to love one's neighbor as oneself (Mark 12:31). There is, he said, no greater command than these (Mark 12:31). Thus he raised the command to love others to the same level as the command to love God. This distinguishes Christianity from various other religions which separate theology and ethics. In such approaches, one's ethic may derive from secular sources; one may, for instance, simply adopt the ethic of the surrounding society. In orthodox or evangelical Christianity, however, the content of theology has a very definite impact upon ethics.

1. John W. Klotz, *Ecology Crisis: God's Creation and Man's Pollution* (St. Louis: Concordia, 1971), p. 5.

Types of Ethical Methodology

Legalism

We need to note that several different types of ethical methodology are currently being practiced by Christians. One general approach may be termed legalism. This attempts to reduce the issues of Christian ethics to laws which dictate behavior. These regulations are understood to be universal and unexceptionable in character. They apply always, everywhere, and to everyone. Often understood to be taken directly from Scripture, these laws or rules are to be followed without question.

Legalism does credit to the fact that biblical revelation is not merely the presentation of the person of God, but also the communication of truth, propositional truth. God has both informed us as to what is truth and given us direction as to what is the good and the right. Legalism also takes into account the absoluteness and supremacy of God. He alone has the authority to prescribe what is true and right. Thus the wishes and claims of humans are not factored into the calculation of what is right.

This approach, however, has two major shortcomings. First, it fails to take into account the specific or localized character of much of the biblical revelation. In many cases, the ethical dictums found in Scripture were not intended as universal statements, but as responses to specific situations. These dictums may not have been given if the situation had been slightly different.

The second shortcoming is the closely related fact that God gave many different commands, some of which applied in some situations but not in others. For Scripture on occasion draws distinctions between actions that fall within the same general class. For example, is it right or wrong to kill another human being? The Bible gives differing answers to that question. On the one hand, God prohibits taking human life in what seems to be a universal statement: "Whoever sheds the blood of man, by man shall his blood be shed; for in the image of God has God made man" (Gen. 9:6). Yet elsewhere killing is permitted. For example, murder could be avenged in kind. Consequently, cities of refuge were established so that persons who had killed unintentionally could escape justifiable retribution (Num. 35:6–15). Further, in cases of war and capital punishment killing another human was not merely permissible, but mandatory. This was a command, not a concession to human sinfulness. It appears from these considerations that either there were many more laws or the law governing the taking of human life was much more complex than formerly believed.

Situationism

In contrast to legalism, a second approach to ethics maintains that there are no absolute or divinely revealed laws. The divine command does not tell us to do a certain thing, but to act in a certain fashion, or to do whatever we do with a certain attitude or motivation. This accounts for the apparent contradiction on a cognitive or propositional basis, for that is not the true locus of the divine will for humans. From this particular point of view have emerged various types of relativistic ethics, the most prominent of which in recent years has been situation ethics.

Situation ethics maintains that nothing is always right or always wrong, good or bad. What makes something good is whether it is the most loving thing to do. If, in a given situation, a particular action is the most loving thing to do, then it is good and right. If, on the other hand, it is not the most loving thing to do, it is bad and wrong. The only thing that is always good is love, and the only action that is always right is action performed in the most loving fashion. This approach places normativeness in an attitude or a way of doing things rather than in specific content or things to be done. God has not revealed what we are to do, but how we are to be.[2]

The value of situationism lies in its having seen the complexity of the moral situation. The apparent contradictions found among the divine commands are indications of the variety of values involved in the typical ethical decision or directive. Situation ethics correctly fixes normativeness in a principle, the principle of love, but makes the mistake of restricting ethical considerations to that one principle.

Principialism

There is a third approach to ethical decision-making which I believe incorporates the strengths of legalism and situationism, while avoiding their difficulties and errors. I would term this approach "principialism."[3] It maintains that the locus of divine revelation and thus of normativeness is the ethical principle. This does not in any sense deny verbal inspiration, but maintains that in matters of ethics the words are the vehicle for conveying the principles which God intends humans to know and honor. The rules given in differing situations varied because different combinations of principles applied. The task of the Christian ethicist is to determine what principles are applicable to the case under consideration and to combine them in such a way as to produce a rule that will govern action in other cases of this type. This means that there

2. Joseph Fletcher, *Situation Ethics* (Philadelphia: Westminster, 1966).
3. Ebbie C. Smith, "The Ten Commandments in Today's Permissive Society: A Principleist Approach," *Southwestern Journal of Theology* 20.1 (Fall 1977): 42–58.

will indeed be an objective good and bad, right and wrong, for each situation, but the rule which expresses them may be much more complex than some have thought.

We will seek to follow principialism in the remainder of this presentation. In chapter 3 we expounded those theological motifs which constitute the values appropriate to ecological ethics. We will now attempt to draw upon those values as principles, and to combine them in such a way as to give us directives for action.

Ethical Solutions and Practical Solutions

In our discussion we must bear in mind the distinction between what we might term ethical solutions and practical solutions. Or we might term them strategic and tactical solutions. An ethical or strategic solution is the state of affairs that we decide would resolve the ethical problem. The practical or tactical solution is the specific action or procedure necessary to bring about the ethical or strategic solution. Sometimes the impracticality of the former makes realization of the latter quite difficult.

A story from World War II illustrates the point. Early in the war, German submarines, frequently operating in wolf packs, were sinking large numbers of American cargo ships, making it difficult to provide our military personnel and our allies with necessary supplies. A great deal of thought and anguish went into attempting to stop this heavy attrition. Finally one man proposed what he thought to be a brilliant solution. "Heat the water of the Atlantic Ocean to 212 degrees," he said, "and when the German U-boats surface, we can simply pick them off with guns and bombs." "That is a brilliant idea," someone responded, "but how would you heat that much water?" "Don't ask me," replied the man. "I just make policy; I don't carry it out." In terms of our analysis, the general value or principle pursued was ending the loss of American cargo ships. The strategic solution was the destruction of the German submarines. The tactical solution was heating the water to force the submarines to surface.

A complicating factor is that working to achieve one value may endanger or diminish another. Single-issue persons seldom see this dilemma. We need to bear in mind that differing with others on the tactical solution does not necessarily mean that we differ on the ethical solution. It may simply mean that we do not think their practical solution effective, or that we espouse principles which we believe will be adversely affected by it.

Let us say, for example, that we have concluded that the pollution of the environment is bad and therefore all smokestack emissions should be reduced immediately. If we were to do that, however, there would be some severe ramifications. Large numbers of persons would become unemployed, and the modifications necessary to reduce emissions would add considerably to the cost of manufactured products. Both of these effects would in turn have significant impact upon the economy. So we must seek to arrive at ethical solutions, and then search for the best possible practical solutions. Our discussion will focus primarily upon ethical solutions, but we will occasionally explore possible practical solutions as well.

Tenets of an Ethic of Ecology

Preservation of the Creation

We must seek to preserve the purity, beauty, and integrity of the whole of the creation. More specifically, we must find ways to reduce (or, ideally, to eliminate) the pollution of our environment, that is to say, of the entire creation. We must endeavor to reduce the harmful emissions into the air, water, and soil. This means that we individual Christians will take great care to ensure that we are not contributing to the pollution of our world and universe. The use of certain substances and the avoidance of others will help to advance the cause. Even if it means forgoing some economic advantage or some item of convenience, we will choose practices and substances which are environmentally healthy.

Personal ecological ethics, what we as individuals do, would be helped to a considerable extent if every Christian in our country took stewardship of the environment seriously. Given the number of Christians, or even the number of evangelical Christians in the United States, there would be a measurable impact upon the environment. Beyond that, however, we must be concerned about our social ethics. In addition to our individual actions, we must be concerned about the actions of the society of which we are a part. Social ethics for the individual Christian consists of efforts to influence what is done on a societal scale.

Influence can frequently be exerted through economic means. Boycotts of certain types of products or of certain corporations which are polluting the environment can be quite effective. Resolutions by national church bodies are not noted for their effectiveness in altering corporate policy, but if they are backed by the members of the denomination who then take action to demonstrate the seriousness of the intention, they can be of considerable influence. Suppose, for example, that the Southern Baptist Convention, having passed in its annual assembly a resolution censuring an objectionable product, notified the manufacturer about this action and urged cessation of distribution. If after adequate opportunity the corporation involved failed to comply, the congregations would be informed. Having already been made aware of the action of the annual assembly, the congregations would be prepared to vote to urge their members to boycott the offending party. The denomination would also, of course, inform the manufacturer's competitors that any attempt to utilize the boycott as an opportunity to raise prices will not go unpunished. Think of the message that would be sent if this scenario actually took place! The sales figures in the sections of the country where Southern Baptists are especially numerous would soon persuade the company to rethink its position.

What of those cases where we object to the practices of all of the companies in a given field? Persuading one manufacturer to change the product, and all the Southern Baptists to patronize that particular brand, would probably not prove successful. For that manufacturer would probably have been placed at an economic disadvantage. Non-polluting products are often costlier to make; that is why they are not made in the first place. So the officers of our hypothetical company would be on the horns of an economic dilemma. They might sell at a competitive price, but they would then experience considerably lower profits or even a loss. That might eventually persuade the corporation to stop manufacturing the product. The alternative would be to raise prices to reflect the increased cost of manufacture. The product, then, would be more expensive than what competitors might have to offer, so persons not involved in the boycott (and, unfortunately, probably some who are) would purchase the competing brands. The whole endeavor seems to be self-defeating.

There may, however, be another approach which would be effective in such a situation. In negotiating labor contracts the United Auto Workers select one of the big three auto companies. If a satisfactory agreement is not reached with that company, there is a strike. Once settlement is reached, the other two companies generally go along with the agreement, but if not, a second company is targeted for a strike. Similarly, if Christians were to single out one manufacturer for a boycott, a strong message would be sent to the others; if it is not effective, the other companies could be boycotted in succession.

In some cases, however, the procedure outlined above does not solve the problem. Different means are then called for. Laws must be passed forbidding objectionable practices. There must also be a commitment to strict enforcement of those laws. It will not always be necessary to outlaw the offending practice or substance. If penalties are attached to the undesirable action, if fees are charged for, say, the disposal of waste, the undesirable action will become more expensive than the desirable alternative, and large corporations will modify their conduct. Here a combination of legal and economic means is being employed.

In seeking to preserve the integrity of the world, we must clearly understand that the term *world* has different senses in Scripture. Christopher Derrick has pointed out that Francis of Assisi was both the least worldly and the most worldly of men.[4] He certainly had learned to lead the separated life. He was a man of simplicity, of self-denial. Yet his love for the world—the created universe and all forms of life within it— is legendary. The created world is not inherently evil, it is inherently good, while the world understood as the system of ungodly values and structures is inherently evil. We must learn to love the former, while hating the latter.

Further, our love for the world in the former sense must be of the right type. It is helpful here to distinguish between love as *erōs* and love as *agapē.* If our love takes the form of *erōs,* then we will want to possess the creation, to exploit it, to consume it. That is the type of love which has contributed to the ecological crisis in which we now find ourselves. If, on the other hand, we love the creation with a concern and care for its welfare, for what we can do to maximize its potential, then our love will be *agapē.* And Christians should be especially distinguished by a preponderance of *agapē* over *erōs* in their relationship to all objects of God's *agapē* love.

Self-Maintenance for the Glory of God

We must act to maintain ourselves for the glory of God. By this is meant our total health, physical, psychological, and emotional, as well as full development of ourselves for the sake of the kingdom of God. We must guard our physical health through such means as careful diet, exercise, and preventive and corrective medicine. The principles of sound mental hygiene will also be included. As an act of stewardship we will develop our gifts and aptitudes through education and practice. This will involve one's occupation, hobbies, and service for the Lord. "Be all that you can be" is not simply the slogan of a branch of the military service. It is a maxim of the believer. Since we are part of the creation, and a very important part at that, we will want to take good care of ourselves. This may seem at first glance to be a self-centered approach, but when properly followed it is a matter of loving oneself not for one's own sake, but for the sake of God.

Conservation of the Resources of the Creation

We also need to commit ourselves to careful conservation of the resources of our creation. This means that we must find ways to use less

4. Christopher Derrick, *The Delicate Creation: Towards a Theology of the Environment* (Old Greenwich, Conn.: Devin-Adair, 1972), p. 78.

of earth's abundance as sources of energy and raw materials for manufacture. All of these resources are finite in amount. When the iron ore within the earth's shell has been mined and removed, there will be no more. When the petroleum, coal, and natural gas deposits have been exhausted, there will be no more. (The processes by which fossil fuels were formed are still occurring, but at a rate so low in comparison with our rate of consumption as to make them virtually negligible.) Aluminum, lead, zinc, and nickel are irreplaceable. Yet by no means can we be certain that once they are gone the human race will no longer need these materials. The Christian has a significant stake in assuring that we not find the machine of the human race attempting to run with some of its crucial gauges registering empty.

There are several steps we can take. One is simple reduction in consumption. There are necessary expenditures (in our society) and optional expenditures. Furthermore, in the class of necessary expenditures there are relatively more efficient and relatively less efficient options. We will need to ask which expenditures are really necessary and to what degree, and then adopt those options which are more efficient. This might mean limiting our trips, buying fuel-efficient automobiles, carpooling, taking public transportation, using refillable or recyclable products, purchasing more durable albeit more expensive items, thus reducing the need for early or frequent replacement. These and countless other possibilities will come to mind.

Another step is to use renewable resources. For example, if we use wood products rather than plastic, the raw material can be replaced. This must, of course, be accompanied by sound methods of forest and timber management. In using renewable resources we will in many cases also be using materials which are biodegradable. A closely related measure is the harnessing of sources of energy which are currently going to waste. We learned rather early in the industrial age to exploit hydroelectric power. Today, however, we use numerous alternative technologies instead. But wherever one finds energy being displayed in nature, there is potential. The wind, for example, is a nearly continuous manifestation of power that simply is wasted. Abandoned windmills across our land testify to wise use of wind power before alternatives were available. I grew up on a farm where we drank and bathed with water pumped by a windmill, and we listened to a radio powered by a storage battery which was charged by a wind-operated generator on our roof. It is not nostalgia, but a concern for the resources of our world, that causes me to call for increased use of wind, tidal, solar, and similar forms of energy.

It may seem that because we Americans are only a small part of the world's population (currently about 5 percent, a figure that is gradually declining), we can do little to affect the situation of the world. Yet let us make no mistake about it: we are the ones most in need of changing our patterns of behavior. When I taught Christian social ethics, the rate of consumption of natural resources and pollution of the environment was forty times greater per capita in the United States than in India. The other developed nations, of course, share this problem, but we head the list. We may take some pride in the fact that we are controlling population growth much better than are the undeveloped and the developing nations, but that is small comfort in light of our rate of assault upon the creation.

One hopeful sign is the recent emphasis on reusing, reprocessing, or recycling materials. Consumer pressure has begun to affect the practices of some corporations; some fast-food chains, for example, have shifted to cardboard rather than styrofoam containers. Municipalities have passed recycling ordinances and set up recycling centers.

It should be noted that we occasionally have the possibility of effecting what could be termed a double-plus solution, reducing both consumption and pollution. One of the tensions of ethics is that sometimes the solution or alleviation of one problem creates or aggravates another. At other times, however, the solution to one problem can contribute to the solution of another. An example is the ordinances banning sanitary landfills from accepting leaves. Placed in plastic bags, leaves do not degrade for many, many years; and in the meantime landfills become exhausted as sources of disposal. Municipal compost heaps, by contrast, can provide fertilizer while avoiding the clogging of landfills. Responsible Christians will support the passage of such ordinances and will cooperate with them fully.

Reduced Standard of Living

For the sake of society and the entire creation, we must be willing to accept a lower individual standard of living for ourselves. Some of the courses of action which we have advocated will add to the cost of things. The cost of recycling will undoubtedly increase the selling price of an item. So we will not be able to afford quite as much as we could before.

Yet our standard of living will not be affected as much as we might think. We should probably focus on the quality of life rather than the standard of living. What is the quality of life when the air is so polluted that on certain days citizens are advised to abstain from vigorous physical activity? What is the quality of life if water pollution results in more deaths, earlier deaths, and poorer health? From the perspective of enlightened self-interest, steps that reduce the standard of living may actually amplify the quality of life.

Another dimension here is the desirability of self-sacrifice. Are we willing to pay more for what we consume, if thereby the health and material well-being of others improve? Are we willing to oppose the policies of multinational corporations which hold down their prices to us by paying an absolutely minimum and impoverishing wage to workers of other countries which supply the raw materials or the finished products? Are we willing to insist that companies guarantee the safety and health of their workers, even if that results in a greater cost to us? Here we are moving toward sharing the wealth and even the health with others, insisting on a little less for ourselves.

Simplicity of Life

Reducing the standard of living means that we should commit ourselves to simplicity rather than materialism. It means getting along with less. This will have three benefits or, perhaps we should say, three beneficiaries.

A simple style of life should first of all be adopted because of what it will do for the creation. We will consume less of its natural resources and pollute it less. For inordinate concern with physical or material objects is the root cause of both overconsumption and pollution.

Moreover, a simple style of life should be adopted for its effect on others. To the extent that we do not consume and do not despoil the creation, its resources are available to others. In view here are not only our contemporaries, but future generations as well. We noted earlier (p. 61) that the creation and stewardship thereof were given to all persons, not just Adam and Eve. None of us knows how many generations there will yet be upon our earth. The less we consume, the more will be left for others. We must make certain that our social ethic functions on at least as high a level as our social etiquette. Certainly none of us would think of taking so much food for ourselves that others at a meal would get none. That is the theory behind seconds: one does not take all one can possibly eat at the first opportunity, but takes an additional amount only after everyone else has been served. Yet if we consume earth's resources mindlessly without thinking about those who are to come after us, we are displaying an even more serious lack of concern for others.

Another suggestion to help solve our problems is that we need to think of the population of the world as being our friends and brothers and sisters. If we see a member of our family or a good friend in need, we are certainly moved and will do something to help. And if we realize that our own actions are the cause of that need, we are seized by a sense of responsibility. That does not necessarily extend to persons far away and of a different culture, however. We do not readily realize that our greed may be contributing to their hunger. We may grieve over the casualties that our forces are suffering in a war, while failing to realize that the casualties on the other side bring the same type of sorrow to their families. We need to pray that God will create in us a sense of unity with all of the human race and, beyond that, with the rest of the creation.

A keen sense of unity with others will transform our attitudes toward material things and their use. Both the Old Testament and the New emphasize a joyful sharing of what one has.[5] We will increasingly appreciate this emphasis as we come to understand that fundamental realities are spiritual rather than material. In the material realm, what I give to others seems to reduce what I have myself. Thus, if I have a hundred dollars and give fifty dollars to someone else, I have only fifty dollars left. If, however, I perform an act of kindness, I do not decrease what I am or have, but increase it. A compliment, a kind word, an act of assistance makes me a better person, brings me happiness in giving happiness to others.[6]

Our efforts in this direction will be aided by a broadened understanding of what salvation essentially is, of what we are really saved from. This in turn will depend upon an expanded concept of sin. Part of what Christ saves us from is selfishness, with its insatiable desires for self-satisfaction. In addition, we are delivered from conformity, the need to keep up with the Joneses. Much of the consumption that is contributing to the ecological problems we face stems from the desire for something simply because others have it. A full-orbed grasp of the depth and scope of salvation will help to make us part of the solution rather than part of the problem.[7]

Finally, we will want to commit ourselves to simplicity of life because of what it will do to us. One of the unfortunate effects of materialism is a loss of enjoyment and pleasure in the little things of life. I have thought about this while riding my bicycle to work and hearing the beauty of birds' songs all around me. Bicycle riding is one of those nearly perfect activities. I can have exercise, transportation, devotions (as long as I do not close my eyes while praying), and entertainment all at once, while saving money and only expending about an additional ten minutes of time per one-way trip. Yet all around me are joggers wearing headphones. I do not know what they are listening to, but they are missing the beauty of the birds' songs, and also endangering them-

5. Ron Elsdon, *Bent World: A Christian Response to the Environmental Crisis* (Downers Grove, Ill.: Inter-Varsity, 1981), pp. 140–41.
6. May Evelyn Jegen, "The Church's Role in Healing the Earth," in *Tending the Garden: Essays on the Gospel and the Earth*, ed. Wesley Granberg-Michaelson (Grand Rapids: Eerdmans, 1987), p. 103.
7. Elsdon, *Bent World*, p. 123.

selves by drowning out the sound of approaching vehicles. The money not spent on a Walkman was in this case money well unspent, for it placed me back in contact with the simple beauty of nature. Persons who depend on video games for stimulation have lost the ability to enjoy the beauty of butterflies and flowers. Greater and greater stimulation, often artificial in nature, is required to find satisfaction. Materialism robs us of a certain element of our humanity.[8]

Christians maintain that the real satisfactions in life are spiritual in nature. That being the case, we really do not need most material things, and the pursuit of them proves stultifying to our development. The liberation theologians have noted that one of the means by which oppressors have kept the poorer classes under control over the years is to tell them that material things are not important, that the spiritual, especially in the world to come, is what is worth pursuing. Yet these oppressors do not hesitate to indulge themselves in the material goods of the present life. We must realize that if we sing, "All that I have is in Jesus," but live as if material consumption is what is most important, the credibility of our testimonies will be severely jeopardized.

Prevention of War

We must also do all that we can to prevent war. There are, of course, abundant reasons on other grounds for seeking to prevent war, but we are thinking here primarily of the ecological reasons. War has always been destructive of the environment, of course. With the growth of modern technology, however, this capacity is greatly multiplied. When Saddam Hussein released a large quantity of oil into the Persian Gulf, the major victims were birds, fish, and other subhuman organisms. The potential for nuclear war raises the specter of a barren landscape, a nuclear winter, wholesale devastation of life.[9] Christians have a major responsibility to do all that they can to prevent war, and should be in the very forefront of efforts to promote peace.

Recognition of the Rights of the Nonhuman Members of the Creation

We must recognize the rights of the nonhuman members of the creation. All creatures are God's creatures, are objects of his love, and are of value to him. We have been placed on earth not only to utilize the rest of creation for our own sake, but also to manage the universe for the

8. Ibid., pp. 4–5.
9. Wesley Granberg-Michaelson, *A Worldly Spirituality: The Call to Redeem Life on Earth* (San Francisco: Harper and Row, 1984), p. 3.

sake of its various inhabitants. We are not the only ones who have divinely bestowed rights.

Let us note, of course, that a human is of greater value than a member of another species. Thus, animal-rights movements that protest the death of animals in research experiments aimed at the eventual sparing of human lives need to seriously reassess their value system. Rights of humans take precedence over similar rights of other creatures, but not all rights of humans take precedence over all rights of other creatures. The destruction of animal life for the amusement rather than the sustenance of humans is not right. Similarly, the destruction of species of plant life for the sake of human pleasure or comfort is not consonant with God's view of the creation.

Here we must accept our responsibility not merely to enjoy and utilize the creation, but to tend, care for, and develop it. We must realize that we are the problem. It is not animals and plants that have caused the ecological damage to our universe; it is we. I once heard a noted theologian say, "If tonight every human being on the earth were to die, tomorrow the entire animal kingdom would rejoice—with the exception of the dog, the Uncle Tom of animals." He was right, of course. For plants and animals would all be better off and would live a better life without us.

Additional Considerations

Emphasis upon Long-Range Concerns

There are two remaining considerations in our ethic of ecology. First, long-range concerns are to dominate in our thinking and action. This in itself has biblical and theological grounding in the Christian revelation. Jesus, for example, urged his hearers not to lay up for themselves treasures on earth, where they would deteriorate or be stolen, but rather in heaven, where they would not be subject to such dangers (Matt. 6:19–21). Paul advises us not to look at the things which are seen, because they are temporary, but at the unseen things, which are eternal (2 Cor. 4:18). James urges us to let perseverance finish its work (James 1:3–4). We are told that a day is like a thousand years and a thousand years like a day with God (2 Pet. 3:8). God does not seem to be in a hurry to accomplish his work. Thousands of years elapsed from the fall to the coming of the Redeemer, and centuries from the giving of the prophecy to its fulfilment. Geology indicates that God did his creative work over what we would deem a long period of time.

The problems that we face in ecology have been in formation for a long time. It should not be surprising if their reversal takes quite some time as well. We should not seek for immediate results or take actions with desirable short-term effects but negative long-term effects. This is not easily done within our society. The present atmosphere emphasizes immediacy rather than deferral. This is seen, for example, in the fact that news reports are live, whereas earlier generations had to wait for hours or even months for reports of some of the most significant events in history. The very structure of society discourages the deferring of satisfaction. A very small illustration will make my point. As a youth, I listened avidly to the radio broadcasts of Jack Armstrong, the all-American boy. Various types of prizes were offered on the program, from bandannas to rings which glowed in the dark to decoders which would enable the listener to unscramble secret messages given at the end of the broadcast. In order to receive these special rewards, one had to send in a certain number of box tops from the cereal that sponsored the program. Collecting them took some time, although I was more fortunate than most, since my aunt, as a cook at a senior citizens' residence, could supply me with box tops by the dozen. Then I would send them in and wait the stipulated four to six weeks for the prize to come through the mail. After four weeks I would eagerly go to the mailbox each day. Finally, gratification would come. Today there are still prizes of this type, but now they are placed in the cereal box! Our ethic will have to go against this trend of our society, but it will be worth the effort.

Types of Motivation

Finally, we need to note the different types of motivation that may be involved in formulating an ethic of ecology. These motivations will in many cases affect the nature of one's conclusions. We will look at three types of motivation in what might be viewed as an ascending order.

The first is direct self-interest. This is the approach that simply seeks self-satisfaction in terms of pleasure, comfort, recognition, or something else relatively immediate. It often is short-range in nature.

Second is enlightened self-interest. This approach recognizes that some actions which on the surface do not seem to work to one's good and one's comfort really do so in the long run, and some of what seems to be good turns out in the long run to be detrimental. Such is the nature of the appeal often made in social ethics. What good does it do for us to save money by driving automobiles without pollution-control devices, if the eventual result will be even more severe restrictions and controls? What good does it do to have lower fuel costs now, if as a result we fail to develop alternative sources of fuel and thus become more vulnerable to price fixing by oil suppliers in the future? Some of these appeals may focus on the welfare of others, but ultimately the concern is not for others but for oneself. While more sophisticated than crude self-interest, enlightened self-interest is not necessarily more unselfish, only more calculating.

The third type of motivation is altruism. One works for the good of others rather than oneself, whether the other is God, other humans, or nonhuman members of the creation. One is concerned for others either because they are deemed to have value in themselves or, from the Christian perspective, because God places value upon them.

We spoke earlier of an ascending order: crass self-interest is the lowest type of motivation, and altruism is the highest. There are two bases for that classification. The first is Lawrence Kohlberg's scale of moral development, which gives evidence of this sort of progression.[10] The second is biblical and theological. In numerous places the Scripture appeals to altruism. Paul urges us not to look to our own interests, but to the interests of others, as did Jesus (Phil. 2:3–5). Jesus recognized that his hearers were at different levels of motivation. On the one hand, his preliminary approach to nonbelievers sometimes involved an appeal to their self-interest. The more mature listeners, however, were called upon to engage in self-sacrificial behavior (Matt. 16:24–25).

A major part of our concern in Christian ethics, then, should be with the person who is the moral actor; our ethics will need to be a character ethics. Some ethical theories have said that a good act requires four components to be truly good. It must aim at a good end, utilize a good means, and be performed by a good person with a good motive. The focus upon the good person fits very well with our understanding of the Christian life. For in Christianity general qualities such as humility and unselfishness are essential, and believers are urged to pursue them diligently. Furthermore, evangelical Christianity emphasizes transformation of the individual—in God's regenerating and sanctifying grace we have a major resource for developing and enacting a worthy ethic of ecology.

10. Lawrence Kohlberg, *The Psychology of Moral Development: The Nature and Validity of Moral Stages* (San Francisco: Harper and Row, 1984).

Part 3

Evangelicalism and the Person of Christ

5

Contemporary
Evangelical Christology

A significant feature of contemporary Christology is the resurgence of vital evangelical Christology, which looks to the Scriptures for its basic content and maintains the doctrinal tenets established as the official position of the church during its earliest centuries. Crucial to evangelical Christology are the biblical reports that the first believers recognized that Jesus was no ordinary person. The deeds he performed and the

Reprinted from *Review and Expositor* 88.4 (Fall 1991). Used by permission.

quality of his teaching soon led them to statements such as "You are the Christ, the Son of the living God" (Matt. 16:16), "My Lord and my God" (John 20:28), and even Peter's "Go away from me, Lord; I am a sinful man!" (Luke 5:8). They had no doubt that he was a human being, as human as themselves, and yet, despite their Hebrew monotheism, they also believed that he was in some sense fully divine, deserving of their devotion and worship, as was Yahweh.

As the church sought to understand more fully the meaning of its belief in this person Jesus, varying interpretations arose. It was necessary to arrive at some standard by which to measure these various constructions. Consequently, a series of ecumenical councils was called during the fourth and fifth centuries, the Council of Chalcedon (451) formulating the most definitive statement. That formula preserved the genuineness and completeness of both the divine and the human natures, their distinctness and yet the unity of the person. Chalcedon became the standard of orthodox belief regarding the person of Christ.

This belief in the full deity and full humanity of Jesus is essential to evangelicalism and its overall doctrinal scheme. Evangelicalism is, at its core, a view of the nature of salvation. According to evangelicalism, salvation involves regeneration, a supernatural transformation based upon Jesus Christ's atoning death and received simply by an exercise of faith in him. This view of salvation presupposes a number of other doctrines, including the sinfulness of all human beings and the penal-substitutionary nature of the atonement. That view of the work of Christ in turn depends upon the orthodox understanding of his person: he was full humanity and full deity united in one person. Thus, just as the church in its first centuries sought to enunciate clearly the doctrine of incarnation in order to preserve the experience of new life that it had found through Christ, so evangelicalism in more recent years has sought to maintain that orthodox doctrine of incarnation it considers indispensable to the new life which it has experienced.

Much of the recent contribution to evangelical Christology has been from biblical (specifically New Testament) theologians. Among them, I. Howard Marshall and R. T. France have been especially significant.[1] Though not as clearly identified with the evangelical movement, C. F. D. Moule has been influential in much evangelical New Testament scholarship.[2] There has also been a flowering of christological work

1. I. Howard Marshall, *I Believe in the Historical Jesus* (Grand Rapids: Eerdmans, 1977); idem, *The Origins of New Testament Christology* (Downers Grove, Ill.: Inter-Varsity, 1977); R. T. France, *The Evidence for Jesus* (Downers Grove, Ill.: Inter-Varsity, 1986).

2. C. F. D. Moule, *The Origin of Christology* (Cambridge: Cambridge University Press, 1977).

among evangelical systematic theologians, including Bernard Ramm and H. D. McDonald.[3]

Problems for Contemporary Evangelical Christology

While seeking to preserve the theological values that the Chalcedonian fathers prized in their day, contemporary evangelicalism faces problems that incarnational Christology did not face in earlier times. Evangelical Christology recognizes that it must respond to these problems if it is to be viable.

The Historical Problem

The first major contemporary problem which was not an issue for Chalcedon is in the area of biblical studies. The rise of historical criticism, especially of the Gospels, has made Christology more difficult. To the extent that the construction of Christology depends upon the Gospels' reports and interpretations of Jesus' sayings and deeds, biblical criticism raises troublesome questions. Much biblical study questions whether the Gospels report Jesus' actual statements and deeds, the tradition about him which arose in the church, or the theological interpretations of the Gospel writers.[4] Evangelicalism has insisted upon an objective Christology that is built on what Jesus actually was, did, and said, rather than on what was believed or taught about him. It therefore has a vital stake in the accuracy and dependability of the Gospel accounts.

The Exegetical Problem

A second problem is of a more exegetical nature: does the Bible actually teach the doctrine of incarnation? The discussion has focused especially upon the issue of the deity of Jesus. This in turn has taken two forms. First is the question whether Jesus actually thought of himself as divine. The question arises because Jesus never made such a claim, at least not in explicit fashion. If he really was divine, ought he not to have made some bold claims to that effect? Second is the matter of the biblical writers' witness to the deity of Christ. Here the case is also not as

---

3. H. D. McDonald, *Jesus—Human and Divine: An Introduction to New Testament Christology* (Washington, D.C.: University Press of America, 1989); Bernard L. Ramm, *An Evangelical Christology: Ecumenic and Historic* (Nashville: Thomas Nelson, 1985); Douglas D. Webster, *A Passion for Christ: An Evangelical Christology* (Grand Rapids: Zondervan, 1987). For a detailed treatment of much of the material in this article, see Millard J. Erickson, *The Word Became Flesh: A Contemporary Incarnational Christology* (Grand Rapids: Baker, 1991).

4. E.g., Norman Perrin, *Rediscovering the Teaching of Jesus* (New York: Harper and Row, 1976), p. 15.

clear as might be desired. Some of the texts formerly considered good documentation for the deity of Jesus are no longer thought to be quite so unequivocal. Indeed, the Scriptures contain very few clear references to Jesus' deity. For example, the prologue to John's Gospel, which in the past was often cited as a prime proof text, has come under suspicion; in fact, the entire fourth Gospel is considered unreliable history and theology.[5] The christological passage in Philippians 2 is thought to be based on an ancient hymn of the church and on the theme that Jesus was the second Adam. The point here, then, would not be that he was uniquely in the form of God, but that, like the rest of us, he bore the image of God.[6]

The Metaphysical Problem

Another difficulty is the metaphysical problem, which arises from the fact that the classic formulation at Chalcedon was enunciated in the categories of Greek philosophy (person and nature). The metaphysical objection takes two contrasting forms. On the one hand, some have argued that the Chalcedonian Christology is not true to the biblical witness. The biblical way of thinking is not metaphysical and speculative. The Hebrews simply did not think ontologically. They thought of Jesus functionally, that is, in terms of what he did, rather than metaphysically, that is, in terms of what he was in some ultimate sense.[7] While some hold that the Chalcedonian construction makes explicit what is implicit within the Scriptures, others find it quite incompatible with biblical thought. Both groups of scholars, however, are convinced that metaphysical thinking like that engaged in at Chalcedon is not found in the Bible itself.

The other form of the metaphysical objection looks forward rather than backward from Chalcedon. Instead of arguing that Chalcedon's metaphysical Christology is not found in Scripture, it contends that the Chalcedonian way of thinking is not compatible with contemporary forms of understanding (actually, some scholars present both forms of the metaphysical objection). In particular, this form of the metaphysical objection rejects substance metaphysics in favor of process metaphysics, which contends that the fundamental unit of reality is not substance but event. Change, rather than permanent qualities, is the basic characteristic of reality. Thus, a Christology based upon the understanding that the nature of things is static is unrealistic.[8]

5. An extreme view is that of David F. Strauss, *Life of Jesus, Critically Examined* (New York: Macmillan, 1892).

6. James D. G. Dunn, *Christology in the Making: A New Testament Inquiry into the Origins of the Doctrine of the Incarnation* (Philadelphia: Westminster, 1980), pp. 98–115.

7. Oscar Cullmann, *The Christology of the New Testament* (Philadelphia: Westminster, 1959), pp. 3–4.

8. Norman Pittenger, *The Word Incarnate: A Study of the Doctrine of the Person of Christ* (New York: Harper, 1959), pp. 146–65.

The Logical Problem

Another area of difficulty is the logical problem. This is not a new issue, having plagued Christian theology throughout its history. The issue has become more pointed in the twentieth century, however, with the emphasis upon analysis of language. The problem is not difficult to see: if Jesus was fully God and fully man, there seems to be an internal contradiction. For if he was fully divine, his knowledge, power, and other capabilities were infinite. On the other hand, if he was fully human, his capabilities must have been limited. How could he be both limited and unlimited, finite and infinite, simultaneously? Is this not a clear violation of the law of contradiction?

There is an additional variety of the logical problem, namely, the mythological issue. In describing transcendent reality in the categories of the tangible, experiential realm, it is necessary to utilize expressions which cannot be taken literally. Some of these are mythological in nature. Drawn from the common culture of biblical times, they may be outmoded, contradictory, or both.[9] They may be internally contradictory, or they may contradict truths established on other grounds.

The Anthropological Problem

Another set of issues involves anthropological complications. On the one hand, postmodernism maintains that a major paradigm shift has taken place, so that the older ways of thinking are no longer applicable.[10] While there are variations, the basic premise here is that the referent of a word is not some external, objective reality, but other words.[11] On the other hand there is universalism, which on the basis of data from various religions has called into question the uniqueness of Christ and the exclusiveness of his work.[12]

The Sociological Problem

Finally, there is what might be called the political or sociological problem: the objection by certain subgroups within society that traditional Christology is in some sense discriminatory against them, or that they cannot relate to the traditional picture of Jesus. This objection has come from several sources: Third World liberation theologies, American black theologies, and feminist theologies. Each for its own distinc-

9. Michael Goulder, "The Two Roots of the Christian Myth," in *The Myth of God Incarnate*, ed. John Hick (Philadelphia: Westminster, 1977), pp. 69–74.

10. Mark C. Taylor, *Erring: A Postmodern A/theology* (Chicago: University of Chicago Press, 1984), p. 6.

11. Richard Rorty, *Consequences of Pragmatism: Essays 1972–1980* (Minneapolis: University of Minnesota Press, 1982), p. xxxv.

12. John Hick, *God Has Many Names* (Philadelphia: Westminster, 1982), pp. 13–60.

tive reasons finds difficulty with a Jesus depicted as white, Western, and male. Some object that this depiction supports hierarchy and thus leads to oppression.[13]

Evangelical Responses to the Problems

The Reliability of the Biblical Sources

In an earlier period, critical scholarship regarding the Bible, and especially the four Gospels, was in general rejected by conservative or evangelical Christology and accepted and employed by liberal Christology. Contemporary evangelical Christology, however, attempts to wrestle with the problems of Gospel criticism, maintaining that when purged of antisupernatural presuppositions which predetermine the results, critical biblical scholarship can be used to develop a rather traditional incarnational Christology. Indeed, many evangelical biblical scholars see themselves as more critical than the radical critics, being willing to submit the methodology itself to critical evaluation and modification.[14] They consider the more liberal biblical scholars to be the conservatives or even reactionaries, clinging stubbornly to outmoded assumptions, while they themselves are the progressives, going on to more current views. These evangelicals are not precritical or uncritical in their approach, but postcritical.

The first major point where evangelical New Testament scholars and Christologists have challenged the more liberal thinkers relates to the dating of certain books. The issue is quite important in regard to the reliability of the Gospels, for a relatively long period of time between the occurrence of the events and the writing of the Gospels would have permitted the growth of the tradition posited by form criticism. The trend in New Testament scholarship has been toward an earlier dating of the Gospels, however. One of the most thorough and surprising treatments has come from John A. T. Robinson, whose *Redating the New Testament* represents quite a change of conviction from his earlier writings, such as *Jesus and His Coming*. Noting how thin was the evidence for late dating and how circular was the argumentation, he found that the disturbance of one piece in the picture, the Gospel of John, caused the whole pattern to dissolve.[15] Whereas some scholars had previously dated John as late as the end of the second century, Robinson began to have doubts, partly through recognizing John's dependence upon the Synoptic Gos-

---

13. Mary Daly, *Beyond God the Father: Toward a Philosophy of Women's Liberation* (Boston: Beacon, 1973), pp. 71–78.

14. E.g., France, *Evidence for Jesus*, p. 103.

15. John A. T. Robinson, *Redating the New Testament* (Philadelphia: Westminster, 1976), p. 9.

pels and partly by observing linguistic parallels to the Dead Sea Scrolls. He began to suspect that the book might have been written before the Jewish revolt of 66–70. That, however, would require either dating the Synoptics even earlier or abandoning the generally accepted view that they were written before John.[16]

Robinson considered the absence of any reference to the fall of Jerusalem, which can be accurately dated at A.D. 70 from secular sources, a very significant factor in dating the Gospels.[17] The omission is especially noteworthy in light of form criticism's argument that the Gospel passages often reflect the *Sitz im Leben* of the church. Other considerations are the abrupt ending of the Book of Acts, the presence in the Synoptic Gospels of apocalyptic portions resembling the material found in Paul's letters to the Thessalonians (which are probably among the earliest New Testament writings), and the silence of the Gospels regarding the death of James, the brother of Jesus.[18] Evangelical scholars have been impressed with this argumentation, coming as it does from Robinson, who is not noted for conservative theological views. While the arguments are primarily negative, or arguments from silence, it should be noted that, given the form-critical *Sitz im Leben* principle, there would be no such silences if the Gospels had been written late.

Contemporary evangelical Christology also argues for the reliability of the tradition. Whereas form criticism has attempted to evaluate from the perspective of a different time and culture the possibility of accurate transmission, evangelicals insist that we evaluate the transmission of the tradition within its Jewish milieu.[19] The "Scandinavian School" of Harald Riesenfeld and Birger Gerhardsson has argued that in the Jewish community the rabbi watched over the memorization of the tradition by his pupils, so that what was passed on was, with respect to both content and form, a fixed body of material.[20] This argument has been criticized on the grounds that it draws upon Jewish rabbinic practices of the second century, which, in the aftermath of the Jewish war, were radically different from those of New Testament times. Later German scholarship, most notably Rainer Riesner, has contended, however, that memorization was a regular part of the Jewish culture of New Testa-

16. Ibid., pp. 9–10.
17. Ibid., p. 13.
18. Ibid., p. 107; cf. the earlier volume, John A. T. Robinson, *Jesus and His Coming* (New York: Abingdon, 1958), pp. 105–11.
19. Peter Davids, "The Gospel and Jewish Tradition: Twenty Years After Gerhardsson," in *Gospel Perspectives*, ed. R. T. France and David Wenham, 6 vols. (Sheffield: JSOT, 1980–1986), vol. 1, p. 75.
20. Harald Riesenfeld, *The Gospel Tradition and Its Beginnings: A Study in the Limits of "Formgeschichte"* (London: A. R. Mowbray, 1957); Birger Gerhardsson, *Memory and Manuscript: Oral Tradition and Written Transmission in Rabbinic Judaism and Early Christianity* (Lund: C. W. K. Gleerup, 1961).

ment times, and thus a likely means of accurately preserving a pre-Easter tradition about Jesus.[21]

Further light has been shed by study of some modern cultures that are predominantly oral. While they are removed in time by many centuries, they are in other ways quite close to the biblical situation, certainly more so than are Western societies or other groups frequently appealed to as parallels. The amazing ability of modern peoples to retain and repeat content with great fidelity argues that highly accurate oral transmission of the gospel message was by no means impossible in ancient times.[22]

Another mark of current evangelical Christology is skepticism about the theory of some of the more radical form and redaction critics, such as Rudolf Bultmann and Norman Perrin, that certain "prophets" within the early church delivered messages purportedly from the risen Lord, which the church then incorporated into the tradition as if they had been spoken by Jesus during his earthly ministry.[23] Thus, some of the words attributed to him are not authentic sayings of the historical Jesus. Even some conservative scholars espoused a form of this theory.[24] Most evangelical Christologists today, however, have major doubts that a group of Christian prophets played such a role in biblical times.[25]

On a more positive note, evangelical Christologists argue that the Gospels are reliable reports of what Jesus did and said, and thus they can be used to construct an accurate picture of the historical Jesus. In making their argument, evangelicals have adopted their own versions of the criteria used by form critics to evaluate whether the claimed sayings of Jesus are authentic. They have tended to be quite skeptical about the

21. Rainer Riesner, "Jüdische Elementarbildung und Evangelienüberlieferung," in *Gospel Perspectives,* ed. France and Wenham, vol. 1, pp. 211–20; a much more detailed argument is presented in his dissertation, *Jesus als Lehrer: Eine Untersuchung zum Ursprung der Evangelien-Überlieferung* (Tübingen: J. C. B. Mohr [Paul Siebeck], 1984), and summarized on pp. 499–502.

22. Albert B. Lord, *The Singer of Tales* (Cambridge, Mass.: Harvard University Press, 1960), p. 123; Jan Vansina, *Oral Tradition: A Study in Historical Methodology* (London: Routledge and Kegan Paul, 1965). My former colleague Herbert Klem knows of African tellers of tales who can recite from memory for two days at a time.

23. Rudolf Bultmann, *The History of the Synoptic Tradition,* rev. ed. (New York: Harper and Row, 1976), pp. 127–28; Norman Perrin, *Rediscovering the Teaching of Jesus* (New York: Harper and Row, 1967), p. 15.

24. Gerald Hawthorne, "Christian Prophecy and the Sayings of Jesus: Evidence of and Criteria for," *Society of Biblical Literature 1975 Seminar Papers,* 2 vols. (Missoula, Mont.: Scholars, 1975), vol. 2, pp. 105–29; Ralph P. Martin, *New Testament Foundations: A Guide for Christian Students,* vol. 1, *The Four Gospels* (Grand Rapids: Eerdmans, 1975), p. 159; E. Earle Ellis, *Prophecy and Hermeneutic in Early Christianity: New Testament Essays* (Grand Rapids: Eerdmans, 1978).

25. David E. Aune, *Prophecy in Early Christianity and the Ancient Mediterranean World* (Grand Rapids: Eerdmans, 1983), p. 245; David Hill, "On the Evidence for the Creative Role of Christian Prophets," *New Testament Studies* 20.3 (April 1974): 272.

utility of the principle most highly touted by Bultmann and Perrin, the criterion of dissimilarity or discontinuity (a statement attributed to Jesus can be considered authentic if it differs significantly from anything that can be found in Judaism or in the early church), particularly if it is the sole principle employed.[26] More positive is the evangelicals' use of the criteria of multiple attestation or multiple forms. The former comes into play when more than one source essentially agree, and especially when their literary independence from one another can be demonstrated; in such a situation there is a fair degree of certainty that the sayings attributed to Jesus are authentic. The latter comes into play when the same saying or motif appears in different classes of Gospel material, as identified by the form critic. The criterion of multiple forms is more difficult to apply than the criterion of multiple attestation, but is a valuable supplement to it.[27]

Other criteria also are utilized. According to the criterion of a Palestinian environment, a saying of Jesus that includes an Aramaic expression is probably authentic. This must be used with a degree of tentativeness, since such an expression might not necessarily go back to Jesus, but to anyone familiar with Aramaic.[28] The criterion of unintentionality applies in those passages of the Bible where it is apparent that something which the church did not intend to emphasize nonetheless shines through.[29] Even more striking are those texts where what is reported does not forward the cause of the church, and may even hinder it.[30] Such references are doubtless authentic. Finally, there is the criterion of causal effect, a special application to history of the principle of sufficient reason. This is the idea that there must have been a cause sufficient in effect to account for the presence of each item within the tradition.[31]

Utilizing all of these criteria, contemporary evangelical Christology maintains that there is demonstrably authentic and reliable material in the Gospels. To reach this conclusion, it is not necessary to resort to the doctrine of divine inspiration of the Scriptures, although evangelicals certainly subscribe to this belief. Nor is it necessary to demonstrate the authenticity of every word ascribed to Jesus. On the basis of the foregoing considerations, it is possible to construct, with a reasonable de-

26. Marshall, *I Believe*, pp. 201–2.

27. Robert Stein, "The 'Criteria' for Authenticity," in *Gospel Perspectives*, ed. France and Wenham, vol. 1, pp. 232–33.

28. Craig Blomberg, *The Historical Reliability of the Gospels* (Downers Grove, Ill.: Inter-Varsity, 1987), p. 247.

29. Marshall, *I Believe*, pp. 205–6.

30. C. F. D. Moule, *The Phenomenon of the New Testament* (Naperville, Ill.: Allenson, 1967), pp. 63, 65.

31. Marshall, *I Believe*, pp. 207–11.

gree of probability, a picture of Jesus that enables us to know who and what he was; indeed, there is enough reliable evidence for us to construct an incarnational Christology.[32]

Special questions have arisen in relation to the Gospel of John. Traditionally, this book was used extensively to construct Christology, for it is the most theological of the Gospels, and focuses especially upon the person of Jesus. Later, however, it fell into considerable disrepute as a historical source. Because of the obvious theological interest of the author and the marked topographical and chronological differences from the Synoptics, it was regarded not as a witness to the Jesus of history, but only to the Christ of faith. Indeed, it was not even referred to as John's Gospel, but rather as the fourth Gospel, a term that Robinson considered an affectation since the Synoptics are not usually referred to by number.[33] That the Gospel of John was not to be relied upon in attempting to construct a Christology became something of a new consensus, a critical orthodoxy so widely held that Robinson referred to it as the traditional view or the "old look."[34]

Over a period of time, however, the question of the historicity of this book was raised anew. One of the first to reopen the subject was C. H. Dodd in 1963.[35] Robinson spoke of straws in the wind, then added quite a number of straws himself.[36] One component in the consensus was the idea that John was dependent upon the Synoptic Gospels. It appears likely, however, according to many current evangelical Christologists, that John's Gospel rests upon a tradition independent of and in many cases more primitive than that of the Synoptic Gospels. The burden of proof has now shifted: it is presumed by many scholars that John, unless proven otherwise, is independent of the Synoptics.

But even if the Gospel of John is not dependent upon the Synoptics, we still expect it to complement, and certainly not contradict, them. The differences between John and the other accounts are well known, however: its selection of material, theological distinctiveness, chronology, historical references, and style. Today's evangelicals insist, however, that no individual area of difference, nor any combination of them,

32. R. T. France, "The Authenticity of the Sayings of Jesus," in *History, Criticism and Faith*, ed. Colin Brown (Downers Grove, Ill.: Inter-Varsity, 1976), pp. 101–43; Stein, "'Criteria' for Authenticity," pp. 225–53.

33. John A. T. Robinson, *Can We Trust the New Testament?* (Grand Rapids: Eerdmans, 1977), p. 26.

34. John A. T. Robinson, *Twelve New Testament Studies* (Naperville, Ill.: Allenson, 1962), pp. 94–106.

35. C. H. Dodd, *Historical Tradition in the Fourth Gospel* (Cambridge: Cambridge University Press, 1963).

36. Robinson, *Twelve New Testament Studies*, p. 94.

presents an insuperable difficulty. Indeed, the chronology of John is in many ways easier to defend than that of the Synoptics.[37]

Not only are the contradictions between John and the Synoptics not as severe as formerly believed, but there are positive indications of the historicity of John's Gospel. It was once believed that John reflects a Hellenistic influence far removed not only geographically, but also conceptually, from the simple world of Galilean fishermen and even pre–Jewish war Palestinian Judaism. That view has been breaking down, however, because of a number of factors and particularly the discovery of the Dead Sea Scrolls. There are definite parallels not only of terminology, but also of ideas.[38] In addition, there have been some archaeological confirmations of John's geographical and topographical references, which are more numerous and specific than those in the Synoptic Gospels. Some of these details would likely not appear in the text if the writer had not been an eyewitness.[39] Thus even the most controversial of the Gospels is clearly a reliable testimony to Jesus.

The New Testament Teaching Regarding the Deity of Jesus

Beyond the question of the utility of the Gospel materials as sources of knowledge of the historical Jesus is the issue of whether the New Testament actually teaches the deity of Jesus. Contemporary evangelicals consider the deity, not the humanity, to be the disputed issue which must be argued. This is not to say that they are not firmly committed to the full humanity of Jesus, but simply that they do not find that issue to be under attack in our day. Docetism is not a very live theoretical option, although some, especially laypersons, may in practice be inclined to it in certain ways.

The question of the New Testament teaching about Jesus' deity is twofold: Did Jesus actually believe in his own deity? Did the New Testament writers clearly affirm the deity of Jesus? Evangelical Christologists do not claim that Jesus ever affirmed his deity in an overt or explicit fashion. They do, however, find implicit claims. One of them is Jesus' use of the expression *Amen* in connection with his sayings. This term was commonly used in the Old Testament by both the individual and the community as a response indicating that a particular prayer or portion of the divine Word was valid and binding upon them. What is unique about Jesus' use of the expression is that he inserted it

37. Blomberg, *Historical Reliability*, p. 169.
38. Leon Morris, *Studies in the Fourth Gospel* (Grand Rapids: Eerdmans, 1969), p. 330.
39. Ibid., pp. 139–214; John A. T. Robinson, *The Priority of John* (London: SCM, 1985), p. 53.

before his own statements. This was an implicit claim that his words were valid and authoritative simply because they were his words.[40]

A second implicit claim to deity is Jesus' use of the expression *Abba* in addressing the Father. This Aramaic term, used within intimate family relationships, has no parallels in the terms used in Jewish prayers for addressing God. An authentic word of Jesus, it expresses his intimate relationship with the Father, into which he also led his followers (see Rom. 8:15; Gal. 4:6). I. Howard Marshall concludes that "in these two words *amen* and *abba* we have indirect indications of Jesus' consciousness of his unique position."[41]

A third consideration is Jesus' use of the expression *Egō de legō* ("But *I* say"). Here Jesus was in effect claiming to set himself over against the law of Moses, distinguishing himself from the rabbis, whose only authority derived from their exposition of Moses. Jesus was claiming to know the will of God which underlay the law and thus to give its true meaning. He did not cite any prophetic inspiration. He appeared to be speaking on his own authority. Here Marshall comments, "He thus spoke as if he were God."[42]

Also noteworthy is Jesus' attitude toward teachers and authorities that might come after him. Whereas none of the prophets, including John the Baptist, regarded himself as the final or supreme authority, Jesus apparently did not expect his words to be supplanted, or even supplemented or interpreted.[43]

Jesus also seemed to have an understanding of himself as acting in the place of God. This is seen both in his forgiveness of sins and in his eating with sinners (which was an implicit acceptance rather than condemnation of sinners). Moreover, his teaching on the kingdom of God pictures his own role in a rather presumptuous way. He is not only the judge but the king. These are strong indications that he thought of himself as equal with God.[44] Such considerations are not unique to contemporary evangelicalism; they have long been used as arguments for Jesus' deity. What is distinctive here is the evangelicals' cognizance of the critical issues involved with the passages cited.

Another implicit claim to deity is found in Jesus' application of the Old Testament to himself. R. T. France has pointed out that Jesus repeatedly applied to himself Old Testament statements about God. The reference to his mission to seek and save the lost (Luke 19:10; cf. Ezek. 34:16, 22), the application to John the Baptist of the prophecies of Malachi

40. Marshall, *Origins,* pp. 58–59 n. 9.
41. Ibid., p. 46.
42. Ibid., pp. 49–50.
43. Ibid., p. 51.
44. Ibid., p. 50.

(3:1; 4:5–6) regarding a messenger who would serve as the forerunner of God's coming in judgment, the characterization of his own words as permanent and indestructible (Mark 13:31; cf. Isa. 40:8)—all indicate that Jesus thought of himself as the one whom the Old Testament spoke of as God. What is most impressive about these claims is that they were not part of "a crusade by Jesus to establish his claim to special status, but rather an assumption of a special relationship with God which does not need to be defended."[45] This so pervades Jesus' teaching and activity that it could be expunged only by a critical approach specifically designed to exclude all such claims, and even then the task would be difficult.

Closely related to Jesus' application of Old Testament statements to himself are instances in which he actually assumes roles assigned by the Old Testament to Yahweh. France identifies a total of thirteen such passages, which he classifies as nonpredictive, messianic, and predictive of the coming and judgment of Yahweh. He contends that Jesus did not claim simply to be doing the work of God, but to be one with the Father.[46]

One other major area which current evangelical Christologists believe bears witness to Jesus' self-understanding as divine is his parables. Philip Payne has done extensive work in this field. He notes two unique features of Jesus' parabolic teaching. One is the references to himself, a practice without parallel in the rabbinic parabolic teaching. The other is the fact that in the vast majority of the parables Jesus depicts himself through images which in the Old Testament refer to God. Payne finds ten such images in twenty New Testament parables, including the images of the sower, the shepherd, and the bridegroom.[47]

Having examined Jesus' self-understanding, we must now investigate whether the New Testament authors confirm it. In other words, do they support his implicit claims to deity?[48] Contemporary evangelicals point out that three categories of texts in the New Testament bear upon this issue. Some passages seem to deny the deity of Christ, for example, his reply in Mark 10:18, "Why do you call me good? . . . No one is good—except God alone," and his plea on the cross, "My God, my God, why have you forsaken me?" (Matt. 27:46; Mark 15:34). Coming from Jesus himself, these statements may not bear directly on the issue at hand. Paul, however, in a number of passages (1 Cor. 8:6; 12:4–6;

45. R. T. France, "The Uniqueness of Christ," *Churchman* 95.3 (1981): 207.
46. R. T. France, *Jesus and the Old Testament: His Application of Old Testament Passages to Himself and His Mission* (Downers Grove, Ill.: Inter-Varsity, 1971), p. 151.
47. Philip B. Payne, "Jesus' Implicit Claim to Deity in His Parables," *Trinity Journal*, n.s. 2.1 (Spring 1981): 3–23.
48. France, "Uniqueness," pp. 204–5.

Eph. 1:17; 4:4–6; 1 Tim. 2:5) appears to draw a distinction between God the Father and the Lord Jesus. Contemporary evangelicals affirm the traditional position that, given the trinitarian view, these texts do not argue against the deity of Christ.[49]

A second set of texts is ambiguous about the deity of Jesus. The uncertainty is of two types: textual (how the Greek text should read) and syntactical (how it should be translated). There are three instances of the former (John 1:18; Acts 20:28; Gal. 2:20) and six instances of the latter (Rom. 9:5; Col. 2:2; 2 Thess. 1:12; Titus 2:13; 2 Pet. 1:1; 1 John 5:20). While we cannot discuss these passages here, many evangelicals are convinced by arguments like those of Raymond Brown, who holds that John 1:18; Romans 9:5; Titus 2:13; 2 Peter 1:1; and 1 John 5:20 probably call Jesus God.[50]

In addition to the probable instances, there are three passages where Jesus is quite clearly referred to as God—John 1:1; 20:28; and Hebrews 1:8–9. It should probably be noted, however, that with the exception of Romans 9:5, these texts are found in the later books of the New Testament. In light of this, some have argued that the claim of the deity of Jesus was a relatively late phenomenon, arising as a result of the influence of Hellenism upon the Christian tradition. Wilhelm Bousset was one of the first to propose this theory. More recently, Ferdinand Hahn, a pupil of Günther Bornkamm's, elaborated and advanced the theory considerably. On the basis of changes he saw in the meaning of the titles of Jesus, Hahn posited three stages between Jesus and Paul: the Palestinian Jewish church, which was Aramaic-speaking and centered in Jerusalem; the Hellenistic Jewish church, which spoke Greek, used the Septuagint, and was more open to Hellenistic ideas; and the Hellenistic Gentile church, which was predominantly Gentile, definitely Greek-speaking, and more influenced by pagan concepts. The idea of the deity of Jesus is a reflection of these pagan concepts.[51]

Contemporary evangelical Christology has made two major responses to the theory of Hellenistic influence on the Christian tradition. One has been to challenge the validity of the three-stage scheme. Marshall has been a leader in this endeavor. He notes that the linguistic and cultural differences between the Palestinian and Hellenistic Jews of the early church were not absolute, so the two groups were not necessarily separated by clear-cut characteristics. In addition, the terms *Hebrew* and *Greek* were used rather loosely. Hellenists were living in

49. E.g., Marshall, *Origins*, pp. 107–8.
50. Raymond E. Brown, *Jesus, God and Man: Modern Biblical Reflections* (Milwaukee: Bruce, 1967), pp. 13–23.
51. Ferdinand Hahn, *The Titles of Jesus in Christology: Their History in Early Christianity* (New York: World, 1969).

Jerusalem and were part of the church from a very early date, so that there may well have been no time when there were no Greek-speaking Christians. And while there were groups with differing views regarding the role of the law and the status of Gentiles, there is no evidence of similar differences in Christology. Marshall believes that the juxtaposition of the two groups from the beginning rules out any stages in christological development.[52]

What, however, of the distinction between Jewish Christianity and Gentile Christianity? Must not this allow for some evolution in Christology? Here the problem is simply the lack of time. Paul wrote his earliest epistles within about twenty years of Christ's death and the events of Pentecost. At most the Gentile mission at Antioch must be dated within fifteen years of the crucifixion; Martin Hengel thinks the time span should be reduced to no more than five years, which simply does not allow for the supposed changes in belief.[53]

Marshall concludes that the three-stage scheme is untenable: not only are the stages too fluid, but the very existence of the third stage is doubtful. The whole theory is a case of circular reasoning in which the facts have been forced into a straitjacket that does not fit.[54] This judgment has been supported by New Testament scholars not identified with the evangelical camp, such as Werner Kümmel and Oscar Cullmann.[55]

The second evangelical response to the hypothesis that the doctrine of Jesus' deity is a Hellenistic import has been to ask whether the doctrine can be found within the tradition at an earlier point. The most significant work done along this line is that of C. F. D. Moule. He distinguishes between what he terms the evolutionary and the developmental views of Christology. The former resembles biological evolution in that mutations occur from which emerge forms radically different from the original; in other words, new species of ideas appear. This is the "history of religions" approach to Christology. In the developmental view, the changes which occur grow naturally out of what was already present in latent form from the beginning. The biological parallel here is the growth of a given member of a species from birth to maturity, not the arising of a new species.[56]

52. Marshall, *Origins*, pp. 37–40.

53. Martin Hengel, "Christologie und Neutestamentliche Chronologie," in *Neues Testament und Geschichte: Historisches Geschehen und Deutung im Neuen Testament. Oscar Cullmann zum 70. Geburtstag,* ed. Heinrich Baltensweiler and Bo Reicke (Zurich: Theologischer; Tübingen: J. C. B. Mohr, 1972), pp. 63–64.

54. Marshall, *Origins,* p. 41.

55. Werner G. Kümmel, *Theology of the New Testament According to Its Major Witnesses* (Nashville: Abingdon, 1974), pp. 105–6, 118–19; Cullmann, *Christology of the New Testament,* p. 323.

56. Moule, *Origin of Christology,* pp. 1–3.

A first consideration in Moule's argument is what he calls "the corporate Christ." Numerous New Testament texts speak of the believer as being "in Christ," a form of expression not used in connection with other (i.e., merely human) leaders. There is, as Moule puts it, a tendency to regard Jesus as a whole, a body, of which we are the parts, the organs.[57] A second consideration is the worship of Jesus by the church. There are indications of a tacit belief in his deity: doxologies that refer to him; prayers directed to him, including the expression *Maranatha* in 1 Corinthians 16:22; and references to him as judge, a role appropriate to deity (these references harmonize with his own teachings).[58] Obviously, the doctrine of Jesus' deity was latent in the tradition from the beginning.

One major issue with which evangelicals have shown a willingness and even an eagerness to wrestle in recent years is the question of whether Philippians 2:5–11 teaches a two- or three-stage Christology. Traditionally employed as a major witness to an incarnational Christology, the three-stage interpretation (preexistence, humiliation, exaltation) has been challenged by a number of scholars, including Ernst Lohmeyer and James Dunn.[59] Dunn contends that the particular background of this passage is a Christology incorporating the theme of Jesus as the second Adam. This theme, Dunn argues, was rather widespread in the period before Paul's writing and pervaded Paul's thinking. Dunn also asserts that the term *morphē theou* ("form of God") in verse 6 is to be understood as a synonym of *eikōn theou*. This is not some preexistent possession of the divine nature, but simply the "image of God" borne by Adam, Jesus as the second Adam, and presumably all human beings. Thus no preexistence is involved, and perhaps no deity either.

Present-day evangelical Christology considers Dunn's case flawed. The identification of *morphē* and *eikōn* as synonyms, while plausible, is certainly not probable, and founders upon linguistic data, particularly as drawn from the Septuagint. Furthermore, the word *morphē* must be seen in its context, where there is a positive parallelism with "equality with God" and an adversative parallelism with "form [very nature] of a servant."[60] Thus, evangelical exegetes like Marshall support

57. Moule, *Phenomenon of the New Testament*, pp. 22–25.

58. R. T. France, "The Worship of Jesus: A Neglected Factor in Christological Debate?" in *Christ the Lord: Studies in Christology Presented to Donald Guthrie*, ed. Harold H. Rowdon (Downers Grove, Ill.: Inter-Varsity, 1982), pp. 17–36.

59. Ernst Lohmeyer, *Kyrios Jesus: Eine Untersuchung zu Phil. 2, 5–11*, 2d ed. (Heidelberg: Carl Winter, 1961); Dunn, *Christology in the Making*, pp. 98–117.

60. Paul Feinberg, "The Kenosis and Christology: An Exegetical-Theological Analysis of Phil. 2:6–11," *Trinity Journal*, n.s. 1.1 (Spring 1980): 29; Robert B. Strimple, "Philippians 2:5–11 in Recent Studies: Some Exegetical Conclusions," *Westminster Theological Journal* 41.2 (Spring 1979): 260; D. F. Hudson, "A Further Note on Philippians ii: 6–11," *Expository Times* 77.1 (Oct. 1965): 29.

the traditional interpretation of a three-stage Christology, according to which the preexistent Second Person of the Trinity became incarnate and then in exaltation returned to his former status.[61]

A Metaphysical Basis for Incarnational Christology

We noted earlier the metaphysical problem which the twentieth century has posed for incarnational Christology. One form of the metaphysical objection is the contention by Oscar Cullmann and others that the New Testament does not witness to an ontological deity of Christ, only a functional deity. Contemporary evangelicals such as Marshall, France, and Richard Longenecker reject this contention. They argue that there were underlying conceptions of an ontological nature which preceded the expression thereof. So while the Christology of the earliest Jewish Christians was primarily functional, "it presupposed and carried in substratum ontological commitments." And while there was a development of the concepts of the earliest Christology, that development was "of the nature of explication and not deviation."[62] Thus the relatively ontological nature of Paul's theological writings and the explicitly ontological character of the Christology of the Fathers at the councils and especially at Chalcedon were not something foreign to the first believers' understanding of Jesus, but merely an unfolding of that understanding. A metaphysical development of one's Christology is not only permissible for Christianity today, it is necessary.[63]

Evangelical Christologists, however, have rejected process Christology, which the second form of the metaphysical objection has suggested as a substitute for the substance metaphysics of Chalcedon. They have engaged in extended criticisms of process Christology.[64] They have been less thorough and explicit in constructing a positive alternative metaphysic. In general, their work has shown less of the older Thomistic type of framework, and more of an ideology that falls where some types of idealism and realism overlap.[65] Clearly, these theologians are convinced that what the Chalcedonian fathers were trying to express must be preserved. On the other hand, the Chalcedonian formulation is not adequate and must be replaced by a more contemporary scheme. As they seek to penetrate the obscurity of the concepts, evangelical Chris-

---

61. I. Howard Marshall, "Incarnational Christology in the New Testament," in *Christ the Lord,* ed. Rowdon, p. 6.

62. Richard N. Longenecker, *The Christology of Early Jewish Christianity* (Naperville, Ill.: Allenson, 1970), p. 155.

63. Ibid.; France, "Worship of Jesus."

64. See especially Royce Gordon Gruenler, *The Inexhaustible God: Biblical Faith and the Challenge of Process Theism* (Grand Rapids: Baker, 1983).

65. Bruce A. Demarest and Gordon R. Lewis, *Integrative Theology*, 2 vols. (Grand Rapids: Zondervan, 1987, 1990), vol. 1, pp. 36–37n.

tologists have received some help from philosophers of religion.[66] In general, the emphasis is more upon a metaphysic of subjects (God is the supreme person; we are subordinate created persons) than of substances. In this sense, the new evangelical metaphysic shows considerable affinity with personalistic idealism, but not the type that regards material objects as unreal.[67]

The Logic of the Incarnation

In the modern world, perhaps the greatest difficulty for the doctrine of incarnation is the logical problem connected with the two natures–one person formula. Consequently, a considerable amount of attention has been given to this area of Christology.

One proposed solution, that of Ronald Leigh, is to view the God-man as possessing one nature. Leigh regards the two-natures doctrine as logically contradictory and therefore impossible to maintain rationally.[68] It is preferable to think of Jesus as falling into two classifications, God and man. As a parallel, Leigh offers the chair desk, which has sufficient characteristics of a chair and sufficient characteristics of a desk to justify including it in both classifications. The most appropriate designation for this piece of furniture, however, is neither chair nor desk, but chair desk, a whole new classification. Note that this new classification is not a genuine *tertium quid*. It includes rather than excludes the qualities of the other two classes. There is a consistency between the characteristics which qualify the object as a chair and those which qualify it as a desk.[69]

Leigh maintains that the analogy of the chair desk helps us to see how Jesus Christ is to be understood. It is appropriate to speak of him as God because he possesses the characteristics essential for being called God. Similarly, it is appropriate to speak of him as human, because he possesses all the qualities necessary for inclusion in that classification as well. Yet he is not some *tertium quid* which is neither God nor human. For these two classes overlap to some extent in that humans were created in the image of God. Jesus was "like the Father *in areas essential to deity* but unlike the Father in some areas nonessential to deity, and like fallen man *in areas essential to humanity* but unlike fallen man in some areas nonessential to humanity."[70] Leigh's argument includes the idea

66. E.g., Stephen T. Davis, "Jesus Christ: Savior or Guru?" in *Encountering Jesus: A Debate on Christology*, ed. Stephen T. Davis (Atlanta: John Knox, 1988), pp. 39–59; Thomas V. Morris, *The Logic of God Incarnate* (Ithaca, N.Y.: Cornell University Press, 1986).

67. Erickson, *Word Became Flesh*, ch. 20.

68. Ronald W. Leigh, "Jesus: The One-natured God-Man," *Christian Scholar's Review* 11.2 (1982): 130.

69. Ibid., pp. 131–32.

70. Ibid., p. 135.

that there are some essential differences between the members of the Trinity. For example, not only did Jesus not know the time of his second coming, but there are biblical texts which imply that the Holy Spirit does not either. Thus Jesus' ignorance is not to be attributed to the incarnation, since the Holy Spirit was never incarnate, but rather is one of the essential differences between the Father on the one hand, and the Son and the Holy Spirit on the other.[71]

While Leigh's suggested solution to the problem has not met with widespread acceptance by most evangelicals, some elements of his proposal have been incorporated into other evangelical Christologies. Seeking to retain the concept of two natures, several of these approaches are variations of kenotic Christology.

Classical kenotic Christology held that Christ gave up some or all of the attributes of deity in order to become human. Gottfried Thomasius, for example, maintained that Christ gave up the relational attributes of deity while retaining the immanent attributes. Stephen Davis has proposed a variation which he characterizes as a kenosis of accidental attributes. He draws a distinction between being truly human and being merely human (i.e., being human without being divine), as well as between being truly divine and being divine simpliciter. What happened in the incarnation was that Christ gave up any divine attributes inconsistent with being human, attributes which must then be accidental, while retaining essential divine attributes. Similarly, he did not assume any attributes of humanity that are inconsistent with being divine, these being accidental to humanity, while assuming those attributes that are essential to humanity.[72]

Another variation is kenosis by addition (the usual form of kenoticism is kenosis by subtraction). This variation states that what we ordinarily mean when we discuss humanity is abstract or "mere" humanity, which has certain qualities such as having come into existence at a particular point in time and being contingent. Incarnate humanity, that is, humanity in union with deity, however, has these qualities only latently, so that such a person may have had a preexistence from all eternity, but of course not as a human. We tend to define humanity from our examination of individual cases, and then conclude that what is true of them is essential to human nature. That is not necessarily so, however. Thomas Morris points out that all the human beings whom we have ever encountered live on the earth, but that living on the earth is not essential to being human.[73] Thus, we should not conclude that every quality found among all humans is part of essential humanity.

71. Ibid., p. 136.
72. Davis, "Jesus Christ: Savior or Guru?" pp. 50–51.
73. Morris, *Logic of God Incarnate*, p. 63.

What happened in the incarnation is that Christ added to his deity the attributes of essential (not abstract) humanity.

It should be noted here that our definition of deity, like our definition of humanity, is often worked out quite abstractly, as if we could know what deity is like apart from the revelation in Jesus Christ. In the incarnation some of the qualities of abstract deity (though not of essential deity) became latent. This means, for example, that Jesus continued to possess the omniscience that pertains to God in the abstract, but that it was latent during his time upon earth. His knowledge was in his unconscious, just as much of what we have experienced is in our unconscious much of the time. Before the incarnation he chose so to limit himself that he had access to that infinite knowledge only when the Father made it available to him.[74]

The Uniqueness of Jesus

Two additional problems remain for evangelical Christology. One is the question of the uniqueness of Jesus. A number of theologians, including John Hick and Paul Knitter, have argued that there is nothing especially unique about Jesus.[75] There are definite parallels in other religions and in the leaders of those other religions, so that it does not make sense to claim that he was a unique incarnation of God. The response of evangelicals has been to argue for Jesus' uniqueness, especially upon the basis of the resurrection. Historical evidences are adduced to support this unusual claim and thus to contend that something was true of him which has not been true of any of the other great religious leaders.[76]

The Universality of Jesus as Savior

The final problem is in a sense the reverse of the previous one. It is contended that Jesus cannot be the Savior of all of humanity. If he was incarnate in a particular human person, he cannot be the Savior of humans who do not share the particulars of that individual, for example, women and blacks. One thrust of evangelical Christology has been to

74. Erickson, *Word Became Flesh*, ch. 22.

75. John Hick, *God Has Many Names;* idem, *God and the Universe of Faiths: Essays in the Philosophy of Religion* (New York: St. Martin's, 1973); idem, *Problems of Religious Pluralism* (New York: St. Martin's, 1985); Paul F. Knitter, *No Other Name? A Critical Survey of Christian Attitudes Toward the World Religions* (Maryknoll, N.Y.: Orbis, 1985).

76. Gary R. Habermas, in Gary R. Habermas and Antony Flew, *Did Jesus Rise from the Dead? The Resurrection Debate*, ed. Terry L. Miethe (San Francisco: Harper and Row, 1987); William Lane Craig, *Assessing the New Testament Evidence for the Historicity of the Resurrection of Jesus* (Lewiston, N.Y.: Edwin Mellen, 1989); Robert Stein, "Was the Tomb Really Empty?" *Journal of the Evangelical Theological Society* 20.1 (March 1977): 25–28.

show that Jesus in his own ministry showed special concern for all social classes and races and both genders. He is especially suited to be the Savior of all.[77]

It will be apparent from this chapter that there has been a shift in orientation in many evangelical Christologies. In an earlier period, attention was frequently focused upon the intramural debates, the issues internal to evangelicalism. The prime concern of current evangelical Christologies, on the other hand, has been to recognize the issues posed from outside evangelical Christianity and then to show the rationality of conservative Christology.

It appears that the future is bright for evangelical theology, as it draws upon the resources of a number of disciplines. Excellent biblical scholarship can be expected from the growing number of exegetes and biblical theologians. In addition, the philosophical resources are increasing. The growing number of religious philosophers who are giving attention to the philosophical issues that relate to the incarnation, and the increased number of conservative and evangelical Christians who belong to organizations such as the Society of Christian Philosophers and the American Philosophical Association, promise to supply useful conceptual tools for relevant and competent expression of incarnational Christology not only now but for some time to come.

---

77. Rebecca D. Pentz, "Can Jesus Save Women?" in *Encountering Jesus*, ed. Davis, pp. 77–91.

6

Is Belief in Christ's Lordship Essential?

The most important and most precious Christian beliefs can become the subject of disagreement and debate. At various times in the history of the church different doctrines have come in for extensive and definitive discussion. In the fourth and fifth centuries it was the Trinity and the person of Christ; in the eleventh and twelfth centuries, the atonement; in the sixteenth century, the nature of justification and the doctrine of the church; in the early and middle twentieth century, the doctrine of revelation. In the past decade, the lordship of Christ has been increasingly debated by evangelical theologians. This debate has far-reaching implications for our perspectives on regeneration, assurance of salvation, and sanctification.

I have sometimes wondered, when studying the theological controversies surrounding the ecumenical councils of the fourth and fifth centuries, just how those disputes arose, and what were the dynamics of the interaction between the adherents of opposing viewpoints. The current debate over the role of the lordship of Christ may give us some

Reprinted from *Southwestern Journal of Theology* 33.2 (Spring 1991). Used by permission.

clues. The "free grace" school of thought, represented especially by Zane Hodges, former professor of New Testament at Dallas Theological Seminary, and the "lordship salvation" view, advocated principally by John MacArthur, pastor-teacher of Grace Community Church of Sun Valley, California, have for several years engaged in debate in print.[1] Whereas in the early Middle Ages such disputes were solved by convening an ecumenical council, twentieth-century Protestants instead conduct their debate in print, allowing the reading public to arrive at their conclusions.

Since several Dallas Seminary faculty and alumni have entered the discussion on Hodges's side, and since MacArthur is a graduate of Talbot School of Theology, one might think this to be merely an internal dispute among theologians in the dispensational tradition. It is more than that, however. The issues involved here are of immense importance. At stake is our understanding of the nature of salvation, including the nature of saving faith. This in turn has significant ramifications for evangelism and for our understanding of the Christian life.

We will begin by outlining Hodges's view as found in his *Gospel Under Siege* and in his response to MacArthur, *Absolutely Free*. An outline of MacArthur's thought as found in his *Gospel According to Jesus* will follow. We will then seek to determine the exact issues dividing the two positions and submit those issues to logical analysis. We will conclude with a few suggestions for advancing the discussion.

Exposition of the Doctrinal Dispute

Before presenting the two positions, let us take a moment to note how each side views the other, and what they feel is at stake. To those who emphasize free grace, the issue is the purity of grace. In their understanding, lordship salvation mixes a requirement of works with faith, thus perverting the pure grace of the gospel. In the view of those who hold to lordship salvation, the advocates of free grace are guilty of cheapening the gospel, so that what they offer is not merely free grace, it is cheap grace. It is not difficult to see why each side sees the debate as crucial, and views the teaching of the other with alarm. They believe the very nature of the gospel to be at stake. In addition, both sides feel that Scripture, as well as the historic belief and practice of the church, clearly favors their own view.

I have often pointed out to students the importance of noting what the parties in a dispute say about their own view. Frequently the two

---

1. It should be noted that MacArthur and others who share his view reject the label of "lordship theology"; see John F. MacArthur, *The Gospel According to Jesus* (Grand Rapids: Zondervan, 1988), pp. 28–29 n. 20.

sides' statements of their own view will be very similar to one another, whereas their characterizations of the opposing view will be sharply different. A legalist views a middle-of-the-road position as antinomianism and therefore treats it as if it were more extreme than it is. Similarly, an antinomian looking at a moderate position believes he sees legalism, and ascribes to it all the characteristics thereof. We will need to sift carefully through the charges and countercharges, and then find our own interpretation.

The "Free Grace" View

An abundance of writings sets forth the position of totally free grace, as its adherents like to label it. Most prominent are the several writings of Hodges.[2] Charles Ryrie took a similar stance as early as 1969.[3] Michael Cocoris has contributed to the literature.[4] Bob Wilkin and the Grace Evangelical Society are major advocates of free grace.[5] Several major doctrinal motifs run through all of their writings:

1. *The simplicity of faith.* Faith is the one and only condition requisite for receiving eternal life. This truth is seen in the simple declarations of what salvation involves. John 5:24 says, "He who hears . . . and believes . . . has everlasting life" (NKJV).[6] The words of Paul to the Philippian jailor were similarly uncomplicated: "Believe on the Lord Jesus Christ, and you will be saved" (Acts 16:31 NKJV).[7] There is no mention of repentance, of good works, of commitment to lordship. It is faith, and faith alone. As Hodges comments regarding Jesus' specification for the Samaritan woman:

> Its very lack of complication is part of its grandeur. It is all a matter of giving and receiving and no other conditions are attached. . . . It must be emphasized that there is no call here for surrender, submission, acknowledgement of Christ's Lordship, or anything else of this kind. A gift is being offered to one totally unworthy of God's favor. And to get it, the woman is required to make no spiritual commitment whatsoever. She

---

2. Zane C. Hodges, *The Hungry Inherit* (Chicago: Moody, 1972); idem, *The Gospel Under Siege* (Dallas: Redencion Viva, 1981); idem, "I John," in *The Bible Knowledge Commentary*, ed. John Walvoord and Roy Zuck (Wheaton, Ill.: Victor, 1983); idem, *Grace in Eclipse* (Dallas: Redencion Viva, 1985); idem, *Absolutely Free* (Grand Rapids: Zondervan, 1989).

3. Charles C. Ryrie, *Balancing the Christian Life* (Chicago: Moody, 1969).

4. G. Michael Cocoris, *Lordship Salvation—Is It Biblical?* (Dallas: Redencion Viva, 1983); idem, *Evangelism: A Biblical Approach* (Chicago: Moody, 1984).

5. Bob Wilkin, review of *The Gospel According to Jesus* by John F. MacArthur, *Grace Evangelical Society News* 3 (Oct.–Nov. 1988): 1–2; idem, "Current Issues in Salvific Repentance" (Paper presented at the annual meeting of the Evangelical Theological Society, San Diego, 17 Nov. 1989).

6. Hodges, *Gospel Under Siege*, p. 10.

7. Ibid., p. 13.

is merely invited to ask. It is precisely this impressive fact that distinguishes the true Gospel from all its counterfeits.[8]

This faith is a matter of believing divinely revealed facts.[9] It is appropriation.[10] Citing 1 John 5:1, Hodges says, "Everyone who believes is born of God. . . . *There are no exceptions at all.*"[11] Distinctions between false faith and genuine faith are inappropriate on two counts. First, they violate common sense. In other areas of human experience we do not talk about false faith.[12] Second, they are contrary to biblical teaching. The Bible knows nothing of an intellectual assent that is not genuine salvation. It instead contrasts faith and unbelief, not true and false faith.[13]

2. *The dispensability of repentance to saving faith.* Perhaps the major point of the emphasis upon the simplicity of faith is that it neither requires nor involves repentance. Repentance is not found in Acts 16:31, nor are repentance and surrender implied in the word *believe.*[14] Repentance is essential to fellowship with God, but not to salvation. Hodges's position is clear: "Though genuine repentance *may* precede salvation . . . , it *need not* do so. And because it is not essential to the saving transaction as such, it is in no sense a condition for that transaction. But the fact still remains that God demands repentance from all and He conditions their *fellowship with Him* on that."[15] Hodges thinks it especially significant that John, who was especially concerned to bring his readers to saving knowledge of Christ (John 20:31), makes no mention of repentance as a condition for salvation. Indeed, Hodges goes as far as to say that John *avoids* the doctrine of repentance.[16] Insisting that one must not only believe but also repent is adding to the gospel of pure grace, complicating and perverting that truth.

3. *Separation of the saviorhood and the lordship of Christ.* The school of free grace makes explicit what has been implicit in the preceding two points. To be saved, one needs only to believe in and trust Jesus as Savior. Commitment to Jesus as Lord is not an additional condition for salvation.

Separation of saviorhood and lordship may seem difficult to sustain in light of the references to Jesus as Lord in connection with prescrip-

8. Ibid., p. 14.
9. Hodges, *Absolutely Free,* p. 39.
10. Ibid., p. 40.
11. Ibid., p. 42.
12. Ibid., pp. 27–28.
13. Ibid., p. 30.
14. Ibid., pp. 144–45.
15. Ibid., p. 146.
16. Ibid., p. 147.

tions for salvation. Notable examples are Acts 16:31 and Romans 10:9–10. Seemingly, salvation requires a commitment to obedience, since the word *Lord* means "one having the right to command." Basically the answer given by the advocates of free grace is that the term *Lord* is misunderstood if taken in this fashion. While the word can and does indeed mean "master" in some New Testament usages, it has many other meanings, including "God" (Acts 3:22), "owner" (Luke 19:33), "sir" (John 4:11), "idol" (1 Cor. 8:5), and even "husband" (1 Pet. 3:6).[17] The references to Jesus as Lord should be understood as references to his deity.[18] Thus commitment to Christ's lordship in the sense of obedience to him is not part of the initial experience of salvation.

4. *The permanence of regeneration.* There is a strong emphasis upon the absolute and irreversible character of the change wrought in a believer by regeneration. There is a permanence to the act of saving faith. Hodges says, "The water of life is received *once* and it is possessed *forever.* It is a forever gift!"[19] A transforming work that cannot be lost is accomplished in the individual. Even if one desired to give back the regeneration once received, it cannot be nullified. Hodges's statement here is a strong one: "Nor is there anything I can do about regeneration once I have received it. By that astonishing miracle I am constituted a child of God. Even if I were to decide I did not want to be His child, it would do me no good. My spiritual birth, like my physical one, is irreversible."[20] Once we have become new creatures, once we have been born again, there is nothing that can be done to change that fact. It is permanent and irrevocable.

5. *Distinction between salvation and discipleship.* In many ways the basic concept is the distinction between salvation and discipleship. This thought recurs frequently in the writings of the advocates of free grace. Hodges says, for example, "But no one can understand the New Testament who does not see the obvious difference between the gift of life and being a pupil of Jesus Christ."[21] This distinction is essential to correct interpretation. In other words, it is a hermeneutical (as well as a theological) principle of great significance.

In making this distinction, the school of free grace is not saying that discipleship is not important, nor that it should not be preached. Rather, discipleship is not a condition for salvation and should therefore not be included in evangelistic preaching. Lewis Sperry Chafer

17. Ryrie, *Balancing the Christian Life*, p. 173.
18. Ibid., pp. 174–76; Livingston Blauvelt, Jr., "Does the Bible Teach Lordship Salvation?" *Bibliotheca Sacra* 143 (Jan.–March 1986): 38–41.
19. Hodges, *Absolutely Free*, p. 57.
20. Ibid.
21. Ibid., p. 68.

wrote, "Next to sound doctrine itself, no more important obligation rests on the preacher than that of preaching the lordship of Christ to Christians exclusively, and the saviorhood of Christ to those who are unsaved."[22] Livingston Blauvelt goes as far as to affirm that if we must acknowledge Christ's lordship, no one can ever be saved, since humans in their natural state are incapable of any good works.[23] (Apparently this spiritual blindness or total depravity does not prevent one from taking whatever steps are involved in believing or exercising saving faith, however.) "To require from the unsaved," says Blauvelt, "a dedication to [Christ's] lordship for their salvation is to make imperative what is only voluntary for believers (Rom. 12:1; 1 Pet. 3:15)."[24]

6. *The nonessentiality of works.* The advocates of free grace insist that we exercise great care in understanding the nature, status, and value of works. For the confusion of works with faith, or the requirement of works for salvation, is a perversion of grace and of the very heart of the gospel. One is not required to perform good works in order to be saved. That should be obvious. Hodges insists, "There are no other conditions. There are no hidden clauses or commitments."[25] Not faith and works, but faith alone, is the basis of salvation.

Subtler than the obvious heresy of requiring good works for salvation is the view that truly regenerate persons, because they are regenerate, will certainly perform good works. According to this view, one who claims to be a Christian but does not perform good works either has forfeited eternal life or never possessed it in the first place. Hodges firmly rejects both of these conclusions, saying of James's statement that faith without works is dead (James 2:17), "Whatever James is saying . . . it can be neither of these ideas."[26]

Hodges acknowledges that James "plainly makes works a *condition* for salvation."[27] This should not be understood as a reference to spiritual salvation, however. Rather, it is to be understood first in light of 2:14, where James denies the ability of faith to save one, which in turn must be understood in the light of 1:21–22, where we are told that doing the word can save one's soul. We have naturally tended to understand the reference to saving one's soul as salvation from hell and damnation. But since one of the consequences of sin is death (1:15), the reference is actually to saving one's life in the physical sense. Hodges says, "It is

22. Lewis Sperry Chafer, *Systematic Theology,* 8 vols. (Dallas: Dallas Seminary Press, 1947–1948), vol. 3, p. 387.
23. Blauvelt, "Does the Bible Teach Lordship Salvation?" p. 38.
24. Ibid.
25. Hodges, *Absolutely Free,* p. 202.
26. Hodges, *Gospel Under Siege,* p. 19.
27. Ibid., p. 22.

easy to see how obedience to the Word of God can 'save the life' from the death-dealing outcome of sin."[28]

Lordship salvation, by contrast, makes works the basis for assurance of spiritual salvation. The presence of works is believed to be an evidence of the new birth. First John is understood as pointing out those works that are indices of the Christian life. Hodges argues that such a view has a very unfortunate result: "If good works are really a condition, or an essential fruit, of salvation, the answer to this question [Can I be sure of salvation?] must be: No. At least it must be 'no' until the hour of one's death. For only then will it be seen—if it can even be seen then!—whether the extent of my works as well as my perseverance in them are adequate to justify the conviction that I am saved."[29] Whether good works are regarded as a cocondition with faith or as an inevitable result of faith, there is no true assurance of salvation.[30] The insecurity of wondering whether one displays sufficient good works to be sure of salvation is agonizing and must be avoided.

According to the position of totally free grace, however, it is possible to know that one is saved, and to know it at the moment of salvation. A perfect example is the Philippian jailor. He was simply told to believe. Those who do so will therefore know that they have been saved, just as the jailor. Having made the prescribed response, he knew he was saved and rejoiced in that fact, as Acts 16:34 makes clear.[31]

7. Distinction between salvation and fellowship with God. The question arises: If works are neither a condition nor an essential fruit of salvation, what roles do they perform? Two should be noted. First, they enable us to maintain fellowship with God. Although not a necessity for receiving salvation, works are required for fellowship with God. It should be apparent that salvation and fellowship with God are two different things, just as faith and acceptance of Christ as Master are two different things. Fellowship with God and with Christ involves repentance and appropriate works.[32] Being *in the faith* is not the same as being born again or justified.[33] Rather, being in the faith means "to be operating and acting within the parameters of our Christian conviction and belief, precisely as Paul claims to be doing in the immediately preceding verses [2 Cor. 13:1–4]."[34] While salvation is not conditioned upon repentance and good works, fellowship is: "But the fact still re-

28. Ibid., p. 24.
29. Ibid., p. 9.
30. Ibid., p. 10.
31. Ibid., p. 13.
32. Hodges, *Absolutely Free*, p. 168.
33. Ibid., p. 200.
34. Ibid., p. 201.

mains that God demands repentance from all and He conditions their *fellowship with Him* on that."[35]

There is, as we have indicated, a second role for works. Hodges recognizes what James has said about being justified by works. This, however, must not be understood as justification before God. Rather, it is justification before humans. Works are the means by which the reality of one's salvation is seen by others.[36]

8. *The indefectibility of the believer's salvation.* The strong emphasis upon the dispensability of works leads to the question of whether it is possible to lose one's salvation. Unlike many Calvinists, Hodges and those who share his theology hold that the faith of true believers can grow cold. Yet this does not mean that they lose their salvation. He says, "The simple fact is that the New Testament never takes for granted that believers will see discipleship through to the end. And it never makes this kind of perseverance either a condition or a proof of final salvation from hell."[37] In Luke 7 John the Baptist has clearly come to disbelieve. And warning passages in the Book of Hebrews describe individuals who had become Christians and then had fallen away. What they had fallen away from, however, was the church, not their salvation: "The Epistle to the Hebrews, therefore, is fundamentally concerned with the problem of those who draw back from their Christian commitment and conviction. Those who do so, of course, abandon the church (cf. 10:25). It is therefore the *visible household of faith* from which they secede. They cannot secede from the family of God, however, and precisely for this reason they are subject to God's discipline."[38]

The "Lordship Salvation" View

Like the advocates of free grace, John MacArthur espouses a dispensational view. MacArthur's position, however, seems in some ways closer to classic Reformed or covenant theology. Witness the fact that prominent covenant or nondispensational Calvinists share his view. Among them are James Montgomery Boice, pastor of the Tenth Presbyterian Church of Philadelphia, a thoroughgoing Calvinist in the classical tradition; J. I. Packer, professor of theology at Regent College, a Reformed Anglican; and John Piper, pastor of the Bethlehem Baptist Church of Minneapolis, a strongly Calvinistic Baptist.[39] Each has indicated his strong approval of MacArthur's position, Packer and Boice in

35. Ibid., p. 146.
36. Ibid., pp. 173–74.
37. Ibid., p. 80.
38. Hodges, *Gospel Under Siege,* pp. 75–76.
39. James Montgomery Boice, *Christ's Call to Discipleship* (Chicago: Moody, 1986); J. I. Packer, *Evangelism and the Sovereignty of God* (Chicago: Inter-Varsity, 1961); John Piper, *Desiring God: Meditations of a Christian Hedonist* (Portland: Multnomah, 1986).

forewords to MacArthur's *Gospel According to Jesus,* and Piper in a very favorable review of the book.[40] The adherents of free grace contend that the shift to the view that faith involves an active obedience took place in the Puritan era and is therefore embodied in the Westminster standards and English Calvinism.[41] It is distinguished from the position of free grace by several motifs:

1. *The identity of salvation and discipleship.* MacArthur insists that there is no twofold nature to the Christian life; one is not called first to salvation and then later to discipleship. According to that scheme, one could be a Christian without being a disciple. MacArthur is clear on this point: "The gospel Jesus proclaimed was a call to discipleship, a call to follow Him in submissive obedience, not just a plea to make a decision or pray a prayer."[42] The invitations issued by Jesus specifically involved discipleship and obedience to the Lord. Those who draw a distinction between faith and discipleship discard the intent of virtually every recorded invitation of Jesus.[43] To respond to Jesus' call is to become a disciple; anything less than that is simply unbelief. It is a cheap and meaningless faith, not saving faith.[44]

In MacArthur's understanding of Scripture, any distinction between disciple and believer is artificial. The two words are used synonymously throughout the Book of Acts (e.g., 5:14; 6:1). Further, separating the two by introducing the concept of nominal or carnal Christian is inappropriate. While there are different degrees of spirituality or of sanctification, the idea of a bare Christianity which involves only belief but not commitment is untrue to Scripture.[45]

2. *The necessity of repentance for salvation.* In sharp contrast to the free-grace theology, MacArthur insists that repentance is an indispensable part of conversion. Repentance was paramount in Jesus' preaching. It was the very note on which he began his ministry (Matt. 4:17). Repeatedly he enunciated the need for repentance, sometimes without mentioning faith. Repentance was also the basic theme of John the Baptist, and it was prominent in the early church's preaching as well.[46]

Repentance has several components. It involves a change of mind *and* an alteration of direction. It means a genuine intention to abandon

40. John Piper, "Putting God Back into Faith," review of *The Gospel According to Jesus* by John F. MacArthur, *Standard* 79.2 (Feb. 1989): 54–55.

41. Hodges, *Absolutely Free,* pp. 32–33; Thomas G. Lewellen, "Has Lordship Salvation Been Taught Throughout Church History?" *Bibliotheca Sacra* 147 (Jan.–March 1990): 58.

42. MacArthur, *Gospel According to Jesus,* p. 21.

43. Ibid., p. 30.

44. Ibid., pp. 30–31. Boice, *Christ's Call to Discipleship,* p. 14, identifies this faith with the cheap grace of which Dietrich Bonhoeffer wrote in *The Cost of Discipleship.*

45. MacArthur, *Gospel According to Jesus,* pp. 24–25, 97–98, 196.

46. Ibid., p. 66.

one's sin. It includes intellectual, emotional, and volitional elements. MacArthur says, "As *metanoia* is used in the New Testament, it *always* speaks of a change of purpose, and specifically a turning from sin."[47]

MacArthur is emphatic that repentance, as a critical element of saving faith, is necessary for salvation.[48] Inasmuch as it was an indispensable part of Jesus' message, it should be of ours as well: "No evangelism that omits the message of repentance can properly be called the gospel, for sinners cannot come to Jesus Christ apart from a radical change of heart, mind, and will. That demands a spiritual crisis leading to a complete turnaround and ultimately a wholesale transformation. It is the only kind of conversion Scripture recognizes."[49]

3. *The inseparability of faith and obedience.* MacArthur goes to great lengths to spell out his understanding of true faith. It is not a humanly produced phenomenon; it is a gift of God, and it includes repentance as a critical and indispensable factor.[50] Most significant of all, however, "the faith God begets includes both the volition and the ability to comply with His will (cf. Philippians 2:13). In other words, faith encompasses obedience."[51] MacArthur quotes with approval W. E. Vine's observation that the Greek verbs *peithō* ("obey") and *pisteuō* ("trust") are closely related etymologically, and that the former denotes the obedience produced by the latter.[52] For Paul, faith and obedience were closely related, and sometimes synonymous (Rom. 6:17). The gospel was something to be obeyed (Rom. 10:16; 2 Thess. 1:8). The goal of Paul's ministry was that others come to obey God (Rom. 15:18), and he wrote repeatedly of the obedience of faith (Rom. 1:5; 16:26). In numerous other places in the New Testament, obedience is treated as synonymous with faith: John 3:36; Acts 6:7; Hebrews 5:9; 11:8. MacArthur even quotes Rudolf Bultmann's article in *The Theological Dictionary of the New Testament* to establish the equivalence of belief and obedience.[53]

Having argued that obedience is equivalent to faith, and having earlier claimed that it is a critical part of faith, MacArthur somewhat paradoxically goes on to contend that it is "the inevitable manifestation of true faith."[54] He draws this conclusion from both negative and affirmative statements made by Paul. Paul wrote to Titus of those who profess to know God, but by their disobedience prove their unbelief (Titus

47. Ibid., p. 162.
48. Ibid.
49. Ibid., p. 167.
50. Ibid., pp. 172–73.
51. Ibid., p. 173.
52. Ibid., p. 174.
53. Ibid., pp. 174–75.
54. Ibid., p. 175.

1:16). Positively, he asserted that righteous living is an inevitable by-product of real faith (Rom. 10:10).[55]

4. *Confession of Christ's lordship as a requisite for salvation.* MacArthur strongly objects to separating Christ's lordship from his savior-hood. Contrary to the view that Jesus called upon unbelievers to accept him only as Savior, and presented the call to acknowledge him as Lord to those who already were believers, MacArthur maintains that Jesus frequently made his lordship the crucial issue in his conversations with unbelievers. Everything he said to the rich young ruler demanded recognition of his lordship. He also indicated that the profession of those who called him Lord but did not obey was inauthentic (Matt. 7:21–23; Luke 6:46–49). MacArthur comments, "He made it clear that obedience to divine authority is a prerequisite of entry into the Kingdom. Clearly, His lordship is an integral part of the message of salvation."[56]

A full understanding of the meaning of the word *Lord* is essential. It is certainly true that the word constituted a confession of the deity of Jesus Christ, as the school of free grace insists. It is not restricted to that meaning, however. "Lord" also means sovereign master. Thomas's confession, "My Lord and my God" (John 20:28), would be redundant if "Lord" were simply a synonym for God. Moreover, the context of Romans 10:9, especially verse 12, makes clear that Christ is "Lord of all." To confess him as Lord is therefore to acknowledge and accept him as Lord of all.[57]

It is impossible to separate Jesus' lordship from his saviorhood. He cannot be Savior without being Lord. "Apart from His lordship, every aspect of His saving work is impossible."[58] The very core of the gospel is at issue here:

> When we come to Jesus for salvation, we come to the One who is Lord over all. Any message omitting this truth cannot be called the gospel according to Jesus. It is a crippled message that presents a savior who is not Lord, a redeemer who does not demonstrate authority over sin, a weakened, sickly messiah who cannot command those he rescues. . . .
>
> He is Lord, and those who refuse Him as Lord cannot use Him as Savior.[59]

This insistence that confession of Christ's lordship is essential to salvation should not be interpreted as works righteousness. It is the Holy Spirit who enables one to confess Jesus as Lord. This is therefore no

55. Ibid., pp. 175–76.
56. Ibid., p. 204.
57. Ibid., pp. 207–8.
58. Ibid., p. 209.
59. Ibid., pp. 209–10.

more a meritorious human work than is believing on him. Both are God's sovereign work in the human heart.[60]

5. *The difficulty of salvation.* MacArthur emphasizes that the Christian life is not an easy life, but a demanding and trying experience. He notes the contrast Jesus drew between the narrow and the broad way (Matt. 7:13–14). Jesus used several figures to depict the contrast: two gates, two roads, two destinations (eternal life and destruction), two groups of travelers (the few and the many). Here MacArthur takes issue with many dispensationalists by interpreting the narrow way not as a reference to the law, but to the gospel. He insists that Jesus had in view the difficulty of the way of salvation.[61]

MacArthur also cites Luke 13:23–30, where Jesus is asked whether there will be only a few who are saved. His reply is, "Strive to enter by the narrow door; for many, I tell you, will seek to enter and will not be able" (RSV). MacArthur points out that the word for "strive" here is *agōnizomai*, which implies an agonizing, intense, purposeful struggle. It is used in 1 Corinthians 9:25 of an athlete striving for victory, and in 1 Timothy 6:12 of the Christian fighting the good fight of faith. Salvation is not easy. The gate is small and few find it.[62] Thus the idea of cheap grace must be rejected:

> The message of Jesus cannot be made to accommodate any kind of cheap grace or easy-believism. The kingdom is not for people who want Jesus without any change in their living. It is only for those who seek it with all their hearts, those who agonize to enter. Many who approach the gate turn away upon finding out the cost. Lest someone object that this is a salvation of human effort, remember it is only the enablement of divine grace that empowers a person to pass through the gate. In the brokenness of divinely granted repentance, in the poverty of a divinely wrought humble spirit, God's power becomes the resource.[63]

6. *Works as the assurance of salvation.* In Hodges's thinking, assurance that one is saved does not depend upon the presence of any kind of works, but rests solely upon God's promise that those who believe are saved. MacArthur's understanding is quite different. It is not wrong to question one's salvation. On the contrary, we are encouraged by Scripture to examine our lives to determine if we are in the faith (2 Cor. 13:5). The Bible indicates that the evidence of God's saving work in a life is the fruit that transformed behavior inevitably produces (1 John 3:10). If faith does not result in righteous living, it is dead and cannot save

60. Ibid., p. 209.
61. Ibid., pp. 179–80.
62. Ibid., p. 182.
63. Ibid., p. 183.

(James 2:14–17). "Professing Christians utterly lacking the fruit of true righteousness will find no biblical basis for assurance they are saved (1 John 2:4)."[64] The mark of a true Christian is perseverance to the end. True believers *will* persevere; turning from Christ or apostatizing is definite proof that one never was saved.[65]

The key to this matter of assurance is a correct understanding of the nature of salvation. It is not only justification. It also involves regeneration, sanctification, and ultimately glorification. MacArthur writes: "Salvation is an ongoing process as much as it is a past event. It is the work of God through which we are conformed to the image of His Son (Romans 8:29, cf. Romans 13:11). Genuine assurance comes from seeing the Holy Spirit's transforming work in one's life, not from clinging to the memory of some experience."[66]

Analysis of the Issues

Both the adherents of totally free grace and the adherents of lordship salvation view the other position with alarm, as a perversion of the true gospel. Hodges sees MacArthur as jeopardizing salvation by grace by introducing the requirement of works for true salvation. MacArthur, on the other hand, views Hodges's position not as free grace, but cheap grace, which actually involves a form of antinomianism.

It may be best to note first those points on which the two views agree. The similarities are more numerous than might be thought:

1. Both are concerned that the Christian have assurance of personal salvation, although they have very different ideas about the basis or locus of such assurance.

2. Both desire to preserve the doctrine of salvation by grace. This is most obvious in Hodges's attempt to exclude any connection between salvation and works. It is also found in MacArthur's insistence that the entirety of the Christian's response to Christ—faith and commitment—is a gracious divine gift.

3. Both believe that discipleship and obedience to the Lord are important. MacArthur contends that they are requisite for (initial) salvation. Hodges emphasizes that the believer should move on to commitment and obedience.

What, then, are the underlying issues that have led to dispute? I believe there are three:

1. *The understanding of the concept of conversion.* Does conversion include faith only, or does it also involve repentance, whether as a necessary accompaniment of faith or a part of it? Hodges holds that faith is

64. Ibid., p. 23.
65. Ibid., p. 98.
66. Ibid.

all that is needed, whereas MacArthur insists upon the necessity of repentance as well.

The difficulty appears to stem in part from the fact that the Bible gives different formulas for conversion, different responses to the query, "What must I do to be saved?" Some passages, emphasized by Hodges, specify that faith is necessary for salvation, but make no mention of repentance. Other passages specify repentance, but make no mention of faith. The question is, How are we to interpret and integrate these passages, which ultimately is systematic theology's task? There are various possibilities:

a. We might regard one of the two sets of passages as primary from a hermeneutical standpoint and interpret the other set in that light. This appears to be the technique which Hodges has followed, elevating the passages where only faith is mentioned to a position of normativeness.

b. We might conclude that there are multiple (or at least dual) ways of salvation. One may be saved by faith or by repentance. The method varies with the individual, so that some need to believe and others to repent. Whatever a given individual lacks is what he or she must exercise.

c. We might conclude that both faith and repentance are necessary to salvation. In those biblical passages where only one is mentioned explicitly, the other is implicit. Repentance and faith would then be complementary aspects of a whole—conversion.

The two sets of passages we have in view can be represented symbolically as $F \supset S$ (i.e., "if faith, then salvation") and $R \supset S$. In actuality, the full biblical formula may well be $RF \supset S$. In those cases where one or the other component is implicit, the formula would be $R(F) \supset S$ or $F(R) \supset S$. It would be instructive to investigate whether the immediate context, the person(s) involved, or some other factor can account for the emphasis upon faith in some texts and upon repentance in others. While the limitations of space prohibit that endeavor here, my preliminary conclusion is that there is some support for such a hypothesis. In addition, the suggestion that faith and repentance are complementary (c) appears to offer a more adequate and accurate account of the data, and with fewer biblical and theological problems, than do the other two possibilities (a and b). At least on this point, then, MacArthur's approach is to be preferred.

2. *The basic element of salvation.* The *ordo salutis* of evangelical theology is a rich and manifold picture, involving such aspects as regeneration, justification, sanctification, and glorification. Different theologies emphasize different aspects of this wonderful reality. Thus, for example, Martin Luther emphasized justification whereas John Wesley put considerable emphasis upon sanctification. Where the emphasis is placed is often an indication of the real character of a particular theology. To oversimplify the matter, we might characterize free

grace as stressing justification, and lordship salvation as emphasizing regeneration.

This characterization, however, deserves elaboration. At first sight it seems inaccurate, especially with respect to free grace. As we have seen, Hodges places great confidence in the permanent effect of regeneration. It is an irrevocable change which one cannot reverse by choice and determination. What is significant for our purposes, however, is that regeneration, according to this way of thinking, does not necessarily produce any discernible change in the behavior of the Christian. A person may be a born-again Christian, yet live in ways that are little if at all different from the unbelievers that constitute society. The crucial point is that the person has received a standing of righteousness before God. Thus it appears that what is most constitutive of salvation is justification. This is not to say that discipleship and sanctification are unimportant to Hodges, but that they are not indispensable components of salvation in its irreducible minimum. When repentance is not regarded as an aspect of conversion, the effect of salvation is to add something to, but not necessarily to remove anything from, what the individual was. The result is a change in one's relationship to God, but not necessarily in one's own nature.

MacArthur, on the other hand, makes much of the changed nature of the individual. Because there has been transformation, at least to some degree, there must inevitably be changed behavior, or good works. This is why good works can be the basis of assurance of salvation. To emphasize this change in internal nature, which leads to changes in conduct, is to emphasize regeneration rather than justification.

It is rather striking that both positions make little reference to union with Christ as a component of salvation. There are numerous references in Paul's writings to the believer's being "in Christ" (e.g., 1 Cor. 1:4–5; 15:22; 2 Cor. 5:17; Eph. 1:3–4, 6–8; 2:10; 1 Thess. 4:16) and "with Christ" (e.g., Rom. 6:4; 8:17; Gal. 2:20; Eph. 2:5; Col. 2:20; 3:1). There also are statements about Christ's being in us (Gal. 2:20; Col. 1:27) or with us (Matt. 28:20; John 14:23). Perhaps most significant is Jesus' teaching about the vine and the branches (John 15:1–11), an analogy of the relationship between himself and the believer.

A good case can be made that union with Christ is an inclusive term for the whole of salvation—justification, regeneration, and sanctification are aspects of it. Thus, justification is not an external transfer of righteousness from Christ to the believer, but a matter of our possessing with Christ his righteousness by virtue of being united with him. Similarly, regeneration is not some abstract occurrence that vitalizes us, but Christ's spiritual vitality in and through us, or, as Paul put it in Galatians 2:20, Christ living in us. We also experience the blessing of adoption by the Father (another topic neglected by both camps) through becoming joint heirs with Christ, with whom we suffer and are glorified (Rom. 8:17).

This emphasis upon union with Christ would appear to favor the theology propounded by MacArthur, since it stresses the lordship of Christ and, accordingly, the vitality of the relationship between the believer and Christ. The emphasis on union with Christ also indicates that other aspects of the *ordo salutis*, such as justification and regeneration, are not as separable from one another as Hodges might suggest, since they are part of a whole. Yet it is my contention that both sides have neglected this important and even basic dimension of salvation, resulting in a somewhat depersonalized and formal understanding of the Christian life.

3. *The relationship between faith and works.* Hodges is rightly concerned to avoid any conception that works are necessary to obtain salvation. Where he differs from MacArthur is on the issue of whether works must necessarily follow salvation. MacArthur insists that if there is genuine salvation, there will be works as evidence. If works are absent, the genuineness of one's salvation is in doubt. MacArthur's position is more a case of "if no works, then no salvation," than of "if works, then salvation." There is a significant difference between these two propositions. To Hodges, however, MacArthur's version of the connection between faith and works seems to involve works righteousness as well. In fact, Hodges assumes that any emphasis upon works as proof of salvation implies that works contribute to salvation.

It appears that some additional analysis is in order. What MacArthur is saying is, "If there is salvation, there will be works. If there are no works, there is no salvation." Logically, this could be depicted as follows:

$$S \supset W$$
$$\underline{\sim W}$$
$$\therefore \sim S$$

This is a logically valid conditional argument—denying the consequent (*modus tollens*). Hodges, however, appears to picture the argument differently:

$$S \supset W$$
$$\underline{W}$$
$$\therefore S$$

This, of course, is a fallacy, the fallacy of affirming the consequent. For W to imply S (i.e., for works to imply salvation) would require a different formula:

$$W \supset S$$
$$\underline{W}$$
$$\therefore S$$

This would be a form of salvation by works, or at least partially by works.

It may be helpful to consider as an analogy the statement, "If there is fire, there is smoke." A valid inference would be, "There is no smoke; therefore there is no fire." On the other hand, "There is smoke; therefore there is fire" does not necessarily hold. There could be other reasons for smoke, such as the release of some chemical into the atmosphere.

To be sure, MacArthur does seem to be saying, "Where there are works, there is salvation." This proposition should be considered in the context of inductive logic, however, in which a hypothesis is verified by accumulating many instances of evidence. This procedure, so widely followed in scientific experimentation, is actually an accumulation of many instances of what in a deductive approach to the formula, "Where there is salvation, there are works," would be the fallacy of affirming the consequent. The more instances that are accumulated, the more probable is the hypothesis.

Unfinished Agenda

Sharpening of the Logic

A number of steps should be followed if the dialogue is to progress in a productive fashion. First, an analysis similar to what we have already undertaken in this chapter needs to continue, with more precise definition of terms and closer attention to the syntax and logic of the arguments. Thus far in our analysis, Hodges has come in for the harsher treatment. Problems in argumentation are not restricted to him, however. MacArthur has been ambiguous in his discussion of the relationship of obedience to faith. He seems to alternate between saying that obedience is synonymous with faith, that it is part of faith, and that it is an inevitable accompaniment of faith. Such fluctuations do not contribute to precise understanding. Similarly, he seems to say both that repentance is part of faith and that it is an invariable companion of faith. This also introduces confusion.

One notable feature of Hodges's presentation is a rather heavy reliance upon the use of analogy. Analogy, unless the correspondence of the parts can be conclusively demonstrated, as in an algebraic equation, serves to illustrate or illuminate, not to argue or prove. Thus it helps us understand the meaning of a concept, but does not offer evidence for its truth. The only exceptions are cases where a concept seems to be either incoherent or internally contradictory and therefore untenable, and an analogy can serve to remove the apparent contradiction, thus making the concept at least potentially true. Hodges, however, seems to use analogies as if they count for the truth of the concept or argument being set forth. This part of his presentation needs refinement, to say the very least.

Further, on both sides there needs to be a careful analysis of some of the distinctions drawn, to see whether they are justified or artificial. Herein lie both the strength and the weakness of much dispensational exegesis and theologizing. Close attention to details, careful detection of subtle nuances, is vital, and is both a science and an art. At times, however, a terminological difference is without warrant made the basis of conceptual differences. The old distinction between the kingdom of heaven and the kingdom of God is an example. Hodges's explanation that James's statements about justification by works refer to justification before other human beings appears to be similarly artificial and strained. There are other examples in the writings of both camps that might warrant further scrutiny.

Lowering of the Emotional Tone of the Rhetoric

It is natural, when proponents of opposing positions believe that an essential element of the Christian message is being compromised or even undermined, to picture the difference of opinion in rather dramatic and absolute fashion. This leads to the suggestion that the other position is heresy, and a tendency to depict the opposition in the worst possible light. More-extreme responses are the inevitable result.

It may be that the two sides in this debate should make an effort to see how close to each other they actually are. If their assignment were to come to agreement, if there were some urgent need for agreement, if their lives depended upon doing so, they might find that they are not so far apart as they think. Perhaps if they sat down and questioned one another in an affirming fashion, each camp trying to determine wording that would make its position more acceptable to the other, an agreement might emerge. Consideration of a mediating position might help. For example, Darrell Bock suggests an alternative which, although he is basically a defender of free grace, comes quite close to MacArthur's position.[67] This is not to suggest that either party should compromise

---

67. Darrell L. Bock, "A Review of *The Gospel According to Jesus*," *Bibliotheca Sacra* 146 (Jan.–March 1989): 37–39.

or concede sincerely held convictions, but that each should consider whether they have overreacted, misunderstood the other, or stated their own view in an unnecessarily extreme or unclear and thus misleading fashion. Dialogue is essential because this dispute has the potential for dividing congregations and the entire church of Jesus Christ, perhaps unnecessarily.

Identification of the Requisites for Salvation

Finally, the proponents of totally free grace and of lordship salvation should concentrate on determining what the precise requisites for salvation are and how much of each requisite must be consciously fulfilled. It is one thing to say that one must acknowledge the lordship of Christ. It is another thing to say that one must consciously understand and adhere to it. It is one thing to be unaware, or at least not consciously aware, of the lordship of Christ, and another to be aware of it and reject it. How explicit must one's awareness be? It is quite possible that a great deal is implicit in a belief in Jesus Christ. James Orr has said, "He who with his whole heart believes in Jesus as the Son of God is thereby committed to much else besides."[68] This is an area which has not yet been adequately examined—a factor which may be contributing to the confusion.

We have seen that the issue is sharply debated. It might be tempting to say, "Let's all work together, since we have the same goal of making everyone a full disciple of Christ. It makes little real difference whether that takes place in one step or two." Yet it does make a difference, for if one is taught that repentance and commitment are not necessary for salvation, it may be difficult to get that commitment at a later point. On the other hand, if the demands of discipleship are laid too heavily upon potential converts, some may never take the first step, especially the perfectionists, who often prove to be the most conscientious Christians once they accept Christ. It is therefore important that the debate continue. If it stimulates all of us to more intensive and careful study of the Scriptures and to theological reflection, it will have contributed positively to the life of the church.

68. James Orr, *A Christian View of God and the World* (Grand Rapids: Eerdmans, 1954), p. 4.

Part 4

**Evangelicalism
and Salvation
and the Christian Life**

7

Will Anyone Be Finally Lost?

There are certain views that seem to keep recurring within Christianity. One of them is universalism, the teaching that all will be saved. While all of its manifestations have shown their own unique variations, this ancient doctrine continues to reappear. In our own day there are specially nuanced versions.

The Traditional Exclusivist Position

From the earliest New Testament times there was an exclusive character to the gospel. John the Baptist preached an austere message of repentance, urging his hearers to flee from the coming destruction. Jesus made clear that he was the only way to the Father: "I am the way and the truth and the life. No one comes to the Father except through me" (John 14:6); and "I tell you the truth, unless you eat the flesh of the Son of Man and drink his blood, you have no life in you" (John 6:53). The disciples enunciated the same thought when Jesus asked his little group if they, like the multitudes, were going to leave him. Peter responded on behalf of the Twelve: "Lord, to whom shall we go? You have the words of eternal life. We believe and know that you are the Holy One of God" (John 6:68–69).

This same narrowness or exclusiveness is found in the church's earliest preaching and teaching. Peter declared, "Salvation is found in no one else, for there is no other name under heaven given to men by which we must be saved" (Acts 4:12). Similarly Paul, writing to the Romans, said, "Everyone who calls on the name of the Lord will be saved" (Rom. 10:13). He then went on to ask, "How, then, can they call on the one they have not believed in? And how can they believe in the one of whom they have not heard? And how can they hear without someone preaching to them? And how can they preach unless they are sent?" (vv. 14–15a). In addition, exclusivism seems to be implied in 1 Corinthians 15:21–22; 1 Timothy 2:5; and Hebrews 9:12.

It was not many centuries, however, before departures from exclusivism began to appear. One of the clearest was the doctrine of *apokatastasis* ("restoration") taught by Origen. He saw the threats of hell as only *remedial*, not *retributive*. He maintained that God is indeed a consuming fire, but that what he consumes is not human souls, but the evil therein. There is, to be sure, an anguish which unbelievers experience, but that anguish is working toward God's final purpose. There will be a time, known only to God, when even the enemies of God will be conquered and subjected. What does this subjection involve? Origen states that "the name 'subjection,' by which we are subject to Christ, indicates that the salvation which proceeds from Him belongs to His subjects."[1] So then, the punishment of the wicked will come to an end, and even they will be "restored" to God's favor.

Over the centuries of the history of the church, as its theologians wrestled with such challenges to the exclusiveness of salvation in Jesus Christ, an orthodox consensus formed. This consisted of a general set of tenets:

1. All humans are sinners, by nature and by choice; they are therefore guilty and under divine condemnation.
2. Salvation is only through Christ and his atoning work.
3. In order to obtain the salvation achieved by Christ, one must believe in him; therefore Christians and the church have a responsibility to tell unbelievers the good news about him.
4. The adherents of other faiths, no matter how sincere their belief or how intense their religious activity, are spiritually lost apart from Christ.

1. Origen *De principiis* 1.6.1, in *The Ante-Nicene Fathers*, ed. Alexander Roberts and James Donaldson, 10 vols. (Grand Rapids: Eerdmans, 1979), vol. 4, p. 260.

5. Physical death brings to an end the opportunity to exercise saving faith and accept Jesus Christ. The decisions made in this life are irrevocably fixed at death.

6. At the great final judgment all humans will be separated on the basis of their relationship to Christ during this life. Those who have believed in him will spend eternity in heaven, where they will experience everlasting joy and reward in God's presence. Those who have not accepted Christ will experience hell, a place of unending suffering and separation from God.

Twentieth-Century Pluralism and Inclusivism

The twentieth century has seen some major alterations. One is the position known as pluralism. Its proponents, including John Hick and Paul Knitter, see all religions as valid means of approaching God.[2] They are not contradictory or contrary, but alternative forms of the same basic truths. A number of arguments are cited in support of pluralism, including Christianity's minority status and lack of missionary success vis-à-vis other major religions,[3] the spiritual nature of all religions,[4] the phenomenological similarity of worship experiences worldwide,[5] and cultural relativity, that is, the fact that our religious views and commitments are in large measure determined by where we were born.[6]

Also gaining in popularity in the twentieth century is inclusivism. This is the idea that Christianity is the true religion and the only means of salvation, but that more persons experience the benefits of Christianity than is usually realized. Contemporary Roman Catholicism has exhibited a tendency toward inclusivism. Vatican II, for instance, distinguished degrees of membership in the church, including non-Catholic Christians, who are "linked" to the church, and non-Christian religious persons, who are "related" to the church.[7] Witness also Karl Rahner's concept of "anonymous Christians."[8]

---

2. John Hick, *God Has Many Names* (Philadelphia: Westminster, 1982); idem, *God and the Universe of Faiths: Essays in the Philosophy of Religion* (New York: St. Martin's, 1973); Paul F. Knitter, *No Other Name? A Critical Survey of Christian Attitudes Toward the World Religions* (Maryknoll, N.Y.: Orbis, 1985).

3. Hick, *Many Names*, pp. 60–61; idem, *Universe of Faiths*, p. 138.

4. Hick, *Universe of Faiths*, p. 130; Eugene Hillman, *Many Paths: A Catholic Approach to Religious Pluralism* (Maryknoll, N.Y.: Orbis, 1989), p. x.

5. Hick, *Many Names*, pp. 62–66.

6. Ibid., pp. 31, 61; Hick, *Universe of Faiths*, pp. 100, 122–23, 132.

7. "Dogmatic Constitution on the Church," in *The Documents of Vatican II*, ed. Walter M. Abbott (New York: Herder and Herder, 1966), pp. 30–35, sections 13–16.

8. Karl Rahner, *Theological Investigations*, 20 vols. (Baltimore: Helicon, 1961–1981), vol. 6, pp. 390–98.

Evangelical Developments

We must ask ourselves whether twentieth-century pluralism and inclusivism have affected evangelicalism. Evangelicals do accept the exclusivistic set of tenets developed by orthodoxy over the centuries. There is, however, a tendency within evangelicalism to adopt unconsciously the views and attitudes of the larger culture.[9] Are we perhaps seeing some erosion of the traditional view of the ultimate condition of the lost, and of the exclusion of those who have not made an overt commitment to Christ? To put it another way, can we identify any evangelical parallels to pluralism and inclusivism?

We should begin by noting that there is no evidence of pure universalism among evangelicals. All are agreed that salvation comes only through Jesus Christ's work, so the greatest departure here from traditional exclusivism would be some variety of inclusivism. Further, no one currently identified as an evangelical maintains that everyone who has ever lived will be saved, that is, will come to receive new life and spend eternity in the presence of God. There are, however, some alterations of a few of the tenets of the orthodox view.

General Revelation and Implicit Faith

The first modification of the traditional position has to do with the efficacy of general revelation. A number of evangelical theologians have observed that there seems to be some basis for what they term "implicit faith" as a grounds for salvation. They point out that God has revealed himself to all persons through nature, their inner sense of morality, and his working in general history. These witnesses to God are available to anyone willing to observe and reflect. The content of this revelation is rather general, however. It includes the existence of God, something about his greatness and holiness, and something about his moral expectations and requirements of humans. This is sufficient to enable them, without recourse to special revelation, to come to the realization of God's existence and holiness and their own spiritual and moral inadequacy. It is argued that if they, recognizing their inability to satisfy God's expectations, then throw themselves upon his mercy, they are exercising implicit faith, and God will justify and regenerate them upon the basis of Christ's atoning work, even though they do not consciously identify Jesus as the object of their faith, and may not even have heard the name of Jesus.

Quite a number of evangelical theologians allow for the possibility of

---

9. James Davison Hunter, *Evangelicalism: The Coming Generation* (Chicago: University of Chicago Press, 1987), pp. 46–49.

implicit faith.[10] The next question is how many people really possess it. Here there is a considerable difference of opinion. Most evangelicals who accept the possibility hold that very few actually come to salvation through this channel. One dissenting voice is that of Clark Pinnock, who presents three arguments in support of the concept of implicit faith.

1. One of the axioms of Pinnock's thought is his conviction of the universal salvific will of God. God wants everyone to be saved. His promises are not tribal or restrictive. There is a global reach to the gospel. This axiom opposes "several strong tendencies in historical theology to narrow God's grace down and restrict his redemptive purposes. There are today, for example, large numbers of evangelicals who, in the *extra ecclesiam nulla salus* tradition, seriously maintain and defend the notion that God will send to hell immense numbers of people who never had an opportunity to call upon the name of Jesus."[11] Contrasted with this narrow view is the biblical scenario, which is "expansive and inclusive. It projects an unnumbered host around the throne of God (Rev. 7:9)."[12]

Pinnock begins by examining what Luke has to say in Acts. Although Luke had a strong belief in the finality of Christ, he also had an openness to people of other faiths. A case in point is Cornelius, whose prayers, according to Luke, God heard. Belief in the finality of Christ did not cause Luke to "close himself off from an ability to relate in an open spirit with people of other religions."[13] Pinnock believes that this openness stemmed from two presuppositions which Luke held and the Bible generally holds. First, Luke believed in a divine revelation accessible to all people everywhere. Second, he viewed history as dynamic rather than static; thus people who do not currently believe may in time change their attitude.[14]

The existence of a universal or general revelation means that knowledge of God is not limited to those places where biblical revelation has gone. Pinnock makes much of the "Melchizedek factor." Abraham rec-

10. Augustus Hopkins Strong, *Systematic Theology: A Compendium*, 3 vols. (Old Tappan, N.J.: Fleming H. Revell, 1907), vol. 3, pp. 842–44; J. I. Packer, "'Good Pagans' and God's Kingdom," *Christianity Today* 30.1 (17 Jan. 1986): 22–25; Clark Pinnock, "The Finality of Jesus Christ in a World of Religions," in *Christian Faith and Practice in the Modern World: Theology from an Evangelical Point of View*, ed. Mark A. Noll and David F. Wells (Grand Rapids: Eerdmans, 1988), pp. 152–68; Bruce A. Demarest, *General Revelation: Historical Views and Contemporary Issues* (Grand Rapids: Zondervan, 1982), pp. 253–62; J. N. D. Anderson, *Christianity and World Religions: The Challenge of Pluralism*, rev. ed. (Downers Grove, Ill.: Inter-Varsity, 1984), ch. 5.

11. Clark Pinnock, "Toward an Evangelical Theology of Religions," *Journal of the Evangelical Theological Society* 33.3 (Sept. 1990): 361.

12. Ibid.

13. Pinnock, "Finality," p. 158.

14. Ibid.

ognized that here was a person who really knew God.[15] Pinnock concludes that general revelation is sufficient to elicit saving faith.

Most evangelicals would contend, however, that general revelation is not effective in producing faith and that, consequently, very few (perhaps no one) will be saved without having explicitly heard the gospel of Jesus Christ. Pinnock's characterizations of this contention are not temperate: "a very closed-minded attitude"; "a strong tradition that refuses to grant any gracious element in general revelation"; "reluctant in the extreme to grant more than a glimmer of hope"; "overcautious, even niggardly comments"; "a brittleness, rigidity, and narrowness in the presence of non-Christian people." He concludes, "The tradition that stems from the 'extra ecclesiam nulla salus est' has a great deal to answer for in terms of turning multitudes away from listening to the Good News."[16] In other words, the church's traditional position not only limits the number to be saved to a relative few, but even reduces that number by driving many to reject the unpalatable message. Pointing to the experience of John Hick, Pinnock declares that "what drives people more than anything else into the camp of theological relativism is the impression they have that the God of orthodox theology is harshly exclusive by nature."[17]

By contrast, Pinnock is more optimistic about the effects of general revelation: "For my part I am bold to declare that on the basis of the evidence of the Melchizedek factor I referred to earlier God most certainly does save people in this way. I do not know how many, but I hope for multitudes."[18] At this point he seems to be saying that these people do indeed receive the salvation that God desires and intends for them, but that they are missing the full value of having a conscious personal relationship with Jesus Christ. For he acknowledges shortly thereafter that

> it is possible . . . to let this insight get out of hand. Although it would be reasonable to call Jethro a pre-Christian believer, it would not be accurate or helpful to call him an anonymous Christian. The evidence does not allow us to say that Jethro enjoyed the benefits that are ours from knowing Christ and had no need of ever meeting Christ in a fulfilled relationship. . . . We cannot say anything that would create the impression that there are some who do not need to repent and believe the gospel.[19]

15. Ibid., p. 159.
16. Ibid., pp. 159–61.
17. Pinnock, "Evangelical Theology of Religions," p. 362.
18. Pinnock, "Finality," p. 164.
19. Ibid., pp. 164–65.

We should note briefly the grounds for Pinnock's conclusion. The view that few are saved is repugnant and morally offensive to him: "Basically I am offended by the notion that the God who loves sinners and desires to save them tantalizes them with truth about himself that can only result in their greater condemnation."[20] In other words, the position that general revelation is not efficacious for salvation seems to contradict the fundamental nature of God. Note that the way in which Pinnock has chosen to spell out the traditional position will lead to rather extreme responses. But does it follow that God delights in the condemnation of the wicked? Is it not possible that God does not delight in the condemnation of the wicked, but grieves over it? And is it not possible that God's basic purpose in giving a general revelation of himself is to help us to believe, but that there may also be the effect of increasing the condemnation of some, many, perhaps even most? Note also that those who are less confident than Pinnock that there will be large numbers who come to faith through the general revelation do not necessarily maintain that there will be none, or even just a few. They simply do not feel that they have adequate basis for concluding that a large number will be saved. Finally, note that if Pinnock's objection to the traditional position on the efficacy of general revelation is valid, it also is a valid objection in regard to special revelation, if the number who are saved is relatively few.

A further word on the view of those who are uncertain that many will be saved through the general revelation is in order at this point. Some of them hold that anyone *can* be saved in this manner; nonetheless, they wonder whether many, or perhaps even any, *are*. This distinction is completely overlooked by John Sanders, who says in regard to my own position, "Given Erickson's view on inerrancy, we can safely conclude that if he asserts that Paul says no one is saved in this way, then he believes that there is no possibility at all and that inclusivism must be false."[21] There is a suppressed premise in Sander's argument, namely, "If it does not happen, it cannot happen." This should be stated and argued. Failure to do so leads Sanders to say, inaccurately, "Perhaps it would be best to conclude that Erickson is in fact a restrictivist who merely uses the language of inclusivism."[22]

2. Pinnock's second argument is biblical precedent or, as he puts it, the Melchizedek factor. There is within the biblical revelation evidence of persons who did come to implicit faith. As Pinnock puts it, "God does have regard for faith in him even when it is forced to rely upon de-

---

20. Ibid., p. 160.
21. John Sanders, *No Other Name: An Investigation into the Destiny of the Unevangelized* (Grand Rapids: Eerdmans, 1992), p. 277.
22. Ibid., pp. 277–78.

fective and incomplete information."[23] He believes that such persons as Melchizedek, Jethro, Job, Abimelech, Naaman, and Balaam all had faith in God, although they lived outside the range of God's salvation. Summarizing Pinnock's view, John Sanders says, "Such 'holy pagans' are cited by the author of Hebrews as being the examples of faith we should emulate."[24]

3. Pinnock's third argument is the specific and direct statements of Scripture. He points to indications that a large number of the saved will be gathered in the end. Objecting to "the scenario that consigns the majority to hell and expects the salvation of only a pitiful few," he comments, "The God and Father of our Lord Jesus is far more generous than that, and his promises are much larger than that. Like Jesus we ought to relish the prospect when the multitudes without number will come from east and west, from north and south, and sit at table in the kingdom of God (Luke 13:29). God's promise to save the race requires the redemption of innumerable people."[25] Also pertinent here is a statement from which we quoted earlier: "Whatever the reasons for this narrowing down of the grace of God in the gospel, the Biblical scenario is expansive and inclusive. It projects an unnumbered host around the throne of God (Rev. 7:9)."[26]

A second facet of the biblical testimony is those passages which speak of God's apparent purpose and intention to save the entire race, the most prominent being Titus 2:11 and 1 Timothy 2:4. There also is Luke's openness to Gentiles as well as his statement, "In every nation any one who fears him and does what is right is acceptable to him" (Acts 10:35 RSV).[27] In addition, Pinnock has recently reversed a position he took earlier and now contends that Matthew 25:31–40 teaches that some will be saved who were unaware of serving Christ: "Serving the poor embodies what the love of God himself is, and it is accepted as the equivalent of faith."[28]

What shall we say to Pinnock's use of Scripture to support his view? There are a number of points where I feel reservation.

1. Pinnock has used Scripture selectively. Although the passages which he cites certainly do speak of large numbers, there are other passages which seem to speak of a small number. Among them are Matthew 7:14; Luke 13:23–27; and possibly even 1 Peter 3:20 and Revelation 3:4.

23. Pinnock, "Finality," p. 163.
24. Sanders, *No Other Name*, p. 259.
25. Pinnock, "Evangelical Theology of Religions," p. 367.
26. Ibid., p. 361.
27. Pinnock, "Finality," p. 158.
28. Clark Pinnock, *A Wideness in God's Mercy: The Finality of Jesus Christ in a World of Religions* (Grand Rapids: Zondervan, 1992), p. 165; cf. Pinnock, "Finality," p. 166.

There is, then, genuine basis for skepticism about the number of those who will believe.

2. There also is some inaccuracy in the use of Scripture. It is true that Luke quotes Peter as saying, "I now realize how true it is that God does not show favoritism but accepts men from every nation who fear him and do what is right" (Acts 10:34–35). This remark occurs, however, in the context of Cornelius's hearing and responding to the gospel. It can hardly be used to argue that a person can be saved simply on the basis of the general revelation. Recognizing this problem, Pinnock comments that, like Abraham and Job, Cornelius "was a believer already and not hell bound. True, he needed to become a Christian to receive messianic salvation, including assurance and the Holy Spirit, but not to be saved from hell."[29] This comment is similar to Pinnock's rejection of Rahner's concept of the anonymous Christian, but here appears to be an ad hoc distinction introduced to bolster the theory.

3. There are a number of problems with the Melchizedek factor. One is that we know so little about Melchizedek. We are told nothing about his background prior to the encounter with Abraham. We do not know whether his spirituality came through general revelation or through some special revelation, as seems to be the case with Abraham, whom Pinnock cites as a similar instance. It is very difficult to conclude from this situation that some people who have only the general revelation are saved.

4. While it is possible that large multitudes come to faith through the general revelation, there is no evidence to that effect in the biblical testimony. The Scripture does not tell us that the multitudes without number who sit at table in God's kingdom are there without the aid of special revelation. Isolated cases cannot lead us to conclude that multitudes are saved without it, although hope for the salvation of multitudes can coexist with a virtual absence of evidence.

5. It is difficult to say precisely what belief the general revelation instilled. Was it just a belief in the existence of God, in which case Pinnock should have cited other examples, such as the pharaoh in the time of Joseph (Gen. 41:38) or Darius (Dan. 6:20)? If no more was entailed and one does not hold that belief in the existence of God is salvific in itself, one cannot argue for the salvation of the unevangelized through general revelation.

6. The examples we do encounter in Scripture came into contact with believers who were bearers of the special revelation. What we have here may well be persons who had been brought to belief in the

29. Pinnock, *Wideness*, p. 166.

existence of God through general revelation and then came to greater faith upon being exposed to the special revelation in oral form.

7. There is also a problem with Pinnock's use of the salvation of Jews before the time of Christ to argue for the possible salvation of persons who since the first coming of Christ have come to believe or to have implicit faith through the general revelation alone. Some evangelicals do believe that those individuals who, like the Jews, have the form of the gospel without its content, in other words, who believe that there is a God, that he is holy, and that they are unable to do anything to negate their sins, and who then cast themselves upon his mercy, are saved. There is a difference, however, in the means by which the two groups arrive at implicit faith. The Jews had God's special revelation. The other group does not. Whereas the Jews had the law of Moses, the others have only the law written on their hearts (Rom. 2:12–18). The difference in the potential efficacy of these two sources of the knowledge of God leads us to be skeptical that large numbers of the second group will be saved.

8. Finally, Pinnock fails to give an adequate description of implicit faith. He likens his view to that of J. N. D. Anderson. Anderson, however, is quite explicit about the nature of implicit faith. It involves a consciousness of one's sin and a casting of oneself upon the mercy of God.[30] This type of detail does not appear in Pinnock. He speaks only of "trusting God" and similarly vague concepts. One could wish for a bit more elaboration of just what implicit faith involves. Without it, Pinnock almost seems to be saying that believing in the existence of God is sufficient.

Postmortem Evangelism

Pinnock does not rest his case with the idea that those who have not explicitly heard the specially revealed gospel during this life will be judged on the basis of their reaction to the natural light which they had from the general revelation. He supplements this idea with that of postmortem evangelism: those who have not heard the gospel during this life will be given a chance to hear it and to respond following this life. This should not be thought of as a second chance, as some have taught. It is only for those who have not had a first chance. This idea, which appeared in Pinnock's writing as early as 1976, has been amplified and developed in recent years.[31] He presents two basic lines of argument in support of this thesis.

30. Anderson, *Christianity and World Religions,* pp. 148–49, 154.
31. Clark Pinnock, "Why Is Jesus the Only Way?" *Eternity* 27.12 (Dec. 1976): 34.

1. Pinnock begins with a logical argument: "If God desires to save sinners, and if sinners have responded positively to the light they have, then it follows that at some point in the future the opportunity to encounter Christ will present itself."[32] He also points out that Jesus stresses that God's judgments will frequently prove surprising. The surprise is likely to work in favor of those who are marginal, in this case the unevangelized.[33]

There is another aspect of the logical argument. God's universal salvific will, his desire to see everyone saved, implies that he "would not send anyone to hell without first ascertaining what their response would have been to his grace."[34] A postmortem presentation of the gospel will enable God to determine how each person would have responded to the gospel if explicitly presented before death, and to judge on that basis.

2. Suspicious of merely logical arguments, Pinnock requires biblical bases as well, and finds them in 1 Peter 3:19–20 and 4:6. He says of these texts, "It seems plausible to suppose that Peter means that the gospel comes to the dead so that they 'might live in the spirit with God' if they respond to the proclamation they hear."[35] This vindicates and makes effective the universality of Christ's redemptive work. Pinnock agrees with the interpretation of these verses by Wolfhart Pannenberg, C. E. B. Cranfield, and G. R. Beasley-Murray: "In this way Jesus triumphs over Satan by taking away from him even those whom the enemy thought were securely his. This is the meaning of the 'descent into hell.'"[36]

Pinnock acknowledges that these verses in 1 Peter are difficult to understand and that his interpretation is far from exegetically certain.[37] In view of that, some would think it better to remain silent and confess ignorance of God's arrangements with other persons. Evangelicals have tended to deny that a postmortem opportunity is biblical. Pinnock differs: "In my view they are unduly cautious. The fact of God's universal salvific will coupled with several broad hints about the postmortem probation are enough for me to hope for such a thing."[38]

We must now examine and evaluate the concept of postmortem evangelism. There are a number of flaws in the argumentation.

32. Pinnock, "Finality," p. 165.
33. Ibid.
34. Pinnock, *Wideness*, p. 168.
35. Pinnock, "Finality," p. 165.
36. Ibid., p. 166.
37. Ibid.; Clark Pinnock, "Why Is Jesus the Only Way?" p. 34; idem, review of *Jesus: The Death and Resurrection of God* by Donald G. Dawe, *TSF Bulletin* 10.4 (March–April 1987): 35.
38. Pinnock, "Finality," p. 166.

1. We begin with the biblical texts to which Pinnock appeals. He is correct in identifying these passages as problematic, for they are indeed that. However, even if for the sake of argument we were to grant that these verses do indeed teach that Jesus descended into hell during the period between his death and his resurrection, they would still not accomplish what Pinnock wants them to accomplish. They would provide evidence for the salvation only of individuals who had died prior to Christ. They would, in other words, validate the Roman Catholic doctrine of *limbus patrum*. They would not apply to persons who came after Christ and did not hear the gospel during their lifetimes. One would have to supply an additional premise, namely, that what was done for those who died before Christ is in principle offered to all other persons. That, unfortunately, the texts in 1 Peter do not teach.

2. The logical argument also needs to be evaluated. The first aspect of this argument ("If God desires to save sinners, and if sinners have responded positively to the light they have, then it follows that at some point in the future the opportunity to encounter Christ will present itself") reduces to a hypothetical syllogism:

> If God loves sinners, he will provide an opportunity in the future for those who have responded positively to the light they have.
> God loves sinners.
> Therefore, God will provide an opportunity in the future for those who have responded positively to the light they have.

Note, however, that the first premise is suppressed. It is not stated overtly nor argued; it is merely assumed. Therefore the conclusion does not follow, for both premises have not been sustained.

The other aspect of the logical argument (God "would not send anyone to hell without first ascertaining what their response would have been to his grace") implies that God does not know what a person's response would have been. This fits with another of Pinnock's theological tenets, that God is not omniscient.[39] That, however, is a statement that not only cannot be established biblically, but is refuted by Scripture. While a few passages, such as Genesis 22:12, seem to support the idea, they are best understood as anthropomorphisms. They are opposed by numerous texts supporting the doctrine of omniscience (e.g., Ps. 147:5; Prov. 15:3; Matt. 10:29–30; Rom. 11:33; Heb. 4:13). Thus this aspect of the logical argument, while valid, does not yield a true conclusion because it contains a false premise.

39. Clark Pinnock, "God Limits His Knowledge," in *Predestination and Free Will*, ed. David Basinger and Randall Basinger (Downers Grove, Ill.: Inter-Varsity, 1986), pp. 141–62.

3. There is also a lack of clarity regarding the relationship between, on the one hand, the knowledge of God gained through the general revelation and the faith resulting therefrom, and, on the other hand, the postmortem opportunity. If the former leads to genuine knowledge of God and a saving relationship with him, is the latter redundant? and, to reverse the question, If the latter is available, is the former needed? Pinnock's answer to the first question would seem to be the more satisfactory, for his rejection of Rahner's concept of the anonymous Christian suggests that one's relationship with Christ is still incomplete after responding positively to the general revelation, and so there remains a need for hearing the message in its full form.[40] The second question seems more telling. If God gives an opportunity after death, is not the predeath opportunity to respond to the general revelation somewhat redundant, and even undesirable? Since the opportunity to hear the gospel post-mortem would doubtless give a better chance for salvation than would the opportunity to believe only the general revelation, would it not be better not to have the predeath exposure to the general revelation? Providing the general revelation seems to make it likelier that some will reject that light and never get the later opportunity. For only those who have not rejected the general revelation get the postmortem opportunity. Would it not be better to make the postmortem opportunity available to all, rather than excluding those who have not responded positively to the general revelation? If God really desires for every one to be saved, why does he jeopardize that opportunity for some? Should not Pinnock be offended by that notion also? Finally, we should note that he does not explicitly discuss whether some will refuse the gospel at the later opportunity, although presumably that is possible.

Annihilationism

Even with the provisions of general revelation and postmortem evangelism, a problem remains. What is to become of those who do not come to belief through having the gospel preached to them either within this life or after death, or through having obtained some knowledge of God from the general revelation? The traditional doctrine is that hell, endless suffering, will be the punishment for their rebellion and unbelief. This view, however, has come under attack over the years; and now, within evangelical circles, a denial of that doctrine is growing. In its place is annihilationism, the doctrine that the lost are destroyed.

40. Pinnock, "Why Is Jesus the Only Way?" p. 34.

Among evangelicals who espouse annihilationism is John Stott.[41] Stott finds the concept of eternal conscious torment emotionally intolerable, but as an evangelical he understands that the issue cannot be settled on the basis of emotions.[42] There must be biblical and theological evidences, and he finds several:

1. The biblical terminology of killing and destruction in regard to the final destiny of the wicked suggests termination, not perpetuation, of existence.
2. The imagery of fire suggests destruction, not endless suffering.
3. Justice seems to require that there be a finite punishment for finite sin, unless the impenitence continues throughout eternity. Otherwise the "eye for an eye" principle would seem to be violated.
4. Eternal existence for the impenitent would contradict those texts that speak of God's complete victory over evil and the final submission of all things to the Lord (e.g., John 12:32; 1 Cor. 15:28; Eph. 1:10; Phil. 2:10–11; Col. 1:20).

It appears that there will be growing controversy over this issue in evangelical circles, with much of the discussion centering upon the meaning of the biblical terms and concepts. Edward Fudge has written a lengthy treatise on annihilationism, which concentrates largely upon the biblical terminology and imagery.[43] Philip Edgcumbe Hughes has endorsed the view.[44] Some denominations which in other respects are considered evangelical hold to various forms of annihilationism, and debate on this point broke out at the Consultation on Evangelical Affirmations in May 1989.[45]

Pinnock has written on the subject of annihilationism a number of times.[46] The most complete treatment thus far is his article "The Destruction of the Finally Impenitent."[47] His point here is to refute the doctrine of endless suffering in hell, which he finds morally offensive and outrageous.

41. John R. W. Stott, "Judgement and Hell," in David L. Edwards and John R. W. Stott, *Evangelical Essentials: A Liberal-Evangelical Dialogue* (Downers Grove, Ill.: Inter-Varsity, 1988), pp. 312–29.
42. Ibid., pp. 314–15.
43. Edward W. Fudge, *The Fire That Consumes* (Houston: Providential, 1982).
44. Philip Edgcumbe Hughes, *The True Image: Christ as the Origin and Destiny of Man* (Grand Rapids: Eerdmans, 1989), ch. 37.
45. *Christianity Today* 33.9 (16 June 1989): 60, 63.
46. E.g., Clark Pinnock, "Fire, Then Nothing," *Christianity Today* 31.5 (20 March 1987): 40–41.
47. Clark Pinnock, "The Destruction of the Finally Impenitent," *Criswell Theological Review* 4.2 (Spring 1990): 243–59.

A first strategy on Pinnock's part is to relativize the teaching of end-less suffering by placing it in historical context. He notes that all doc-trines undergo a certain amount of development over time, and that the doctrine of hell is no exception. Indeed, it exemplifies this principle well. Like other doctrinal formulations, it reflects historical and cul-tural conditions prevailing when it was developed.[48] In particular, here, as in so many areas of doctrine, it was Augustine who established the church's way of thinking.[49] Just as we do not hesitate to maintain that Augustine's formulation was wrong in a number of other areas, so we should be prepared to be skeptical of his view here as well, to con-sider whether the Christian tradition has gone wrong in this teaching of the endless conscious suffering of the finally impenitent.[50]

Pinnock immediately acknowledges that he does not approach this matter calmly. Indeed, he wonders, "How can anyone with the milk of human kindness in him remain calm contemplating such an idea as this?"[51] He recognizes that his unease plays into the hands of critics like J. I. Packer, who faults those who hold Stott's view for displaying a sort of moral superiority, when they may actually be driven by secular sentimentality rather than spiritual sensitivity. But, asks Pinnock, if sentimentality drives Stott, what drives his opponent? Hardhearted-ness and the desire for eternal retribution?[52] Pinnock is quick to say that he considers the concept of hell as endless torment of body and mind "an outrageous doctrine, a theological and moral enormity, a bad doctrine of the tradition which needs to be changed."[53] Inflicting this sort of cruel unending punishment is "more nearly like Satan than like God, at least by ordinary moral standards, and by the gospel itself."[54]

Pinnock believes that morally sensitive people will be offended by the teaching of endless torment. His own view is that the finally impen-itent will suffer extinction and annihilation. He sees this idea as a nec-essary bulwark against universalism. For if the traditional view of hell as endless torment is the alternative to universalism, then "universal-ism will become practically irresistible in its appeal to sensitive Christians. . . . If the only options are everlasting torment and univer-salism, then I would expect large numbers of sensitive Christians to choose universalism."[55]

48. Ibid., p. 243.
49. Ibid., p. 244.
50. Ibid., p. 249.
51. Ibid., p. 246.
52. Ibid.
53. Ibid., pp. 246–47.
54. Ibid., p. 247.
55. Pinnock, "Fire, Then Nothing," p. 40.

Although unable to approach the issue calmly, Pinnock does feel able to deal with it rationally. He gives five major reasons why he holds to the doctrine of annihilation:

1. There is a strong biblical witness to the effect that the fate of the finally impenitent is irreversible destruction. This is found even in the Old Testament, in such passages as Psalm 37:2, 9–10, 20, 38, and Malachi 4:1. John the Baptist said that the wicked are like chaff to be thrown into and burned with unquenchable fire (Matt. 3:10, 12). While Jesus' teaching about the afterlife is sketchy, he made similar allusions (Matt. 5:29–30; 13:30, 42, 49–50). He also referred to him who can destroy both body and soul in hell (Matt. 10:28). Paul speaks of such destruction in Romans 1:32; 6:23; 1 Corinthians 3:17; Galatians 6:8; Philippians 1:28; 3:19; and 2 Thessalonians 1:9. Destruction is also spoken of as the end of the wicked in Hebrews 10:39; 2 Peter 2:1, 3, 6; 3:6–7; Jude 7; and Revelation 20:14–15.

Pinnock concludes that there is adequate textual basis for belief in the annihilation or destruction of the wicked. Indeed, he finds this view better supported biblically than is the traditional position of eternal torment: "I think it is outrageous for traditionalists to say that a biblical basis for the destruction of the wicked is lacking. What is in short supply are texts supporting the traditional position."[56]

2. Pinnock believes that the doctrine of hell rests upon the illegitimate introduction of Greek philosophical conceptions into biblical interpretation. Introduction of the Greek belief in the natural immortality of the soul meant that belief in annihilation had to be rejected. If souls are immortal, then we are left either with universalism, the doctrine that all souls will be saved, or with the notion of hell as everlasting torment. Pinnock, however, points to Paul's teachings that God alone has immortality (1 Tim. 6:16) and that he gives everlasting life to humanity by grace (1 Cor. 15:51–57; Phil. 3:20–21; 2 Tim. 1:10).[57]

Some persons who reject hell term their view conditional immortality. Although Pinnock agrees that humans are not inherently immortal, he does not use that term. Conditional immortality is a necessary but not sufficient condition for his view. For while annihilation would be possible given conditional immortality, endless suffering might still occur, if God gave the wicked everlasting life and also condemned them to torment.[58]

3. The idea of everlasting punishment is intolerable. It makes God cruel and merciless, a bloodthirsty monster. It raises the problem of evil

56. Pinnock, "Destruction," p. 252.
57. Ibid., pp. 252–53.
58. Ibid., p. 253.

to impossible dimensions, especially if accompanied by the doctrine of predestination.[59]

In light of its repugnant character, some have attempted to modify the extremity of the idea of eternal torment. One effort was the postmillennial eschatology of Charles Hodge and B. B. Warfield, according to which most persons will be saved; accordingly, not many will go to hell. This is not a very helpful solution because very few today accept the postmillennial view, and because even on these grounds tens of millions would still suffer everlasting torment.[60]

Another approach is to redefine hell, thus reducing the moral problem. One who has done this is C. S. Lewis, who in *The Great Divorce* pictures hell as almost pleasant, although a bit gray. Pinnock rejects these "revisionist" views of hell, which in effect "take the hell out of hell." They emasculate the biblical warnings against hell, and fail to take seriously the Bible's imagery of burning fire. Pinnock prefers to address the traditional view.[61]

4. A further problem centers upon the nature of divine justice. What possible purpose could be served by unending torment? This would amount to pointless suffering without any resultant good. There also is the problem of the disparity between infinite suffering and the finite sins for which it is deemed to be the punishment. Infinite suffering for finite sins is out of keeping with the love of God as revealed in the gospel.[62]

5. Pinnock's final objection to the traditional doctrine of hell is its metaphysical dualism. Heaven and hell go on alongside each other forever. How can this be reconciled with the promises that God is to be all in all (1 Cor. 15:28) and is going to make all things new (Rev. 21:5)?

These are the major arguments which Pinnock advances in favor of his position. He also feels it necessary to explain away those texts which are generally proposed in favor of the traditional position:

1. In Mark 9:48 Jesus says, "Their worm does not die, and the fire is not quenched," imagery taken from Isaiah 66:24. There is, observes Pinnock, no hint of endless torment here. It is the worm that does not die, and the fire that is not quenched. They destroy the wicked rather than torment them eternally.[63]

2. In Matthew 25:46 Jesus says, "They will go away to eternal punishment, but the righteous to eternal life." Pinnock acknowledges that this text can be read as supporting unending torment. He contends,

59. Ibid.
60. Ibid., p. 254.
61. Ibid., pp. 245, 254.
62. Ibid., pp. 254–55.
63. Ibid., p. 256.

however, that Jesus is not defining the nature of eternal death and eternal life in this text. He is simply saying that there are these two destinies. The traditional view would require inserting the term *conscious*. The text, then, explicitly teaches only the finality of the judgment, not its nature.[64]

3. The parable of the rich man and Lazarus (Luke 16:19–31) depicts the rich man suffering torment in the flames. Two considerations nullify the alleged pertinence of this passage to the issue under consideration, however. First, the mention of Abraham's bosom alerts us to the fact that we are here dealing with imagery, not literal description. Second, the story refers to the intermediate state between death and the resurrection, not to the final state of hell. It is therefore irrelevant to our consideration.[65]

4. Two passages in the Book of Revelation speak of Satan, the false prophet, the beast, and certain evildoers as being tormented in fire and brimstone forever (Rev. 14:9–11; 20:10). Pinnock, however, points out that only in the first case are human beings mentioned, and it appears likely that the reference is to the moment of their judgment, not to an everlasting condition, the smoke going up forever being the testimony to their final destruction.[66]

In the light of all of these considerations, Pinnock holds that his view is better supported by Scripture and theology than is the traditional view. Neither side has unambiguous support, nor should we expect to find such, since the Bible is not concerned to deal with the issue as precisely as we might wish. Pinnock finds it amusing that the traditionalists claim that they alone hold to the infallibility of the Bible, as evidenced by their maintaining the tenet of endless torment. In actuality, says Pinnock, their view has very little biblical support.[67]

We must now evaluate annihilationism. We should first note that many, perhaps all, who hold to the traditional doctrine of hell as endless punishment share the anguish felt by Pinnock and Stott. It is doubtful whether anyone who believes in hell as endless suffering rejoices in that thought. It is profoundly disturbing to all sensitive Christians to think of anyone's missing the opportunity of eternal salvation and being endlessly separated from God, whatever the nature of that state, but especially if it involves pain, anguish, and suffering. Nonetheless, there are a number of points at which we must express reservation with the alternative view presented by Pinnock and Stott.

64. Ibid.
65. Ibid.
66. Ibid., p. 257.
67. Ibid.

1. Traditionalists conclude that Scripture teaches the idea of a hell of endless conscious suffering; they consequently must either adjust their feelings to this conclusion or live with the tension between them. On the other hand, Pinnock and Stott are not convinced of this interpretation. Indeed, Pinnock thinks the biblical support for the traditional position is rather flimsy at best. Some of the passages traditionally regarded as teaching the doctrine of hell cannot, however, so easily be dismissed. In particular, the parallel between eternal life and eternal punishment in Matthew 25:46 is problematic. Note that the verse does not speak of eternal death, which could be interpreted as a death from which one would never come to life again. That would be quite compatible with annihilationism. Rather, it is punishment that is eternal. That seems to say that the punishment continues unendingly. A number of scholars of significant standing in New Testament studies have argued for that conclusion. Robert Gundry puts the case well: "The parallel between eternal punishment and eternal life forestalls any weakening of the former."[68]

Another problem is that Pinnock's use of texts referring to destruction assumes that destruction must mean cessation of existence. That hardly follows, however. Scripture speaks of buildings and cities that are destroyed without being utterly obliterated. An example is the destruction of the temple (Matt. 26:61; 27:40). It would therefore seem natural to interpret the references to destruction in the light of Matthew 25:46 rather than vice versa. It appears that Pinnock's use of biblical data may have been rather selective.

2. There also seems to be a breakdown in the logic of the annihilationists. A case in point is their ignoring the parallelism in Matthew 25:46.

In addition, there are logical difficulties with Pinnock's basic argument. Here, as in the case of postmortem evangelism, we find an enthymeme at a crucial point. His argument seems to proceed somewhat as follows:

The Bible teaches the destruction of the unrepentant wicked.
Therefore, the Bible teaches the annihilation of the unrepentant wicked.

He has apparently identified destruction with annihilation. So then, the argument actually takes the form:

68. Robert H. Gundry, *Matthew: A Commentary on His Literary and Theological Art* (Grand Rapids: Eerdmans, 1982), p. 516; see also Murray J. Harris, *Raised Immortal: Resurrection and Immortality in the New Testament* (Grand Rapids: Eerdmans, 1983), pp. 182–84; and even John A. T. Robinson, *In the End, God* (New York: Harper and Row, 1968), p. 131 n. 8.

The Bible teaches the destruction of the unrepentant wicked.
Destruction means annihilation.
Therefore, the Bible teaches the annihilation of the unrepentant wicked.

Note that the second premise has not been established. Unless it is proved, we have here another fallacy, the informal fallacy of begging the question *(petitio principii)*.

3. Pinnock has a tendency to state the opposing position in the most extreme, objectionable, and hence vulnerable fashion. Thus he focuses his attention on the traditional belief rather than on what he sees as attempts to soften the view of hell or, as he puts it, to "take the hell out of hell." We must ask, however, why this must be done. Is it not possible to concentrate instead on the permanent content of the doctrine, thus treating as dispensable the imagery and form absolutized by Augustine and others?[69] The particular tactic of holding one's opponents to an extreme form which many of them explicitly reject seems especially inappropriate.[70]

4. There appears to be in annihilationism a powerful nonobjective factor which leads to logical and exegetical tendentiousness. Pinnock defends passionately his right not to be calm, and Stott essentially does the same thing, although not as emphatically. There is an intimation that one should be emotive about theology, and especially about a subject like the final states.

Pinnock and Stott do make a very important point. Scholars who engage in scientific exegesis or scientific dogmatics sometimes appear almost bored with what they are doing. That most surely is a defective type of scholarship, a point we do not have space to elaborate on at this time. The crucial consideration here is the particular object of one's emotion. It is important to be very passionate about determining the truth and the significance of an issue. It is also important to be passionately concerned about acting on the truth, the conclusion of the argument, once arrived at. Problems occur, however, when one is passionately committed to arriving at a particular outcome. This impedes the quest for truth. It makes one of the possible conclusions more appealing than the others, and thus tends to lead to a biased interpretation of the evidence.

An analogy would be a medical doctor. She should be very passionate about the practice of medicine, so that the surgery or the diagnostic test she is performing, rather than her investments or the tennis match

69. Millard J. Erickson, "Principles, Permanence, and Future Divine Judgment: A Case Study in Theological Method," *Journal of the Evangelical Theological Society* 28.3 (Sept. 1985): 317–25.
70. See Pinnock, "Destruction," p. 248.

she hopes to play afterward, is foremost on her mind. She also should be passionately concerned about the welfare of her patient. During the surgical procedure or the test, however, she must not be so emotionally desirous that the patient not have a malignancy that she fails to see the telltale signs of cancer. That emotion must be brought under the control of reason, or the welfare of the patient will be compromised.

Pinnock's passion, I believe, has prejudiced his treatment of Matthew 25. It also is evident in his characterization of those who feel that the general revelation is not likely to be efficacious for the salvation of many. He leaves the impression that they have it within their capacity to make salvation or at least annihilation available to unsaved persons, but stubbornly refuse to do so. Not only is such caricaturing of an opponent's position in poor taste, it does not contribute to careful definition of terms and issues, and thus does not really advance the cause of truth.

Also to be noted is the way in which Pinnock responds to criticisms of his own position. He speaks of "dirty-tricks tactics" used against annihilationism.[71] In reference to Adrian Rogers's and Robert Morey's interpretations of his view, he asks, "What does this tell us about the condition of evangelical theology that such a distorted evaluation of a fellow evangelical's work would be possible?"[72] He also speaks of "the emotion and stubbornness one encounters around this subject."[73] He psychoanalyzes the motives of his opponents, while objecting emotionally to their treatment of his own view.[74] This is further indication that emotional considerations have colored the rational at this point.

In actuality, the opponents with whom Pinnock interacts do not rejoice in the lostness and everlasting punishment of the wicked. They also grieve at the prospect.[75] But despite their wishes, they find the Bible to teach eternal torment and therefore must find a way to bring their emotions into line with the biblical witness rather than the reverse. For this they should be commended. Their willingness to let the biblical witness overshadow their desires is evidence of its truth. A principle sometimes employed in textual criticism seems applicable here: the more difficult or unlikely reading is probably to be preferred, for it is less likely to be a scribal emendation. Similarly, a conclusion

71. Ibid., p. 249.
72. Ibid., pp. 249–50.
73. Ibid., p. 258.
74. Ibid., pp. 257–58. Sanders (*No Other Name*, p. 136, n. 7) treats Pinnock's critics in similar fashion, charging that one of them engages in innuendo while expressly denying that Pinnock is a universalist.
75. E.g., Harold A. Netland, *Dissonant Voices: Religious Pluralism and the Question of Truth* (Grand Rapids: Eerdmans, 1991), p. 264.

that goes against the scholar's wishes probably rests on strong supporting evidence.

One other sign of emotive factors is the categorical fashion in which Pinnock deals with the issues. The most evident case is his statement regarding postmortem evangelism: "Of one thing we can be certain: God will not abandon in hell those who have not known and therefore have not declined His offer of grace. Though He has not told us the nature of His arrangements, we cannot doubt the existence and goodness of them."[76] A similar tendency appears in his discussion of the final state of the impenitent. One would like to see the carefully qualified statements that often appear in scholarly discussions of difficult subjects, such as "It appears that . . . , " or "The balance of evidence appears to favor . . . , " or "Here is a passage which frankly presents difficulties for the view we are advocating." Such temperate statements appear to be absent from his writing.

5. There is a lack of self-criticism in Pinnock's writing. A most notable example comes in his correct and helpful observation that theological positions are historically conditioned, and that this applies especially in eschatology. What is disappointing is Pinnock's apparent lack of awareness of any historical conditioning of his own view. It is as if the final, nonconditioned position has been reached. Another example appears in his contention that the doctrine of eternal torment is based on the Greek belief in the immortality of the soul. What is missing from the discussion is any evidence of self-interrogation regarding the philosophical basis of annihilationism. Certainly, philosophical influences did not end with the Middle Ages. Failure to ask such questions makes the influence of presuppositions more subtle and thus more effective. It is sometimes suggested that, as a countering factor, more evidence should be required for the position one favors than seems necessary, on the assumption that one's presuppositions will tend to make the supporting evidence more cogent.[77] This type of approach seems absent from Pinnock's work.

The Future of the Issue

Finally, we need to consider where the issue of the destiny of the unevangelized is likely to go in the future. Will we see a move toward a more complete version of universalism, even within evangelicalism? One possibility is that some of the evangelicals mentioned in this chapter may themselves move in that direction. It must be said in the clearest possible terms that Clark Pinnock, John Sanders, and John Stott are not

---

76. Pinnock, "Why Is Jesus the Only Way?" p. 34.
77. Millard J. Erickson, *Christian Theology* (Grand Rapids: Baker, 1986), p. 57.

universalists or even closet universalists or semiuniversalists. The question is, however, whether they or others might move closer to universalism in the future.

One can imagine that Pinnock might move closer to universalism, since he has both adopted positions which he had earlier repudiated and rejected views which he had earlier held.[78] His earlier positions were held as emphatically as are the later. And so, although at present he most emphatically rejects the idea of universalism, it is not unthinkable that he might change his convictions at some future point. This is not intended as an ad hominem argument, but as a basis for speculation. It must be said, however, that, given the force of his apparent conviction, a future move toward universalism seems relatively unlikely.

But what about the next generation of believers, pastors, and theologians? They may enter the intellectual arena less certain of Christ's exclusiveness than are present-day evangelicals. They may extend the logic Pinnock has used in arguing for annihilationism. For example, they might ask, is it not abhorrent that some individuals should simply cease to be for all eternity? How can a good and loving God condemn anyone to extinction? This is, it should be noted, the very type of argument used by universalists to contend for their position. Nels Ferré, for example, in describing a God who would send persons to hell uses terms strikingly similar to those used by Pinnock.[79] Ferré, however, believes that the doctrine of God requires not annihilationism, but the emptying of hell.[80] Probably he would regard the doctrine of annihilation as, to use Pinnock's terminology, "taking the hell out of hell." Thus, with the same major premise ("God, being love, does not want to send anyone to endless punishment"), but with a change in the minor premise, based upon a slightly different assumption (in contrast to Pinnock's premise "If God does not want to send anyone to endless punishment, he must annihilate the impenitent," Ferré submits that "If God does not want to send anyone to endless punishment, he must save all"), and perhaps a more logical inference from the considerations, Ferré comes to a different conclusion. It would not be surprising, given the ways in which some other schools of thought have developed, if the next generation of evangelical theologians, not possessing quite the

78. Compare, for example, the view of biblical infallibility and inerrancy that is espoused in, on the one hand, Clark Pinnock, *Biblical Revelation: The Foundation of Christian Theology* (Chicago: Moody, 1971) and idem, *A Defense of Biblical Infallibility* (Philadelphia: Presbyterian and Reformed, 1967), and in, on the other hand, idem, *The Scripture Principle* (San Francisco: Harper and Row, 1984).

79. Nels F. S. Ferré, *The Christian Understanding of God* (New York: Harper, 1951), p. 228.

80. Nels F. S. Ferré, *Christ and the Christian* (New York: Harper, 1958), p. 247; idem, *Evil and the Christian Faith* (New York: Harper, 1947), p. 118.

same emotional attachment to certain conclusions, were to take Pinnock's position one step further.

A word of caution is in order. It is one thing to speak emphatically about one's sense of injustice and moral outrage over the idea of God's condemning persons to hell. If, however, one is going to describe sending persons to endless punishment as "cruelty and vindictiveness," and a God who would do so as "more nearly like Satan than like God," and "a bloodthirsty monster who maintains an everlasting Auschwitz," he had better be very certain he is correct.[81] For if he is wrong, he is guilty of blasphemy. A wiser course of action would be restraint in one's statements, just in case he might be wrong.

81. See Pinnock, "Destruction," pp. 247, 253.

8

Are Signs and Wonders for Today?

Exposition of the Signs and Wonders Movement
    Basic Tenets
    Analysis
Evaluation of the Movement
    Positive
    Negative

Since about the year 1970, a new charismatic movement has been developing in conservative Christianity. As the third in a series of such movements to develop in the twentieth century, it is sometimes referred to as the "third wave." The first, old-line Pentecostalism, is identified with specific denominations, such as the Assemblies of God and the Church of God of Cleveland, Tennessee. It emphasizes all of the charismatic gifts, such as speaking in tongues, healing, exorcism, even raising the dead in some cases. Most of its adherents are drawn from the lower socioeconomic classes. Old-line Pentecostalism dates from the early years of the twentieth century, although there certainly were forerunners. Second in the series is neo-Pentecostalism or the charismatic movement. Arising after World War II, it cuts across various denominational lines. Often drawn from higher socioeconomic and educational groups, its adherents can be found in some of the most liturgical denominations. The third wave, unlike its predecessors, does not emphasize the baptism of the Holy Spirit. Instead it stresses healing and special insights, which it calls the "word of knowledge."

Another designation of the third wave is the "signs and wonders" movement. This emphasizes its tie with New Testament Christianity: the preaching of the apostles in the Book of Acts was accompanied by certain miraculous signs which served as evidence of the divine origin of their message. A closely related concept is "power evangelism": proclamation accompanied by miracles makes ministry effective. Yet another designation is "The Vineyard," after a group of churches affiliated with the movement.

The first real leader and still the acknowledged chief of the new charismatic movement, which is closely allied with the School of World Mission at Fuller Theological Seminary, is John Wimber. A course he taught there entitled "Signs and Wonders" first alerted the theological world to the existence of this new movement. In this chapter we will examine and expound the movement, analyze its presuppositions and arguments, and then submit it to a thorough evaluation.

Exposition of the Signs and Wonders Movement

Basic Tenets

1. The signs and wonders movement places heavy emphasis upon the kingdom of God. Wimber gives credit to George Ladd for calling his attention to this important doctrine and helping to shape his particular formulation of it. Wimber maintains that we are caught between two ages, the present evil age and the age to come.[1] Here he employs an analogy suggested by Oscar Cullmann—the period between D-Day (the Normandy invasion) and V-E Day, the day of the final victory of the Allied forces in Europe nearly a year later. We are living between the first coming of Christ, when the decisive events determining the outcome of the cosmic spiritual struggle took place, and the second coming, when everything will be accomplished. The outcome has already been determined, but the final events have not yet occurred.[2] We are in the interlude between the inauguration and the consummation of the kingdom of God.[3] The kingdom, then, is both present and future.

The idea of God as king runs throughout the Bible. He set up his court on Mount Sinai, granting a vision of himself reigning in glory. The prophets Isaiah, Ezekiel, and Daniel saw visions of the Lord lofty and exalted.[4] In the person of Jesus, the kingdom of God came in power. There was always a twofold pattern in Jesus' ministry: first proclamation, then demonstration. He first preached repentance and the good news of the kingdom of God. Then he performed miracles—casting out

1. John Wimber and Kevin Springer, *Power Evangelism* (San Francisco: Harper and Row, 1986), pp. 3–5.
2. Don Williams, *Signs, Wonders, and the Kingdom of God: A Biblical Guide for the Reluctant Skeptic* (Ann Arbor: Servant, 1989), pp. 107–8.
3. Wimber, *Power Evangelism*, p. 6.
4. Williams, *Signs, Wonders*, pp. 27–30.

demons, healing the sick, raising the dead—thus proving that he was the presence of the kingdom, the Anointed One.[5]

We also find in the Bible a series of power encounters between the kingdom of God and the kingdom of evil. Perhaps the most dramatic Old Testament instance is the contest between Elijah and the prophets of Baal on Mount Carmel. Even what seem to be victories for the forces of evil turn out to be victories for God instead. The foremost instance of that principle is the crucifixion of Christ, which proved to be the very basis of victory over satanic power.

Power encounters with Satan pervaded Jesus' public ministry. After his baptism, he submitted to a series of temptations by the evil one. Shortly thereafter, when he was teaching in the synagogue at Capernaum, a demon-possessed man challenged him. Jesus cast out the demon. That evening, he again drove out demons and healed many of various diseases (Mark 1:34). Such power continued to be exercised following Jesus' ascension. At Pentecost it was demonstrated impressively. Wimber states that "power is present when people are united in purpose and language."[6] What had occurred at Babel with the separating of nations and languages was reversed at Pentecost with the gift of tongues. Afterwards, Paul prevailed in his struggles against evil. A case in point is his victory over Elymas the sorcerer (Acts 13). In all of these encounters, the power of the kingdom of God was triumphant over the kingdom of Satan.

2. We have already anticipated the second major tenet of the signs and wonders movement: the reality and power of Satan in the world. While there is no thorough and systematic treatment of evil, the Bible everywhere recognizes its presence. The activity of Satan is traced from Genesis 3, where the serpent tempts Eve, to Revelation, where the serpent of old is identified as the devil. In the interim the effects of his revolt against God are seen, for instance, in Israel's struggles with idols, the occult, and demon powers.[7]

The role of Satan is twofold. He is the individual tempter. Thus he is seen seeking permission to tempt Job (Job 1:6–12). He also deceives the whole earth, commanding his fallen angels in the revolt against heaven (Rev. 12:7–9). He was once a highly exalted supernatural being who had access to God's intimate council, but he rebelled against God and took a host of angels with him. Together they now constitute a counter-kingdom, an evil kingdom.[8]

5. Wimber, *Power Evangelism*, p. 6.
6. Ibid., p. 22.
7. Williams, *Signs, Wonders*, pp. 56–57.
8. Ibid., p. 57.

The Bible sees struggles with corrupt earthly kingdoms as struggles with the satanic kingdom, which controls them. Thus Isaiah shifts his oracle of judgment against the king of Babylon to address Lucifer, the power behind the king; and Daniel has a vision in which the prince of the kingdom of Persia, an evil angel, is overcome by the angel Michael. Such wars are always the kingdom of God against the kingdom of Satan. The struggle is "sacred" rather than "secular." The appearance of the kingdom of God in Jesus has changed the status of the evil one and his kingdom in this world, however. Jesus spoke of seeing Satan fall from heaven like lightning (Luke 10:18), and John informs us that although "the whole world is under the control of the evil one" (1 John 5:19), the "Son of God appeared . . . to destroy the devil's work" (1 John 3:8).[9]

3. The power of the kingdom of God did not belong only to Jesus, but it was given to and exercised by the apostles, and it has also been given to the church down through the ages, including us today as well. This is clearly seen in the Great Commission, where Jesus' command to go and make disciples of all nations is prefaced by the statement, "All authority in heaven and on earth has been given to me." Wimber comments, "*All* authority is in Christ, so anything that he commands us to do, we have access to the power required to do it." Note that this power carries over to us: "Clearly the early Christians had an openness to the power of the Spirit, which resulted in signs and wonders and church growth. If we want to be like the early church, we too need to open to the Holy Spirit's power."[10]

The ability to minister the word effectively because of the display of signs and wonders is what Wimber and other leaders of the third wave term power evangelism. In all of their writings, personal anecdotes are interspersed with biblical texts. Again and again they tell of cases where their ability to do marvelous works has resulted in large numbers of conversions.

In many ways the situation which we face today is no different from that faced in biblical times and, particularly, the situations in which Jesus ministered. There is a strong presence of satanic power in the world today, a sharp opposition to our endeavor to serve Christ. We dare not disregard so much spiritual power of an evil nature. We must expect severe conflict as we seek to carry out the task. Yet the very power that Jesus exercised is available for the spiritual conflict today. That power is his to dispose, and he has authorized all of his followers, including us, to wield it.

9. Ibid., pp. 57–58.
10. Wimber, *Power Evangelism*, p. 31.

The need to emulate the Savior cannot be overstated.[11] Jesus always combined message and ministry. He preached release to the captives, setting free the demonized. This must also be true of us. Jesus told his disciples that they were to do the works which he did, and even greater works than he did. Wimber says, "Clearly Jesus envisioned a group of people—his disciples—who would perform not only the same but even greater miracles than he did. . . . It was Christ's intention that the kingdom of God be spread by others in the same way that he did it—through power evangelism."[12] That power did not end with the apostles. It was found in the next generation as well, as Hebrews 2:3–4 indicates.[13]

4. Sadly, the church today, or at least a significant segment of it, is not engaged in the sort of power ministry that Jesus conducted. It is not that the church is unsuccessful in its attempts, but that it is not even attempting power evangelism. The church does not think this is its task today.

For the absence of power evangelism there seem to be two major reasons, which may well be intertwined. One is theological. Many Christians hold a theology that denies the possibility of miracles in our time. Among them are dispensationalists, who believe that miracles, especially the charismatic gifts, ceased with the apostolic age.[14] That conviction caused a dilemma for many of the advocates of signs and wonders, who were themselves dispensationalists. The issue still affects countless dispensationalists, as evidenced in the recent Dallas Seminary case in which three faculty members were dismissed because they would not categorically reject the possibility of such gifts occurring today.[15] Also denying the possibility is a large group of Christians who are not dispensationalists, but who follow the classic argument formulated by B. B. Warfield in his treatise *Counterfeit Miracles*. He contends that the purpose of miracles was to substantiate and authenticate the ministry of Jesus and the revelation found in the Bible. Now that Jesus' ministry is complete, the miracles have served their purpose and are no longer needed. Consequently, they are no longer occurring.[16]

---

11. Williams, *Signs, Wonders*, p. 128.

12. Wimber, *Power Evangelism*, p. 50.

13. Williams, *Signs, Wonders*, pp. 129–33.

14. Wimber, *Power Evangelism*, p. ix; Charles Kraft, *Christianity with Power: Your Worldview and Your Experience of the Supernatural* (Ann Arbor: Servant, 1989), pp. 2, 3, 72.

15. Randy Frame, "Three Professors Part Paths with Dallas," *Christianity Today* 32.2 (5 Feb. 1988): 52–53.

16. Benjamin B. Warfield, *Counterfeit Miracles* (New York: Scribner, 1918)—reprinted as *Miracles: Yesterday and Today, True and False* (Grand Rapids: Eerdmans, 1953).

The other reason for the absence of power evangelism could be termed either the philosophical problem or the anthropological problem. Most Christians share the Western worldview, which precludes miracles. They do not attempt to perform signs and wonders because, consciously or unconsciously, they do not believe that such phenomena can occur.

That miracles do not fit within the worldview of most Christians is the major thrust of Charles Kraft's *Christianity with Power*. Kraft, who is by training an anthropologist, distinguishes between REALITY, what is actually there or what God sees, and reality, how human beings understand the universe. The fact that different people see things differently suggests that there are differences in their reality.[17] There are several ways of reacting to these differences: dogmatists simply insist that their view is right and that all who differ with them are wrong; the idealist or intuitivist contends that there really is no REALITY, and that reality is whatever one says it is; the agnostic contends that if there is a REALITY behind the reality we perceive, we cannot know it.[18] Kraft believes that it is better to distinguish between REALITY and reality. Such a position has two advantages: it has the potential for lessening dogmatism, and it encourages us to learn from others. We must realize that our experience of REALITY passes through several filters before forming our personal reality. These filters include our worldview, the limitations of our experience, our personality or temperament, our will, and sin.[19] Because the church fails to see the REALITY behind its view of reality, it fails to practice power evangelism.

5. The church has been severely hampered by its worldview. By "worldview" we mean "the culturally structured assumptions, values, and commitments underlying a people's perception of REALITY."[20] For example, we are accustomed to thinking of the world with the Northern Hemisphere on the top; any other version of the globe would appear strange to us. Beyond that, we Westerners have been taught to believe only in visible things. The only exceptions are invisible things which scientists have told us exist, such as radio waves. For centuries a supernaturalistic perspective was part of the worldview of northern Europeans and all those who emigrated to America for religious freedom. Following the Reformation, however, the revolt against the church gradually broadened, first to oppose any institutionalized religion, and then any form of supernaturalism. The Enlightenment was the fullest expres-

17. Kraft, *Christianity with Power,* pp. 12, 17.
18. Ibid., pp. 12–14.
19. Ibid., pp. 15–22.
20. Ibid., p. 20.

sion of this mentality.[21] Today, even Western Christians for the most part reflect the values of the Enlightenment:

a. *Naturalism.* We divide the world into natural and supernatural components, and disregard the latter. When something happens, we ask, "What caused it?"
b. *Materialism.* We prize material objects and measure wealth by the amount of them one possesses.
c. *Humanism.* We focus on human accomplishments and abilities.
d. *Rationalism.* We gain our knowledge of reality through reason.
e. *Individualism and independence.* We stress the individual and regard groups as mere abstractions.
f. *Openness to change.* We seek new experiences in hopes of continued beneficial results.[22]

Christianity that reflects the values of the Enlightenment proves to be powerless, however. Kraft tells of his experiences as a missionary in Nigeria, where he was helpless to minister to the deepest needs of his people because he had never prayed for miracles such as healing. In practice, he says, Enlightenment Christianity is tantamount to deism. It tries to make God predictable and thus controllable.[23]

There are several marks of Enlightenment Christianity:

a. *A pervasive rationalism.* Our apologia for Christianity consists largely of rational proofs of what God has done in the past. We pray for guidance, but then rely on our own reason. Even the Bible is approached rationalistically.
b. *An emphasis on doing things decently and in order.* Worship services are strictly controlled, so that there is no possibility of speaking in tongues, revelations, or other activities that might be considered disorderly.
c. *Lecture-centered church meetings.* Following the Enlightenment assumption that what people need most of all is information, we employ a monological form of communication. Even hymns are designed to convey information.
d. *A de-emphasis of the value of experience.* Even though we interpret the Bible rationalistically, tending to reject what we cannot explain or have not experienced, we are nevertheless suspicious of the validity of experience as a measure of truth.

21. Ibid., pp. 24–26.
22. Ibid., p. 40.
23. Ibid.

e. *A tendency to think of God's Word as limited to writing.* We down-play the dynamic character of revelation and thus have a static view of God's interaction with us.

f. *A scientific approach to ministry.* We look on missions and evan-gelism primarily as a matter of knowledge and technique.

g. *Dependence on doctors rather than God.* When we are ill, we turn to medicine more quickly than to God, probably rationalizing that God has provided the medical means. This is evidence that we ei-ther doubt God's care or are practical deists.

h. *Secular social programs.* We set up programs which collect from the rich and give to the poor as efficiently as possible. These pro-grams, however, often are impersonal and fail to emulate the spir-itual ministry which Jesus practiced.[24]

What is the solution to this situation? Kraft proposes two steps. We must first give up our insistence upon understanding everything. We have a tendency not to believe what we cannot understand. That is a practice we must give up, for it prevents us from trusting God.[25] Sec-ond, we must learn to listen to God. This is not something that most of us are good at. Kraft likens our prayers to one end of a telephone con-versation. We say what we have to say, then hang up. Similarly, in wor-ship we sing a hymn and then hang up without waiting for an answer. Kraft has found that God will show his will directly. For example, God has frequently shown him to whom to minister, and even the specifics of what to minister about.[26]

6. A significant part of the signs and wonders movement is the word of knowledge. This is what Kraft has experienced and is in many ways similar to the revelatory dimensions of Pentecostalism and charismatic Christianity. It is, in particular, the directing of the believer to someone who has a special need, and even identifying what that need is, whether physical (e.g., healing) or spiritual (e.g., forgiveness).

The proponents of the signs and wonders movement have given an-ecdotal evidence of the word of knowledge. A typical experience is re-counted by Wimber. While on a plane trip he happened to look over at the man across the aisle. He seemed to see the word *adultery* on the man's face. He did not actually see it there, but he saw it with his mind's eye, so to speak. Aware that Wimber was staring at him, the man asked, "What do you want?" Wimber replied, "Does the name Jane mean any-thing to you?" It turned out that Jane was the name of a woman with whom the man was having an affair. God also directed Wimber to in-

24. Ibid., pp. 41–47.
25. Ibid., p. 48.
26. Ibid., p. 49.

struct the man that if he did not break off the affair, he would die. In addition, the man was to inform his wife about the affair. As a result of this experience, both the man and his wife accepted Christ during the flight.[27]

The word of knowledge may take other forms. Sometimes it is an instruction as to the portion of a person's body that is in need of healing. The word itself may come as a strange pain or a hunch.[28] Usually these directions from the Lord prove correct, although Kraft says he has learned to be cautious since he has occasionally been wrong (he once felt he had a message about a grandchild for a woman who it turned out was not a grandmother).[29]

7. The signs and wonders movement insists that experience is relevant in doing theology. A contrast is frequently drawn between personal experiences and the restrictive straitjacket of conventional orthodox theology. For example, Don Williams, a New Testament professor with a Ph.D., describes how one day, while reading the Bible, he began to have physical sensations such as tingling and an increased pulse rate. He then had an experience of being anointed by the Holy Spirit. Joy exploded within him, and he began to speak in tongues. Having been taught that we receive complete filling by the Holy Spirit at the time of conversion, he thought that a second experience of the Spirit was unbiblical. He recalls, "My experience now simply did not fit my old theology."[30] This experience was to have a far-reaching effect upon his whole approach to the study and interpretation of Scripture, which he had termed the scientific approach: "An essential part of my encounter with the Holy Spirit and resulting experience was the further breaking up of my scientific bias. Suddenly, I had been catapulted over the laws of reason and nature into an experience of the living God which was congruent with Jesus' anointing by the Spirit at his baptism and the apostles' anointing by the Spirit at Pentecost."[31] This testimony is most impressive, given Williams's qualifications. It is also paralleled in the writings of Wimber and Kraft.[32] Clearly, experience has become for them a powerful factor in determining biblical interpretation and in formulating theology.

8. The signs and wonders movement has a specific understanding of the nature of God and of his method of working. Kraft points out that many people consider God a harsh, judgmental being, along the lines of

27. Wimber, *Power Evangelism*, pp. 32–35.
28. Kraft, *Christianity with Power*, pp. 2, 158.
29. Ibid., p. 160.
30. Williams, *Signs, Wonders*, p. 14.
31. Ibid., pp. 15–16.
32. Wimber, *Power Evangelism*, pp. 23–27, 43; Kraft, *Christianity with Power*, p. 44.

the celestial policeman that J. B. Phillips spoke of. Kraft cites a woman who always sees God with a stick in his hand.[33] This is a misunderstanding of the nature of God. God is instead "a lover, an accepter, a forgiver." While he is hard on hypocrites such as the Pharisees and others who use their power and position to oppress others, he is patient and forgiving with sinners and those in need. Although there are indications of God's judgment (e.g., the threat against the life of the adulterer whom Wimber met on the plane), the emphasis is upon the love and mercy of God.

Moreover, God deals with people directly. An example is the word of knowledge. He frequently gives us understanding of a biblical passage or shows us the specific needs of others. His acts are not restricted to the events that are recorded in the Bible. On the contrary, he tends to work directly in meeting human needs today. Accordingly, whereas some Christians regard medical science as God's way of providing for human physical needs, the signs and wonders movement prefers to turn to God for healing.[34] He is a God who answers prayers, often on a direct and individual basis.

9. What we are called to do is to minister in power. Healing is a manifestation of that power.[35] This means that traditional ministry, including both apologetics and pastoral care, has changed. Traditionally, apologetics has sought to respond to problems which people have with respect to the Christian faith. One major issue is the problem of evil, specifically, how can a good and loving, all-powerful God permit suffering, including suffering by good people, Christian believers? The popular expression of this issue is, "Why do bad things happen to good people?" The conventional response has been theodicy—attempts to explain away the problem, or at least to alleviate it somewhat. The signs and wonders movement, however, advocates an approach somewhat like the solution which Jürgen Moltmann once proposed. Instead of explaining, or explaining away the problem, it is to be disposed of by actually removing it. Suffering which has been removed does not need to be accounted for.[36]

A similar approach is advocated for the dimension of pastoral care. Frequently pastors seek to find ways to enable us to live successfully with suffering, to endure it. Thus the report of the Fuller Seminary faculty committee appointed to study the issues growing out of Wimber's

33. Kraft, *Christianity with Power*, p. 74.

34. Ibid., p. 46.

35. Tim Stafford, "Testing the Wine from John Wimber's Vineyard," *Christianity Today* 30.11 (8 Aug. 1986): 18.

36. Jürgen Moltmann, "Theology as Eschatology," in Jürgen Moltmann et al., *The Future of Hope: Theology as Eschatology*, ed. Frederick Herzog (New York: Herder and Herder, 1970), pp. 46–47.

"Signs and Wonders" course includes a chapter on "The Place of Suffering in Christian Experience." It states, "We believe that suffering is an inescapable ingredient of, and not the exception in, Christian living."[37] That this bears upon the seminary training of pastors is affirmed in the report: "Therefore, we seem summoned to prepare those who suffer to receive that triumphant form of healing available to all God's hurting children—redemptive suffering. Faith in God's perfect goodness amid the pains and losses we devoutly wish to go away—this, too, is healing quite wonderful, not spectacular to be sure, but real, and in the long run as divine as any healing can be."[38] Williams disagrees vigorously. He grants that we are called to suffer, since Jesus called his disciples to suffer. Williams maintains, however, that "we live in a kingdom come and coming where God's reign is actually breaking in upon us. To stress suffering at the expense of healing is to deny the pragmatic reality of the kingdom in our midst."[39]

Analysis

We have seen something of the ideological system of the signs and wonders movement. We now need to do a bit of analytical work, determining just how this view should be classified, what its major concepts are, and how they relate to some other movements. Our analysis will examine both the presuppositions and the arguments employed.

1. A first characteristic of the signs and wonders movement, theologically, is a rather sharp transcendentalism. By this we mean an emphasis upon the independence of God from natural processes or the laws of nature. Advocates of the movement have characterized Enlightenment Christianity as a practicing deism. In contrast, they believe in a God who is active within our world, working miracles. Note, however, that this is still a basically transcendent God who works only occasionally or periodically. Though he may do so fairly frequently, he must, in order to work, break into the world. Other than those occasions he is not really present. He does not work through such means as medicine or counseling. The signs and wonders movement, then, seems to assume an either/or approach. One relies either upon medicine or upon God. It cannot be both at one time. Thus Kraft sees as a symptom of Enlightenment Christianity the tendency to think of medicine and doctors before one thinks of God. The feeling is that "though God can heal, medicine and doctors are more dependable."[40] This seems to indicate a definite

---

37. *Ministry and the Miraculous*, ed. Lewis B. Smedes (Pasadena: Fuller Theological Seminary, 1987), p. 51.
38. Ibid., p. 56.
39. Williams, *Signs, Wonders*, p. 126.
40. Kraft, *Christianity with Power*, p. 46.

disjunction between medicine and God's working. To think of medicine as something God has given is a rationalization, according to Kraft.[41]

The notion that the signs and wonders movement assumes an either/ or approach may seem somewhat illegitimate in view of Wimber's employment of Paul Hiebert's concept of the "excluded middle." Western Christianity has a tendency to separate the supernatural (God and the angels in heaven) from the natural (the realm of ordinary occurrences and human relationships). This dichotomy, however, excludes the middle— gods living within trees and rivers, demons, the Holy Spirit, and signs and wonders.[42] Note that there is a considerable difference between the middle ground of what Wimber terms the Christian worldview, which has a great deal of affinity with animism, and an immanental theology which views God as working through natural processes.

2. There is a definite epistemological presupposition as well: the Christian has direct access to God. Classical Reformation orthodoxy had seen the grounds of authority as involving both an objective element, the permanent truths revealed and preserved in the Bible, and a subjective element called illumination, God's creating in us an understanding of that revelation and a conviction of its truth. Illumination does not communicate new information, but only makes understandable the cognitive dimension which is already present. Similarly, God's guidance of individual believers does not refer to the revelation of new information, but to help in discerning the significance of certain information already possessed. The signs and wonders movement, however, sees the Holy Spirit as imparting an understanding of special gifts which seems virtually to contradict rational interpretations of Scripture. It also sees God as revealing new information about people, their needs and problems, as well as their sins.

3. There is also a definite understanding of history. Some theologians ("transformers") believe that the world has changed in such a way that the actual content of the Christian message must be altered if it is to be understood. Others ("translators") agree that the world has changed, but maintain that all that is needed is a different way of expressing the old message. In the signs and wonders movement, however, we find a non-dialogical approach. No restatement of the biblical message is necessary. All that is needed is a replay of the biblical events, or of something similar, and people will believe. For there has been no really significant change between the world of biblical times and the present world, at least none that cannot be bridged by in effect bringing the present time back into the biblical world.

41. Ibid.
42. Wimber, *Power Evangelism*, pp. 74–81.

4. The signs and wonders movement holds to a partially realized eschatology. Many of the benefits which an older evangelicalism had consigned to the eschaton are considered to be realizable in the present. Among them are the overcoming of physical illness, the restraining of spiritual evil (or the evil one), and even raising the dead. We have here, as it were, an attempt to experience the millennium now.

5. There is a rather privatistic and individualistic conception of the Christian life. While there is a considerable emphasis upon ethics, it relates basically to personal rather than social righteousness. There is, in other words, a considerable separation here between personal piety and public morality. In this respect, the signs and wonders movement is more like classical fundamentalism than like the evangelicalism that experienced a resurgence following World War II.

6. The signs and wonders movement also practices a characteristic hermeneutic. For Wimber and his followers, there is no problem of two horizons. There is only one. There are not a meaning then and a meaning now. Nor is there a need for distinguishing between "meaning" and "significance," to use E. D. Hirsch's terms.[43] Because the meaning then is also the meaning now, there is no difference in application. Whatever the disciples were commanded to do, we also are commanded to do. That we are a different type of audience separated from the disciples chronologically and geographically is inconsequential.

This is a macrohermeneutical assumption. The essence of dispensationalism, after all, is the recognition of different periods in God's working; some portions of Scripture apply to certain periods (dispensations), other portions to other periods. And so some advocates of the signs and wonders movement have abandoned dispensationalism. In so doing, they also seem to have adopted a hermeneutical stance which is almost diametrically opposed to that of dispensationalism. For all of Scripture, in their view, seems to apply to all periods of time.

7. Finally, there is a christological assumption with clear ecclesiological implications. The signs and wonders movement puts emphasis upon the humanity of Christ, the points of commonality, rather than the difference, between him and us. Accordingly, the movement calls us to continue his actions and ministry. It is not merely that we can do what Jesus did. Wimber reads this as a command: we *must* do what Jesus did. We are called to carry on his ministry literally.[44]

43. Eric D. Hirsch, Jr., *Validity in Interpretation* (New Haven: Yale University Press, 1967), p. 8.
44. Stafford, "Testing the Wine," p. 18.

Evaluation of the Movement

Positive

We must now attempt to offer some evaluation of this dynamic movement within current evangelicalism. We will first note its positive aspects:

1. There is a considerable element of truth in the diagnosis of the naturalistic tendencies of Enlightenment Christianity. Most evangelicals believe in the supernatural, or at least in the recorded miracles of biblical times. There is, however, a sort of practical naturalism with respect to the here and now. This is akin to the distinction which I sometimes refer to as official and unofficial theology. Officially we believe that God is all-powerful, and that he can and does perform miracles. Unofficially, however, many evangelicals tend to act as if God does not or will not work to resolve their present problems miraculously. It is easier to believe that God did miracles two thousand years ago, or that he is now doing them eight thousand miles away, than to expect miracles here and now.

Naturalism also shows itself in the belief that we can program results in our ministry. Modern techniques of marketing research leave little room for the unpredictable, and sometimes there is little reliance on prayer. The methodology of ministry often has more in common with Madison Avenue than with the Sea of Galilee.

2. The signs and wonders movement has also called our attention back to the role of the Holy Spirit in the interpretation of the Bible. Sometimes exegesis has become quite mechanical. Some even affirm that, all other things being equal, the unbeliever is likelier to interpret certain passages correctly than is the Christian.[45] The notion of the Bible as a fixed book whose meaning can be extracted by the application of correct interpretational devices is an overextension of the biblical doctrine of revelation.

3. The proponents of signs and wonders have correctly pointed out that demonstration of the Christian faith is often more powerful than an argument for its truthfulness. Whether or not their identification of the proper form of demonstrating the Christian faith is correct, they have at least pointed out that sometimes our arguments are attempts to shore up what should be experienced.

4. Another positive feature is the recognition that the message of Jesus is not exclusively spiritual. It concerns the whole person. Just as

---

45. Daniel P. Fuller, "The Holy Spirit's Role in Biblical Interpretation," in *Scripture, Tradition, and Interpretation: Essays Presented to Everett F. Harrison by His Students and Colleagues in Honor of His Seventy-fifth Birthday*, ed. W. Ward Gasque and William Sanford LaSor (Grand Rapids: Eerdmans, 1978), pp. 189–98.

Jesus cared about the physical needs of the suffering, so also should we, if we are truly his disciples.

5. Also commendable is the criticism of the ministerial approach which tries to reach the unsaved by stressing what they will receive. While such an approach may be an appropriate point for an initial contact, it in effect is counterproductive to repentance, which involves turning from self-seeking and striving instead to do God's will and glorify him.

6. The movement has correctly observed that much of the action we see around us today is not rationally based or motivated. An example is the widespread use of drugs by young people. This is actually quite irrational, inasmuch as they are trading away their future for the sake of a temporary but intense experience. Rational appeals do not carry much weight with them. They simply do not care about the future. What matters is the present. If ministry is to reach people today, it must take this irrational dimension into account.

7. Finally, the signs and wonders movement has correctly pointed out that contemporary evangelicalism has to a large degree conformed its moral convictions and lifestyle to society. The influence of secular society can be seen in the evangelicals' present understanding of family life, their television viewing, and perhaps most of all, their ready acceptance and even championing of the materialistic approach to values.[46] Recent research indicates that this trend is likely to accelerate in the future.[47]

Negative

We have looked at the strengths and commendable features of the signs and wonders movement. There are, however, a significant number of issues on which I have some major reservation:

1. Perhaps most central is the epistemology or the logic of the argument. To a large degree, this is an argument from personal subjective experience. As such, its competition is not rational arguments, but arguments of its own type, or arguments from personal experience. Here we encounter the difficulty of how to choose among them. What does one do with the claims of the New Age movement? Or of Muslims, who are increasing in number even in the United States? Without objective grounding, this becomes a shouting match—"I know that you are wrong" or even "I have just had a revelation that your revelation is false." Eventually, shouting matches become shoving matches or shooting matches.

46. Wimber, *Power Evangelism*, p. 36.
47. E.g., James Davison Hunter, *Evangelicalism: The Coming Generation* (Chicago: University of Chicago Press, 1987), pp. 73–74.

In a sense, subjectivity is a problem with most Pentecostals, and the reason why non-Pentecostals become so frustrated when trying to interact with them. In my first pastorate, for example, there were some old-style Pentecostals. I was talking with one of them on the telephone, discussing a certain biblical passage. It seemed to me that the Bible quite clearly supported the position which I was taking. He retorted, "The problem is that you are not as spiritual as I am. If you were as spiritual as I am, you would see that this is what the passage means." I did not continue the conversation, for that would have been futile. Actually, I knew what my reply should have been. I should have said, "I am *more* spiritual than you are, and I can see that *this* is what the passage means." I did not, however, have the stomach for that type of dialogue. This is intended as an illustration of the point, not an argument. The problem with anecdotal argument is that it can readily be countered by another anecdote. Such arguments are weak because of their subjectivity.

2. There is a strange anthropological naiveté or perhaps even an anthropocentrism about the movement. That appears in the absolute confidence placed in signs and wonders as practical proofs of the position being maintained. As the Fuller report correctly points out, however, the presence of such wondrous works is not unique to Christianity. They can be found in other world religions, and in many folk religions as well.[48] Indeed, the wise men of Egypt matched Moses miracle for miracle up to a certain point. And Christ warned that the false Christs and false prophets who will come in the last times will perform signs and miracles (Matt. 24:24). It is therefore not merely a question of whether the signs and wonders within Christianity are more effective than are those of other religions in establishing their respective truth claims. It is also a question of whether the signs and wonders are genuine rather than spurious, and come from God rather than from Satan. By ignoring this issue the signs and wonders movement shows itself to be both anthropologically and theologically naive. It is quite incredible that Kraft, with his background in anthropology, fails to deal with it.

3. In contrast to the modern scientific worldview, Kraft expounds and Wimber advocates a Third World type of perspective which they identify as supernaturalistic. Yet what is actually being propounded is a prescientific or premodern worldview. That raises the question, Is it really possible and desirable to turn back the clock and ignore the scientific revolution? What would seem to be needed, if we are to avoid writing off large numbers of people today, is an approach that recognizes the validity and utility of science within proper limits. What is actually happening, however, is that in the interest of advancing faith,

48. *Ministry and the Miraculous*, ed. Smedes, p. 58.

Kraft and Wimber may be recommending superstition. The view they seem to endorse includes animism as well as true supernaturalism. There is no particular spiritual merit in that.

What is particularly disturbing about Kraft's approach is that he seems uncritical of his own worldview. He assumes that his worldview is that of Scripture. That may not be so, however. His worldview may simply be the set of presuppositions through which he views Scripture and cultural data. His failure to recognize that his worldview is not necessarily the biblical teaching and to critique it accordingly is particularly distressing in light of his anthropological expertise. What is actually needed is a philosophical critique of the presuppositions of his anthropological method. In other words, his discussion of worldviews should have been placed in a broader context.

4. The signs and wonders movement seems to elevate a secondary factor, namely physical health, into a primary role. The Fuller report refers to "the narcissistic assumption that health is the highest of all goods."[49] To be sure, the proponents of the movement are careful to point out that signs and wonders are just that—they dispose people to respond to evangelism. Yet the miracles also seem to be valued for themselves. Williams, for example, depreciates the Fuller statement regarding the primacy of forgiveness over physical health by pointing out that forgiveness is nowhere included in the Gospel summaries of the ministry of Jesus.[50]

5. There is an apparent exclusiveness to the signs and wonders movement, which gives the impression that it is the only appropriate approach to the Christian life and that all the others are somehow deficient. This means that the efforts of many Christians from the present and from the recent and remote past who have been thought of as doing God's work, especially in evangelism, have been subbiblical. This criticism of the movement has been raised by J. I. Packer as well as by the faculty members at Fuller.[51]

6. There seems to be such an emphasis upon the unusual and spectacular that the more usual manifestations of spiritual force tend to be overlooked. Indeed, there is a virtual denial that the less spectacular are also God's doing. But this is to neglect the biblical witnesses to the immanent working of God, for example, Joseph's word to his brothers, "You intended to harm me, but God intended it for good" (Gen. 50:20), and Peter's statement to the Jews, "Now, brothers, I know that you acted in ignorance, as did your leaders. But this is how God fulfilled what he

49. Ibid., p. 60.
50. Williams, *Signs, Wonders*, p. 126.
51. See Stafford, "Testing the Wine," p. 21; Ben Patterson, "Cause for Concern," *Christianity Today* 30.11 (8 Aug. 1986): 20.

had foretold through all the prophets" (Acts 3:17–18). The Fuller faculty report calls attention to the healing work of God in hospitals established by Christians and to the effect of spiritually motivated social-reform movements, which have together alleviated more suffering than did all of Jesus' direct works during his lifetime.[52]

The problem with an approach that emphasizes the spectacular is that it overlooks and thus fails in some cases to utilize God's blessing. The Fuller faculty statement says, "We reject these views, not because they make too much of God's occasional demonstration of power, but because they make too little of God's constant presence and power."[53] Packer puts it this way:

> I would honor God by articulating the victory in another way. Christ enables us to be more than conquerors under pressure. We seek the strength to cope with divinely permitted circumstances. There are many of us for whom the role model is Joni Eareckson rather than John Wimber. We see the powers of the kingdom operating, but mainly in regeneration, sanctification, the Spirit as a comforter, the transformation of the inner life, rather than in physical miracles which just by happening prevent much of the other kingdom activity whereby people learn to live with their difficulties and glorify God.[54]

The emphasis upon the spectacular is not surprising in our culture. People become profoundly upset by a plane crash which kills a hundred people, but are undisturbed when five hundred persons are killed on the highways during a holiday weekend. Baseball fans are much more stirred by a long bases-empty home run than by a walk followed by a stolen base, a fielder's choice, and a sacrifice fly, even though the end result is the same in both cases—one run. In California, with its glitzy atmosphere, it is not surprising that the spectacular approach is popular. Is this, however, just one more case of Christianity's being conformed to its culture?

What is true on the positive side of the calculation is also true on the negative side. The emphasis upon demon possession and exorcism may well lead to a complacency regarding less dramatic forms of satanic activity. There are undoubtedly countless cases where Satan works quietly, persuasively, and appealingly, unrecognized but causing great harm. In fact, he may be more effective when we are not alert to his presence and activity. By emphasizing the spectacular, then, the signs and wonders movement may well be fostering the devil's work.

52. *Ministry and the Miraculous*, ed. Smedes, p. 31.
53. Ibid., p. 48.
54. Quoted in Stafford, "Testing the Wine," p. 22.

7. A certain amount of selectivity is involved in the claim that Jesus entrusted to us the authority to carry on the same ministry that he did, and that we not only are enabled but are actually expected to do so. Certain of Jesus' feats were not copied by the disciples in his time, and are not today. Examples are the walking on water (though Peter did so at Jesus' bidding) and the feeding of the five thousand through the miraculous multiplication of the loaves and fishes. Certainly, given the amount of poverty and starvation in the world, one would expect to see a duplication of this miracle if it were possible.

8. The signs and wonders movement has distanced itself from the larger issues of social ethics. In this respect, it resembles the older fundamentalism. It ignores social issues despite the considerable biblical testimony regarding God's concern for justice (e.g., Amos 8; James 2:1–9; 1 John 3:17). The Fuller faculty statement says, "Signs and wonders cannot point credibly to the redemptive power of Christ unless they happen in a living context of concern and passion for peace and justice. Without authentic passion for those fundamental social realities of the kingdom of God, evangelical ministries famous for performing miraculous healings will lack credibility among discerning men and women."[55]

9. We spoke earlier of the tendency toward superstition. Kraft's discussion of the "empowerment of words and objects" is more suggestive of superstition and magic than of Christian faith and miracles.[56] Similarly disconcerting to many of the Fuller faculty is C. Peter Wagner's suggestion that Christians would be wise to exorcise demons from their homes, especially if they have visited pagan temples in foreign lands, where demons might have attached themselves to their persons or luggage.[57]

10. The signs and wonders movement is a triumphalist approach to the Christian life. Apparent failures, then, present a problem. And Wimber does admit to failures, at least in principle. The cases of the sick or disabled who are not healed was foremost in the minds of many of the Fuller faculty. Does Satan win them? "If so," says Ben Patterson, "then Satan holds a commanding lead in the game, because the majority of people who are prayed for do not, in fact, get well physically."[58] This creates subtle pressure to see miracles where there are none. Indeed,

---

55. *Ministry and the Miraculous*, ed. Smedes, p. 60.

56. Kraft, *Christianity with Power,* pp. 161–63; for an evaluation see Patterson, "Cause for Concern," p. 20.

57. C. Peter Wagner, "Can Demons Harm Christians?" *Christian Life* 47.1 (May 1985): 76; for the Fuller faculty reaction see George Marsden, *Reforming Fundamentalism: Fuller Seminary and the New Evangelicalism* (Grand Rapids: Eerdmans, 1987), p. 294.

58. Patterson, "Cause for Concern," p. 20.

some faculty members were outraged at what they felt were wild, unsubstantiated reports coming out of the "Signs and Wonders" course.[59]

11. A closely related criticism is the limited efficacy of the healing ministry. When asked how many really spectacular healings had been seen, Wimber replied, "Very few." Many of the healings involve leg lengthening, which, as Kraft concedes, is in the milder forms a matter of relaxing the back muscles.[60]

We are not attempting to dispute or explain away the miracles claimed by the movement, although its argument would be more impressive if more clearly nonpsychosomatic healings were to occur. Rather, our question is, "Why are only certain types of healings performed and not others?" When asked about the repertory, one minister in the movement said simply, "We don't do kidneys. We don't do fractures. We do leg lengthening." A colleague of mine, whose fractured wrist did not heal normally, gave the best one-line response to the signs and wonders movement I have ever heard. Holding up his cast, he asked, "Where are those signs and wonders people when you really need them?"

The signs and wonders movement will be with us for some time. We must make sure that we not suppress any genuine working of the Holy Spirit, but we must also be certain that we maintain a full and balanced Christian life. We will surely need to pray for great wisdom.

59. Ibid.
60. Kraft, *Christianity with Power*, p. 91.

Part 5

Evangelicalism and Its Future

9

Is a Shortage of Clergy Coming?

Could a Shortage of Clergy Occur in the Near Future?
Will a Shortage of Clergy Occur in the Foreseeable Future?
Implications of the Coming Shortage

It is interesting to observe what happens when a traffic light turns red, particularly on those roads where there is considerable distance between traffic signals. Some drivers continue to keep their foot on the gas pedal, in some cases even accelerating. When they get almost to the light, they slam on their brakes. Others, at the first sign of the change to red, take their foot off the gas, gradually decelerating and coasting up to the intersection. The latter group economize on gasoline and on brake linings, and actually average a higher speed, approaching and then going slowly through the intersection when the light turns green, which takes less time than stopping and then accelerating. One very good measure of driving skill is how often one has to stop or, more concretely, how long one's brake linings last. What we are referring to here is *vision*, the measure of how far ahead one looks while driving. Some people look only about ten feet beyond the hood of their car, while more skilled drivers look far ahead. This skill not only is an economizer and a timesaver, but also helps avoid accidents.

Vision, the ability to look ahead, is essential in all areas of life. Unfortunately, in the life of the church there are people who do not plan very far ahead. They fail to anticipate and prepare for changes. They also fail to recognize changes that have occurred in the world and to adapt to them. These people proceed as if the present situation is the final one. In their desire to be current, they frequently condemn themselves to not being current in the future. In this chapter we will try to anticipate what the near future holds for one particular aspect of church life: Will there be an adequate supply of clergy? And if not, what are the implications?

Could a Shortage of Clergy Occur in the Near Future?

The church has always been and always will be concerned about its leadership. It may seem that there is no real cause for concern here. For there seems to be a surplus of full-time clergy. Most denominational officials (other than in the Roman Catholic Church) can testify that they are deluged with applications from persons wanting to procure positions in the congregations within their jurisdiction. This would seem to be a blessing, for churches can be selective in calling pastors, thus by a sort of ecclesiastical Darwinism obtaining the best leadership available. Certainly the possibility of a shortage should not concern us for many years to come, or at least for the foreseeable future.

Is this really the case, however? Or is it possible that the same problems which the Catholic church faces might come to plague other denominations as well? This seems unlikely in the judgment of most persons. Yet we might observe from some other professions that shortages can quickly develop from what seem to be surpluses. A few years ago, in the midst of a glut of elementary- and secondary-school teachers, it seemed as if there would never be a problem. Yet in various parts of the country and in certain specialties shortages are appearing and spreading into allied areas. The oversupply of instructors in higher education seemed even greater, yet we are now being warned of a coming shortage there as well. At times there is a great glut of nurses, and then a shortage reappears. Similar cycles appear in engineering. Because of a scarcity of jobs, young people in high school are counseled not to consider engineering. As a result, fewer persons enter the profession; and when normalcy in the job supply returns, there are not enough engineers to go around. We are now hearing of a shortage of physicians, which is spreading from rural to metropolitan areas. As unlikely as it may currently seem, we may someday find an insufficient number of attorneys as well.

Will a Shortage of Clergy Occur in the Foreseeable Future?

At this point I am going to hazard a prediction, a prediction that has encountered incredulity virtually everywhere I have voiced it. I may well be mistaken on this matter, and if so, I would be very pleased to acknowledge my error. I predict that relatively soon, possibly before the year 2000, we will see a shortage of capable and qualified clergypersons.

There are several considerations that have led to this audacious thesis, the first two of which relate to demographics.

1. On the basis of statistics from a number of denominations, we can anticipate within the next ten years an especially large number of ministers to retire. One major denomination projects that approximately one-third of its pastoral force will retire in the coming decade.[1] This will call for more than a normal decade's worth of pastoral recruits in the next ten years, if the present situation is to be maintained.

In any normal situation, of course, approximately one-fourth of all pastors will retire in a given decade. This simply follows from the fact that pastors have traditionally entered the ministry at about age twenty-five, having spent four years in college and three to four years in seminary. With retirement usually coming at age sixty-five, one-fourth retire per decade. There are indications, however, that an unusually large percentage of the active clergy are approaching sixty-five. Some of this may be attributable to the large number of military veterans who enrolled in colleges and seminaries in the late 1940s and early 1950s. The enrolment at many seminaries peaked during that period, sagging back to lower figures before the surge which began about 1965.

2. In general, churches and Sunday schools are experiencing the effects of the second wave of the baby boom; that is to say, members of the baby-boom generation are now having babies of their own. Church nurseries are once again becoming filled. While youth programs are in most cases still struggling for participants, better times are definitely coming in most churches and for most youth pastors. Youth ministry, in other words, is definitely a growth industry. What all of this means for our purposes is that as the second wave reach adulthood, they will ordinarily be ministered to by the generation in between the two baby booms. Thus we will have a mismatch: larger numbers to be ministered to and fewer persons to do the ministering.

3. A factor which will come into play more gradually, but have longer-lasting effects, is a reduction in the length of the typical career. There are at least three causes. First is the phenomenon of the seminary student who is embarking on a second career. Since many seminarians are anywhere from ten to twenty years older than were their counterparts a generation ago, they will have a shorter period of time in which to serve following graduation. Their careers will span three or perhaps only two decades.

A second cause is the prolonged period that seminary study itself takes. Whereas a generation ago the majority of students completed the

---

1. Cynthia Snider, "Who's Waiting in the Wings?" *American Baptist* 187.6 (Nov.–Dec. 1989): 34.

bachelor or master of divinity degree in three years, the average is now in excess of four years, and moving toward five. Although the increase is small, it will have some effect.

A third cause is the accelerating attrition among pastors. More and more do not persist in the ministry until the customary retirement age of sixty-five. In some denominations the problem is large-scale. In the Southern Baptist Convention, for example, an average of 116 pastors are involuntarily terminated by their congregations each month.[2] This translates annually to 5 percent of the entire senior pastoral force of the denomination.

Part of the increase in terminations stems from a greater tendency to criticize the pastor instead of affirming and encouraging him. Whereas in earlier periods there was a loving appreciation for the ministry of pastors, now there is a tendency to regard them as employees and to set performance standards which they are to meet. Rural congregations of an earlier time realized that results do not always directly correlate with effort. Farmers understood that they were not responsible for a crop failure which resulted from drought or a hailstorm. With increased urbanization and the upward mobility of congregations and especially of evangelicals, however, management by objectives with strict expectations of performance has become the fashion. Managers who are held to strict accountability on their jobs tend to transfer such standards to their pastors, not realizing that working with volunteers is quite different from working with subordinates.

Contributing also to the increased expectations of the pastor is the parishioners' exposure to a variety of ministries. A churchgoer who sits through a reasonably well done sermon may have watched two or three religious telecasts before coming to church. Those presentations are carefully prepared and professionally produced. It may be difficult to avoid comparing them to the worship service of the local congregation, which of course does not have the same resources available.

A further reason for the attrition is the increased complexity of pastoral ministry in the present day. Pastoral ministry has always been one of the most demanding professions, since it involves so many roles and requires such a variety of skills. With the changes in our society in the past decade or two, the demands have increased. There are new, multiplied, or aggravated social problems to deal with, such as marital difficulties and substance abuse, especially among young people. And then there are changes in church life, in many cases the results of societal changes. It has been clearly documented that members of the baby-

2. Presnell H. Wood, "The Call of God in Finding, Keeping a Preacher," *Baptist Standard* 104.11 (11 March 1992): 6.

boom generation, unlike their parents, do not make long-term commitments to an organization, company, or brand.[3] This of course carries over to commitment to a given denomination or a given congregation. Moreover, because of a general shift of values toward materialism and a preference to give to specific challenges rather than ongoing projects, there is a decline in financial support at a time when the church's clientele are expecting more services. In addition, volunteerism is declining, at least in part because of the preponderance of families where both the husband and the wife work. These and many other factors have made the pastor's task more difficult than ever.

One other factor is contributing to the accelerating attrition. In the past it was customary for a pastor who was experiencing difficulty with his congregation to move to another congregation. There he began with a new lease on life, so to speak. But with the current oversupply of pastors, there are fewer opportunities to change churches. This means that a pastor must often stay beyond the optimum time for making a change. Then tensions may build to the point where either the pastor feels he cannot continue and resigns, or the congregation takes action to terminate him. One might think that the eventual result would be a reduction in the oversupply of pastors, and thus a reopening of the door for some to return to the pastorate. Those who have left the ministry in this fashion are, however, unlikely to return. They may have come to enjoy some of the perquisites of ordinary employment, or they may still recall too vividly the trauma of their termination. They are, in other words, lost to the ministry forever, thus contributing to the coming shortage. (While we have used the masculine pronoun throughout this discussion because males still constitute the majority of clergypersons, there is no reason to believe that circumstances will be any different for female clergy in this respect.)

It has been the hope of some who are engaged in theological education that the influx of individuals seeking a second career would decrease the rate of attrition from the ministry. Presumably, being older, more mature, with life experiences that would be transferable from other occupations, they would be relatively immune to the ravages of parish life that lead to pastors dropping out of the ministry. In actuality, these hopes have not been substantially realized. There does not seem to be a significantly different attrition rate for ministers who entered seminary directly after high school and college and for those who embarked on a second career. Apparently some of the latter were not outstanding successes in their earlier vocation. Others came with a somewhat idealized understanding of what ministry would be like, and

3. Leith Anderon, *Dying for Change* (Minneapolis: Bethany, 1990), pp. 81–83.

found themselves both disillusioned and somewhat less able to adjust than are younger persons.

We can anticipate that the rate of attrition will increase, and rather markedly in the case of certain subgroups. The rate of attrition coupled with the high cost of theological education will result in a less well prepared clergy. One trend which is building momentum is the declared intention of a number of larger churches, or megachurches as they are now known, to train their own leadership. This type of preparation will be less extensive, of course, and will also lack much of the theoretical basis taught in seminary. It will be highly geared to ministry in the specific local congregation providing the training. Eventually, however, as with every other type of ministry, there will come a time when one should move on to another position. Some individuals will probably return to the lay vocation from which they were originally recruited. Those who move on to another congregation may well find that the techniques that were designed for a highly contextualized situation do not transfer especially well to another situation. Never having been taught the theoretical basics that would enable them to adapt, they will be unable to develop an appropriate ministry. It will be necessary to repeat the training process in one's new church, if that is possible, or run the risk of failure or even dropout.

Another problem is the mismatch between those individuals who have taken shortcuts to ministry and the persons to whom they are to minister. With the increasing level of education of laypersons, and especially the upward mobility of evangelicals in recent years, a higher level of preparation for the clergy would seem to be in order. This has been the church's response in the past, repeatedly upgrading the amount of education required, particularly as the church sought to recover from the disastrous experiences of fundamentalism. A reversal of this trend, conflicting with the trend among laypeople, would seem to portend a greater level of conflict, frustration, failure, and dropout.

4. In addition to the reduction in the length of the typical ministerial career, we are already experiencing a decline in the number of persons entering the ministry. Most people outside of theological education may not be aware of this development, since the statistics seem, upon superficial analysis, to indicate otherwise. In fact, until the fall of 1989, the total enrolment of all schools in the Association of Theological Schools in the United States and Canada had been increasing every year since 1969.[4] On the other hand, there has been a steady, if unnoticed, decline

---

4. *Fact Book on Theological Education for the Academic Year 1987–88*, ed. William Baumgaertner (Pittsburgh: Association of Theological Schools in the United States and Canada, 1988), p. 1; *Fact Book on Theological Education for the Academic Year 1990–91*, ed. Gail Buchwalter King (Pittsburgh: Association of Theological Schools in the United States and Canada, 1991), p. 25.

for several years in the number of students who are actually preparing for pastoral ministry as such.

One of the reasons for the misunderstanding of the statistics is that students are taking longer to complete their seminary education; in other words, they are taking fewer courses per term. This is a result of many factors, including the families that the older students have to support. Consequently, a given student may be counted in enrolment statistics four, five, or more times, rather than three, resulting in inflated enrolment figures. If the average length of time to acquire a master's degree in divinity increased from three to four years, enrolment figures would increase $33\frac{1}{3}$ percent, but there would be no corresponding increase in the number of graduates. It is important to note the equivalent of full-time enrolment rather than head count. Here it will be seen that there has actually been a decrease.

Also to be noted is that a large number of students are not working toward a master of divinity degree, nor are they enrolled in some other standard program preparatory to the ministry. Many students are in nonprofessional programs, working toward, for example, a master of arts in theological studies. They are studying simply to give themselves a better preparation to serve as lay Christians or, in some cases, to prepare for further graduate studies and eventually for teaching. Others are enrolled in specialized programs such as counseling, church music, and Christian education. Consider also that anyone studying for a doctor of ministry degree is already engaged in professional ministry. Graduates from that program do not increase at all the pool of available pastors. Enrolment figures must therefore be evaluated by noting the number of persons enrolled in the standard preparatory program. Here there has been a continuing decline.

5. Not only are fewer persons currently enrolled in seminary programs that prepare one for the ministry, but fewer young people are considering a pastoral career. This trend, which has already begun, will probably continue. The percentage of college freshmen considering religious vocations has declined from a generation earlier.[5] In this respect, religious vocations are experiencing the same fortunes as are the other helping professions. There is a shift of interest toward fields such as business and toward making money as con-

5. In recent years the percentage of college freshmen indicating an interest in a ministerial career has held constant at 0.2 percent, and for all other religious careers at 0.1 percent—"Fact-File: Views and Characteristics of This Year's Freshmen," *Chronicle of Higher Education* 33.18 (14 Jan. 1987): 39; and "This Year's College Freshmen: Attitudes and Characteristics," *Chronicle of Higher Education* 37.20 (30 Jan. 1991): A30.

trasted with serving humanity or God.[6] There is some indication of a reversal in this trend, but that will not affect the number of seminary graduates and thus the supply of clergypersons for several more years.[7]

Young people's lack of interest in religious vocations is to some extent a reflection of their parents' attitudes. Whereas middle-class evangelicals used to encourage their children to go into the ministry, that has changed. Once the highest status achievable by young people in evangelical circles was to become foreign missionaries or pastoral ministers. Because the evangelical faith was close to the hearts of the parents, they experienced great joy when their children sensed and followed a divine call into the ministry. This frequently represented the answers to prayers, sometimes prayers which had been offered since before the birth of the child.

Today, however, most parents have different aspirations for their children. Absorbing society's criteria of success, they hope that their children will enter business or one of the highly paid professions. In particular, many modern evangelicals urge their children to consider medicine or law rather than the ministry.

But the change in middle-class attitudes is not limited to the parents and their children. Traditionally, the most significant influence in a decision to go to seminary was the encouragement of one's pastor. That is changing, however. Whether out of a sense of disillusionment with their own experience in the ministry, or for some other reason, a considerable number of pastors are no longer making such recommendations.[8] A study of Southern Baptist pastors revealed a significant decline in the number of those who invite their young people to consider the ministry.[9] Not surprisingly, then, the percentage of "preacher's kids" who de-

6. Alexander W. Astin, director of the Cooperative Research Program at UCLA, says, "Our data indicate that materialism still reigns." The program's survey of college freshmen in 1987 showed that 24.6 percent hoped to pursue careers in business, up from 11.6 percent in 1966, the first year of the survey. "Being very well off financially" was one of the top personal goals of 75.6 percent of those polled, nearly double the 1970 figure of 39.1 percent. See "Freshman Interest in Business Careers Hits New Level, and Money Remains a Top Priority, Study Finds," *Chronicle of Higher Education* 34.19 (20 Jan. 1988): A34.

7. By the fall of 1990, the number of freshmen who had a goal of being well off financially had dropped slightly for a second straight year (after seventeen consecutive years of increase) to about 74 percent, and the number of those interested in a career in business had dropped for a second consecutive year to 18 percent—"Record Number of Freshmen Plan to Join Protests on Campuses, Survey Prior to Gulf War Shows," *Chronicle of Higher Education* 37.20 (30 Jan. 1991): A32.

8. "Ministerial Encouragement," *Christian Century* 108.16 (8 May 1991): 513.

9. John Dever and Ron Dempsey, "Summary and Conclusions, Phase II, Part 1 Research," in *Quality in Southern Baptist Pastoral Experience* (Louisville: Southern Baptist Theological Seminary, 1989), pp. 26–28.

cide to enrol in seminary is significantly lower today than was the case a generation or so ago.[10]

It is little wonder that idealistic young people today are inclined to turn to some form of service other than the ministry. While the desire to serve others is there, the pastoral ministry is less likely to be chosen as a channel for fulfilling that desire. Young people are disillusioned by the increasing conflict and general stress within the ministry. As they see pastors beset by criticism and forced to deal with petty matters in the church, more young people are concluding that they can better serve the Lord by not holding a position of pastoral responsibility. Take as an example one evangelical church where the pastor came under considerable criticism and left to take a call elsewhere after three years. The next pastor served for eight years, then was terminated by the congregation shortly before he reached sixty years of age. It would be very difficult to go to that church and speak to the youth groups about the romance of the ministry.

Not only may it be difficult to survive in the pastorate, but it may not provide the opportunity for real and effective ministry. Increasingly churches are moving in the direction of big business, with emphasis upon programing, marketing, and the like. The pastors of such churches are really chief executives, grand promoters.[11] There still are sensitive, caring persons who feel called to what the pastorate traditionally was: a ministry of preaching and teaching the Bible, and of caring for the spiritual and to some extent the emotional needs of people. The pastorate, at least of large "successful" churches, resembles this ideal less and less. Individuals who feel called to a caring, nurturing ministry will look for opportunities elsewhere, perhaps in the chaplaincy or in teaching.

I am reminded of a story which has been told about Marilyn Monroe, a story I have never been able to verify. Quite depressed a short time before her death, she expressed a desire to have a clergyman come to talk to her. Asked whether she wanted a "big operator" or a "man of God," after a moment's reflection she indicated her preference for a man of God. In the past, individuals fitting that description were considered prime candidates for the pastoral ministry, but that may be changing.

Besides young people, another source of candidates for pastoral careers may be drying up. I am referring to those who enter the ministry

10. We noted earlier that only 0.2 percent of college freshmen show an interest in a career as a minister, and 0.1 percent in some other religious vocation. Since 1.0 percent of college freshmen have a parent in the ministry, we can conclude that no more than 30 percent of preacher's kids have any notion of carrying on the family vocation—and even that figure rests on the obviously erroneous assumption that all those who are interested in a ministerial career are preacher's kids. For documentation see n. 5.

11. Anderson, *Dying*, p. 159.

as a second career. When going to seminary at a relatively late age came to be perceived as a possibility, there was a large backlog of persons in their thirties and forties who were interested. Now, however, many of them have already been enlisted. Just as the market for a new product may initially be very good but eventually become saturated, so the number of older persons who may be possibilities has partially diminished. We can expect the number of older persons entering the ministry to grow at a slower rate or, what is more likely, to decline somewhat.

6. There is another reason why the number of persons entering the ministry will decline. Over the years, seminary tuition, which at one time was nonexistent, has been increasing. Now it is not uncommon for annual tuition for a full-time student at an evangelical seminary to exceed $5,000. Such charges are not uncommon at other types of professional schools, of course. The difference is that the potential for earnings in most professions is such as to make repayment of educational loans possible. The salary of most pastors, however, especially in the early years of ministry, is too limited for them to pay off their debt. Moreover, because seminary is graduate education, many entering seminary are already saddled with a large indebtedness for their college years. In some cases, the spouse also brings indebtedness from college.

In light of his overhanging debt, a seminary graduate may feel that he cannot afford to accept the salary offered by a church. Attempts to negotiate an adequate salary may be misunderstood and result in his being rejected for the position on the grounds that he is materialistic and greedy. Or perhaps one may enter the pastoral ministry for a time, and then leave because of the financial burden of the educational debt. An increasing number of mission boards will not appoint a person with heavy debts. If one attempts to avoid such a situation by working more while in school and not taking loans, the length of time required to complete seminary may diminish the prospect for service following graduation. Further, in an increasing number of cases financial problems place excessive strain upon marital and family life.

The impact of the financial burdens of seminary training reminds us of the commercial featuring the mechanic who, having just completed an overhaul of an automobile engine, points out the consequences of not changing the oil filter often enough: "You can pay me now, or you can pay me later." Similarly, if the church does not more adequately support its seminaries and those who go to seminary to prepare for the ministry, it will have to pay graduates more. If it is unwilling to do so, as seems increasingly to be the case, it will find that there simply are not enough qualified and dedicated persons available to serve in the ministry. More and more, seminary education is beyond the reach of potential pastors. As much as they would like to serve the Lord in pastoral ministry, they feel either that they cannot afford to enter seminary or that, if they can, their financial situation upon graduation will disqualify them for any kind of effective ministry thereafter.

7. There is one more long-range factor which will contribute to the coming shortage. I refer to the increasing crisis of seminaries. Part of this is financial in nature. As individual congregations struggle to meet their budgets, and as mission agencies fall into greater financial difficulty, the seminaries, as well as other institutions of Christian higher education, are among the first to be neglected. Historically it can be argued that the growing separation between the churches and the seminaries is due to the churches' abandonment of the seminaries, not vice versa. Because seminaries have been forced to find other sources of support, their ties to sponsoring church bodies have been loosened.

Today a number of evangelical seminaries are in growing financial straits, which at some point will spell peril. There is also a general decline of morale among seminary faculties. The seminary has become the whipping boy, the scapegoat for many of the church's problems. If pastors are not as capable as desired or lack some spiritual qualities, that is the fault of the seminaries, even though the seminaries had those individuals for only a relatively short period of their lives, and the opportunity for nurturing them came when their psyches were relatively fixed. Given this perception, it will become increasingly difficult for seminaries to attract and retain faculty who will have the optimum effect upon students. Many pastors loudly proclaim that the solution is for seminaries to appoint practitioners to their faculties, rather than holders of Ph.D. degrees. But those same pastors lose enthusiasm for the idea, at least as it affects them personally, when they hear the prospective salary. In approaching a gifted pastor to join its faculty, one seminary in effect said, "Wouldn't you like to come and teach preaching to future pastors for $30,000, instead of doing it yourself as a full-time pastor for $70,000 a year?" The man replied, "The Lord be with you till we meet again!" Or consider the case of a full professor who belonged to a church which called as its youth pastor, at a salary several thousand dollars higher than what the professor was being paid, a young man who a year earlier had sat in his classroom. It was demoralizing, to say the least, to realize that the church of Jesus Christ considers a beginning youth pastor more valuable than an experienced seminary professor.

The element of criticism also makes it difficult to acquire first-rate faculty. I once attempted to recruit a capable, gifted, experienced scholar and teacher who was a true churchman with a pastoral heart. His personal convictions and style were in no way controversial. He had taught at a Christian liberal-arts college, then at its sister seminary, and was now once again teaching at a liberal-arts college. He expressed, however, his disdain for seminary teaching and his preference for college teaching, where he did not have to put up with the "hassle" from the church.

Perhaps the most significant factor affecting the future of the seminaries is the tendency of megachurches and some other congregations as well to turn elsewhere for their trained leaders. Under these conditions, some seminaries will have difficulty remaining in existence, and many others will find it impossible to maintain the quality of their programs. Yet the time will come when the church will again realize its need of seminaries. If it fails to learn from history, and specifically from the mistakes of fundamentalism, it will repeat those mistakes and learn some painful lessons experientially. Someone has said, "Experience is the best teacher; it ought to be—it's the most expensive." Then, having in the past cavalierly dissipated the hard-won advances in theological education, and having in many cases actually lost its seminaries, the church will seek to rebuild. In the interlude it will face a shortage of capable leadership.

Rebuilding, however, will be a costlier process in every way than retaining the seminaries would have been. Regaining health is more difficult and expensive than preserving it. Preventive maintenance of a building or an institution is often much cheaper than restoration. Failure to foresee the future has resulted in great pain later on. We have seen school districts close buildings after the baby boom, and in many cases sell the properties, often at bargain prices. Then, apparently unforeseen by school leaders, rising enrolments after the second wave of the baby boom required new buildings, often necessitating acquisition of new property. That has been a more costly process than retaining the old buildings would have been. It is frequently accompanied by the pained howls of enraged taxpayers and in some cases rejections of referenda on bonds. One also thinks of what happened to streetcar systems throughout the United States. Encouraged in part by the persuasive efforts of the bus division of the General Motors Corporation, city after city replaced its streetcars with buses, which were considered in many respects to be greatly preferable. Tracks were paved over or, in some cases, torn out of the streets and sold for scrap. In recent years, however, as the shortage of fuels and the polluting effects of internal combustion engines upon the environment have become more obvious, some cities have begun investigating the possibility of light railways, and a few have begun installing new lines. This, however, is proving to be extremely costly. The dismantling of a system is costly, but the rebuilding of it later is considerably costlier. So the reestablishment of seminaries for the preparation of ministers is going to be a difficult, painful, and expensive task.

Implications of the Coming Shortage

We must now investigate the implications of the anticipated shortage of clergypersons. Specifically, we must ask who will be most seriously affected by it. Will it be the more liberal, mainline churches, or will it be the more conservative, evangelical churches? A case can be made for either answer.

On the one hand, one might argue that the conservative churches will feel the pinch more than will their liberal counterparts for the simple reason that more positions are and will be available among the conservatives. For example, the missions programs of conservative denominations, as well as independent conservative missions, have grown markedly in recent years, and presumably will continue to do so. At the same time, the missions programs of mainline denominations have been undergoing severe contraction.[12] A similar situation exists in regard to pastoral positions in local churches. The growth in both the size and number of conservative congregations is far outstripping the more liberal churches. Most new churches are started by conservative or evangelical groups. On this basis one would tend to say that in the years ahead the need for pastors and missionaries will be greater among evangelicals than among the more liberal churches.

There is a counterargument which we must note, however. The conservative churches are producing considerably more volunteers for ministry than are the liberal churches. This trend also has been in place for some time and presumably will continue. On the basis of this trend alone, one would anticipate a greater supply of evangelical clergypersons than of more liberal ministers. If we ignore the issue of demand and also assume that ministers will fit their congregation's theological persuasion, it would seem that the shortage will be more severe among liberal churches than among conservative congregations.

There are other issues which must be taken into consideration. We must ask who the clergypersons will be. Specifically, it appears that the percentage of women among them will be larger than has been the case in the past. This trend has shown itself even in evangelical schools. That suggests that the number of women available to assume leadership roles in the churches will increase. It is at this point that variations may occur. Those denominations or congregations that are less open to having women pastors, or at least are perceived as being less open to women, may well find themselves in a difficult situation. In this respect, conservative churches may suffer more from the shortage of

12. James Leo Garrett, Jr., "'Evangelicals' and Baptists—Is There a Difference?" in James Leo Garrett, Jr., E. Glenn Hinson, and James E. Tull, *Are Southern Baptists "Evangelicals"?* (Macon, Ga.: Mercer University Press, 1983), p. 81.

clergy than will the liberals. Unable to find a position in a church of their own theological persuasion, conservative women may well be found in the pulpits of liberal churches.

Another consideration is that the majority of seminaries that belong to the Association of Theological Schools in the United States and Canada are evangelical. A report of the task force on globalization to the biennial meeting of the association in 1990 spoke of the "preponderance of institutions within ATS with fundamental 'evangelical' commitments."[13] Beyond that, the enrolment at evangelical schools is on average larger than that at the more liberal institutions. Indeed, with one or two exceptions, every seminary with an enrolment in excess of seven hundred students is an evangelical school.[14]

Given the fact that well over half of the seminary students in the United States and Canada are studying at evangelical schools, an interesting situation could arise as the shortage becomes real. If evangelical seminaries continue to enrol large numbers of students, possibly more than evangelical churches and agencies need and can absorb, they may have a singular opportunity. If there are not enough liberal candidates, there may be little choice but for liberal congregations to call (or executives of liberal denominations to appoint) conservative or evangelical pastors. If these individuals are willing to serve within such a context, they have the potential for significantly altering the face of American Christianity. For at the grassroots or lay level there is evidence that, in general, church members even in mainline denominations are more conservative than their pastors, who in turn are more conservative than are the denominational executives, those who exercise political influence. Thus the evangelical message may be better received than one might expect. In addition, we may be nearing a time when people will find the evangelical message to be more in tune with their experience of the world and life than is the typical message from liberal pulpits. In this respect, the situation may be something like that in Karl Barth's little mountain parish in 1919.[15] Even denominational executives who do not accept the theology of evangelical pastors notice when the churches of those pastors grow in a fashion not true of churches served by non-evangelicals. As one evangelical pastor in a mainline denomination said, "The people are tired of the liberal saw that does not cut." Con-

13. "Addendum: Executive Summary, Report of the Task Force on Globalization" (Report delivered to the Thirty-seventh Biennial Meeting of the Association of Theological Schools in the United States and Canada, Montreal, 1990), p. 83.

14. Association of Theological Schools in the United States and Canada, *Bulletin* 39 (1990), Part 4, *Directory for the Academic Year 1991–92*, pp. 4–65.

15. Thomas F. Torrance, *Karl Barth: An Introduction to His Early Theology, 1910–1931* (Naperville, Ill.: Allenson, 1962), pp. 16–17, 33–47.

sider as an example that fellowship groups of evangelicals are becoming increasingly influential within mainline denominations.

One may regard the prospect of a coming shortage of clergypersons with skepticism, with anxiety, or with anticipation. Those who are wise and who trust in the providence of God will find, even in situations of apparent adversity, opportunities for advancing the kingdom of God. May we, when we find ourselves in such situations, heed our Lord's exhortation to be "wise as serpents, and harmless as doves" (Matt. 10:16 KJV).

10

Contemporary Evangelicalism: Old Fundamentalism or New Modernism?

The Fundamentalist-Modernist Controversy

Perhaps the most conspicuous feature of American theology during the first quarter of the twentieth century was the dispute known as the fundamentalist-modernist controversy. It rent many major denominations, made headlines in the secular media, created animosity among Christians and fellow church members, and set in motion trends which were to continue to the present time.

In many ways, the fundamentalist-modernist controversy was a struggle over which pole of the Christian faith was to be emphasized: authoritativeness or relevance. The fundamentalists, being conservatives, chose to emphasize the authoritative elements of the Christian faith. The modernists were more concerned about making the faith intelligible and even acceptable to persons of their time, even if that meant altering or adjusting the content.

Characteristics of Fundamentalism

The fundamentalists were convinced that the Christian faith is, if not identical with, at least inseparably connected to and dependent upon certain doctrinal tenets. Focus on these tenets led many to discover that they had more in common with persons from other denominations than with certain members of their own. From this discovery and various Bible conferences came lists of basic doctrines known as fundamentals, which became rallying points for those of conservative persuasion. In order to preserve this faith, they found it necessary and desirable to resist and reject certain trends within the current culture. They rejected, for example, certain theories propounded by science, especially evolution. They also rejected certain social practices, such as the drinking of alcoholic beverages. Thus, on the one hand, there were attempts to require denominations—and especially their appointees to foreign missions and theological seminaries—to hold to certain doctrinal positions. On the other hand, there were attempts to legislate what could be taught in the public schools, and to regulate public morality. As a result, a number of states forbade the teaching of evolution, and the federal government enacted Prohibition.

Several of the fundamentals—such as the holiness of God, the sinfulness of humans, the substitutionary atonement of Jesus Christ—converged to create a strong emphasis upon evangelism. There was a belief that the world was becoming worse spiritually, and that it would be delivered from this evil only when individuals were converted to Jesus Christ and regenerated. Consequently, fundamentalists worked hard at evangelism, centering their efforts in the local church building in many cases. Drawing heavily upon the revivalistic tradition of the American frontier, Sunday sermons frequently were geared to presentation of the gospel of individual regeneration. Many messages (and in some congregations all messages) ended with an invitation to come forward and accept Christ. The Sunday evening service was frequently the "gospel hour," with a heavy dose of preaching on sin and salvation. In addition, the fashion within fundamentalist churches was to have special evangelistic crusades or revival meetings in the spring and fall. There would be preaching every night and twice on Sundays by an imported evangelist.

Frequently the preaching in fundamentalist churches was quite highly emotional and had relatively little intellectual content. Indeed, there was a rather strong anti-intellectual tone to much of the preaching and the entire religious practice. The music was also rather simplistic, centering upon the personal experience of the individual believer. Accordingly, fundamentalism drew heavily from the less educated, the lower socioeconomic classes.

The anti-intellectual bent was reflected in the training of the clergy. As fundamentalists lost control of one after another of the denominational seminaries, they found themselves in need of some means of training their clergy. Bible institutes grew up, often as safe havens where young people could go to study. Although originally designed to prepare lay leadership, Bible institutes now became the means for preparing clergy. Usually involving only three years of study beyond high school, not building upon a college education in liberal arts, and often staffed by faculty members who had limited graduate training, this type of shortcut ministerial preparation contributed to the growing anti-intellectualism within fundamentalism. For the most part, these schools had no accreditation and even shunned such as being of the world. Faculty members who wished to pursue further education often sought a doctor of theology degree from one of the conservative seminaries that had been founded as protests against and alternatives to schools now gone liberal.

Fundamentalists were thoroughgoing supernaturalists. They believed in miracles; they expected supernatural working from God. There was a disdain for modern technology and methodology. Distrustful of the social sciences, fundamentalists were likelier to pray about a matter than to develop a program based upon a demographic study.

In stressing the supernatural, fundamentalists neglected the social application of the gospel. Because, as we observed in chapter 1, liberals were emphasizing the social gospel, fundamentalists withdrew from activities aimed at bettering the human condition. In so doing, they neglected a basic dimension of what had been vital evangelicalism.

A related feature of fundamentalism was separatism. Believing that the world is evil, and that both those who involve themselves in it and even any individuals who associate too closely with them are in danger of hell, fundamentalists withdrew not only from unbelievers, supposed heretics in the church, and certain practices and places, but also from participation in the institutions and processes of society.

Finally, fundamentalism was heavily influenced by certain strong personalities. Among the best-known fundamentalist leaders were J. Frank Norris in Fort Worth, William B. Riley in Minneapolis, and Thomas T. Shields in Toronto. Local churches frequently centered upon the personality, preaching, and leadership of their pastor.

Characteristics of Modernism

We should also observe a number of the characteristics of traditional modernism. One is that it was less doctrinally oriented than was fundamentalism. This is part of what made modernism more difficult to identify. Its theologians did not issue lists of their basic beliefs, as did the fundamentalists. Nor did they ordinarily specify the beliefs which they rejected. They simply were not as concerned about matters of doctrine as were the fundamentalists. Their relative lack of interest derived from two of the major sources of nineteenth-century German liberal theology. Friedrich Schleiermacher declared in his *On Religion: Speeches to Its Cultured Despisers* that religion is not a matter of belief or of action. Rather, it is a matter of feeling, especially the feeling of absolute dependence. Albrecht Ritschl, following more closely the thought of the philosopher Immanuel Kant, located the domain of religion in value judgments and thus ultimately in ethics. American liberalism tended to blend the two views, favoring feeling over belief and insisting upon the necessity of ethical action. Beliefs and doctrines took a second place at best.

A second feature of modernism was its affirmation of contemporary culture. Rather than resisting new intellectual and cultural developments, modernism accepted them as good and made them normative for Christian life and thought. There was little sense of an antithesis between revealed truth and natural truth. Thus, on the one hand, there was little inclination to criticize such scientific propositions as biological evolution; and, on the other, there was a positive acceptance of secular learning, much of which modernism assimilated into its system of beliefs.

Modernism also was basically anthropocentric. Its emphasis was considerably more upon humans and their needs than upon God and his glory. This showed itself in a number of ways. First, instead of looking to some divine revelation, modernism considered humanity the judge of truth. Human reason and experience took priority over the Bible as the criterion of truth. Second, modernism was at least as concerned about the relationship between human and human as about the relationship between humans and God. Third, it was very much geared to the satisfaction of human needs. Wrongs against humans seemed to preoccupy the modernists more than did offenses against God.

Similarly, there was a strong fixation upon the temporal as opposed to the eternal. The here and now was of prime importance. Any disruptions of what were considered ideal conditions for life here on earth caused great concern.

Modernism tended to downplay sin. Whereas sin was a very prominent feature of fundamentalist theology, it played only a very small role in the theology and strategy of the modernist. The seriousness of sin was de-emphasized by denying that we have any real responsibility for our own sin. Sin was thought of not so much as a radical corruption of nature that we inherited from Adam as a result of the fall, but as an indication of the incompleteness of the evolutionary process, or as the result of a poor social environment. Humans were thought of as deprived rather than depraved.

While fundamentalists were supranaturalists, looking for God to work directly and miraculously, the modernists had naturalizing tendencies. For solutions they looked to human effort in science and social engineering.

Current Evangelicalism in Relation to Fundamentalism and Modernism

When we look at contemporary evangelicalism, do we see any of the traits of either of these movements of the past? Bear in mind that we are speaking only in broad terms and general description. Some characteristics may be true of only a portion of evangelicalism. For, to a very real extent, evangelicalism is more diverse now than it was earlier in this century. Nonetheless, there are some general marks of portions of current evangelicalism that are reminiscent of fundamentalism and others that are reminiscent of modernism.

Similarities to Fundamentalism

We will note first the similarities between current evangelicalism and the fundamentalism of the early twentieth century. In some cases they are quite striking. Many of them clearly contrast with the variety of evangelicalism that developed in the United States following World War II.

1. There is a resurgence of anti-intellectualism. One of its manifestations pertains to academic standards. Among the factors which hurt fundamentalism in its quest to influence society was the inferior education that its schools offered to its young people. Many of the schools possessed no accreditation, and many of the leaders had an academic background quite inferior to that of their more liberal counterparts. By contrast, one feature of evangelicalism in the middle part of the twentieth century was a struggle for academic respectability, for accreditation of its scholastic enterprise. Thus the early leaders of the "new evangelicalism" pursued graduate degrees at some of the most prestigious universities in the country. Evangelical colleges worked hard to obtain accreditation from their regional accrediting association. Evangelical seminaries applied for membership in the Association of Theological Schools in the United States and Canada. Bible institutes became Bible colleges and then liberal-arts colleges. Christian day schools upgraded their standards and sought accreditation. Churches required prospective pastors to be seminary graduates.

Yet we find today an interesting paradox. Just when evangelicals are reaching their goals, increasing numbers of them are abandoning those goals. The megachurches (generally those churches with over two thousand persons in attendance at Sunday morning worship services) are turning away from accredited seminaries as sources of ministerial leadership. The senior pastors of these churches believe not only that they can do a better job of training their staff, but that they can do so more quickly and economically. They believe that the type of education one receives in a seminary (usually conceived of as an ivory tower) does not really prepare one for ministry as it is today, at least not for ministry in a megachurch.[1] They care little about degrees and accreditation. And so, at a time when the members of evangelical churches are moving upward in educational profile, they are being ministered to by clergypersons with less educational preparation than in the past. To be sure, this dissatisfaction with seminary education has been registered primarily by the megachurches, but their percentage of the total of Christian worshipers will increase in the years ahead.

The tendency toward taking educational shortcuts shows itself in another phenomenon, the doctor of ministry degree (D.Min.). This degree is intended to prepare one for a more effective ministry. It is not intended to prepare a person to teach in higher education. The aim is a worthy one, and some programs of excellent quality have emerged, although others have proven to be quite weak.

One test of the D.Min. degree is what the graduates of the program do afterwards. If the program has really accomplished its purpose, they will have had their appetite for learning and for professional growth whetted, and will continue their education for the remainder of their lives. In many cases, however, this is not happening. A large number of persons who have received the degree are now content to continue in ministry without ever taking additional training. Either they believe that they have learned all that needs to be or can be learned, or else they were primarily interested in acquiring the title of "doctor."

Indirectly, the D.Min. degree is having at least two adverse effects upon the overall quality of ministerial preparation. First, theological schools are directing increasing amounts of energy toward the D.Min. program, sometimes at the expense of other programs. This is producing a dilution of the first-level courses.[2] Second, a considerable number of

1. "Seminaries and/or Teaching Churches: A Report," *NAPCE Newsletter* (North American Professors of Christian Education), Summer 1991, p. 1.

2. To counteract this effect, the Association of Theological Schools now recommends that D.Min. courses be taught by regular faculty as part of their normal teaching load rather than as an overload; see the Association of Theological Schools in the United States and Canada, *Bulletin* 39 (1990), Part 3, *Procedures, Standards, and Criteria for Membership*, p. 45.

persons expect that they will be able to teach at the seminary level with only a D.Min. degree. Some who have the ability to pursue a Ph.D. are instead taking the D.Min. route, probably at least in part because of the logistical convenience of such a program. A professor at one school which offers a Ph.D. in preaching told me that the D.Min. had virtually decimated their Ph.D. program. As a result of this trend, any committee searching for candidates with a relevant academic doctorate to fill a faculty position in the discipline of preaching has a very difficult task.

Anti-intellectualism shows itself in other ways as well. There is a tendency not to wrestle with the really difficult issues of the Christian faith. While there still are pulpits where strong expository preaching prevails and great doctrinal issues are set forth, their number is in general declining. There are conferences on Reformed theology and on eschatology, but they are in general secondary to conferences dealing with practical issues—self-image, family relationships, and even sex life.

Pragmatism is, in a sense, an anti-intellectual philosophy. It is less concerned with whether an idea or proposition corresponds with the actual state of affairs than with whether it "works."[3] Increasingly, evangelicalism is becoming pragmatic. It does not ask so much whether ministry is doctrinally sound and in keeping with the basic theological position of the church, but what results it is providing.

2. Some of contemporary evangelicalism also shows a strong emotionalism. This can be seen in the current trends in evangelical music, where we find a narrowing of the focus. The broad themes of theology are neglected in favor of a few highly specific ones, which are sung in seemingly endless repetition. The repetition, apparently aimed at stirring up the emotional response of the worshipers, has little rational effect. In an earlier age, a church member could gain a fair knowledge of theology through the church's songs. Now, however, there is a much narrower repertoire. As someone has said, "Psalms is a very important part of the Bible, but it's not the only book in the Bible."

The preaching also seems increasingly geared to emotional response. In part this is related to what Ann Douglas has called "the feminization of American culture," including "the feminization of the American clergy."[4] The result is an emphasis upon feelings rather than intellect, and upon counseling and pastoral care rather than upon exposition and instruction.

3. William James, *Pragmatism: A New Name for Some Old Ways of Thinking* (New York: Longmans, Green, 1949), p. 58.

4. Ann Douglas, *The Feminization of American Culture* (New York: Knopf, 1977), pp. 80–164, especially pp. 141–64.

3. Contemporary evangelicalism has to some extent returned to a particular type of evangelism. An old definition characterized an evangelistic sermon as "three jokes and a deathbed story." Unfortunately, that quip was often true. I made a point recently of attending one of the "new look" evangelical churches, which has designed a very contemporary service to attract unchurched people. The senior pastor, who founded the church and around whom much of the ministry revolves, was on vacation, so another member of the staff preached the sermon. It proved to be a rather conventional biblically based message. But as the preacher approached the end of his message, he told an anecdote from his pre-Christian days. He was in the basement of his home when fire broke out. As he tried to make his way through the smoke to the only exit, the lights went out, making escape even more difficult. The tension built as he told the story. If it had not been told in the first person, the audience would have been breathlessly wondering, "Will he make it, or will he die in the flames?" As I sat there engrossed with the story, suddenly the thought struck me, "This is the old fundamentalism. Under these very avant-garde clothes, this is the old fundamentalism and the old evangelism. He is telling the deathbed story." Once again rational argument was being supplanted by an emotional manipulation of the moment. Although there was no traditional invitation to come forward during the closing hymn, there was an invitation to come up to the "bull pen" at the conclusion of the service.

4. A closely related consideration is that current evangelicalism resembles fundamentalism in its strategy of evangelism. Fundamentalism concentrated on attracting non-Christians to its evangelistic services. Members were encouraged to bring along their unbelieving friends, so the church could take care of evangelizing them.

Midcentury evangelicals adopted a different strategy of evangelism. Reasoning that unbelievers would be wary of coming into a Christian house of worship, they concluded that the church must go out to where the unconverted are. Adopting the model presented in the New Testament and especially in the Book of Acts, the congregation came to church to be edified and trained. They then went out from the assembly to those who were in need of salvation. Whether evangelism took the form of confrontation or friendship, it aimed at getting the church to the world, rather than bringing the worldly into the church to be converted.

Current evangelicalism tends to reverse this pattern, to revert to the type of evangelism found in fundamentalism. The aim is to alter the church services so that "seekers" (the new term for unbelievers) will feel comfortable and be attracted to them. Employing modern media to show seekers how the Christian faith relates to their needs, the Sunday morning service is geared to evangelism rather than to worship and instruction.

5. Another trend of present-day evangelicalism is a decline in social concern. One of the great clarion notes on which the new evangelicalism was founded was an appeal to restore the social application of the gospel, a theme which had been a conspicuous facet of evangelicalism in the latter half of the nineteenth century, that is, prior to the polarization that took place on this issue in the fundamentalist-modernist controversy. Carl Henry's *Uneasy Conscience of Modern Fundamentalism* (1947) was an early and pointed expression of this concern. In 1971, he published *A Plea for Evangelical Demonstration*, which reiterated many of his earlier emphases. When I read it, I thought at one point, "He's forgotten that he already wrote this book, and has written it again." Actually, the church had not changed much, so the message was still needed and was being repeated in a somewhat different form. The need for that message may be as great within segments of evangelicalism today as at either of those points in the past.

It is not that there is no ethical emphasis or activity anywhere within evangelicalism. In some cases and places, there is a great deal. The focus is upon one or two typically conservative issues, however, such as abortion and prayer in public schools. Some of the broader concerns about race and poverty are conspicuously absent.

Part of the lack of interest in broad social issues is attributable to the widespread popularity of the church growth movement, which emphasizes the homogeneous unit: we are most effective in reaching those of our own socioeconomic and cultural group.[5] Thus, instead of reflecting the diversity of the church universal, local churches increasingly are becoming homogeneous or monolithic wholes. A typical congregation's marketing team, after doing its research, might conclude that their target group should be upper-middle-class whites. They would probably sell their property in a first-ring suburb and move to a rapidly growing suburb farther out, populated almost exclusively by their type of people. While persons from other groups would not be told that they are not welcome, those with any social sensitivity would quickly feel out of place. If they lack an automobile, they would find the church inaccessible; if they do own one, they could tell by a glance around the church parking lot that they are somehow out of place.

To repeat: It is not that today's evangelical church, and particularly the megachurch, is not concerned about human problems and needs. It is very much so. Indeed, its ministry is largely built upon human prob-

5. Donald A. McGavran, *Understanding Church Growth*, 3d ed., rev. and ed. C. Peter Wagner (Grand Rapids: Eerdmans, 1990), pp. 163–78.

lems and needs.[6] One hears, however, very little from such pulpits about the great social ills of our time. Concerns of this nature are as absent as they were at the height of the fundamentalist movement.

6. A further characteristic found within contemporary evangelicalism is its supranaturalism. In view here is the so-called third wave of Pentecostalism, which, as we saw in chapter 8, is also referred to as the signs and wonders movement, power evangelism, and the Vineyard. This group places much less emphasis upon speaking in tongues than do old-line Pentecostalism and the charismatic movement. It concentrates instead upon healing and prophecy, such as the word of knowledge. Thus it is clearly a supranaturalistic movement. It finds the cause of much illness (and of other ills in the world) in the activities of demonic forces, and seeks to cure that illness by casting out evil spirits. The word of knowledge is often a special revelation from God that virtually contradicts the conclusions of scientific study. The third wave faults much contemporary Christianity for being captive to a modern Western worldview which precludes belief in miraculous workings. Thus the third wave is both supranaturalistic and anti-intellectual.[7]

7. Like fundamentalism, evangelicalism tends to be built around certain individual personalities. This is the era of the evangelical superstar. Increasingly, evangelicals look to a few gurus, often with their own radio or television program, to define belief and practice.[8] Large churches are built around the personal charisma of the senior pastor.[9] Very few of those churches operate democratically. Usually the pastor and a small group of elders, often strongly influenced or even selected by him, make the major decisions.

Similarities to Modernism

Are there any characteristics of current evangelicalism that display similarity to early modernism? Although somewhat less obvious, there are several.

1. Perhaps the most apparent similarity to modernism is the willingness and even eagerness to accommodate to certain features of contemporary society. This may seem strange on first reflection. The accommodation to modern culture by liberals in the early twentieth

6. Leith Anderson, *Dying for Change* (Minneapolis: Bethany, 1990), pp. 84–86.
7. Charles Kraft, *Christianity with Power* (Ann Arbor: Servant, 1989), pp. 41–47.
8. During the ten-year period from 1981 to 1991, 35 percent of all titles on the bestseller lists of the *Bookstore Journal*, which reflect the sales of Christian books at approximately six hundred retail bookstores in the United States and Canada, were by Chuck Swindoll; another 26 percent were by James Dobson (Jack Nickolay, "Christian Best-Sellers: Trends and Observations" [Unpublished paper, Bethel Theological Seminary, St. Paul, Nov. 1991], p. 8).
9. Anderson, *Dying*, p. 52.

century related to the philosophy or natural science of the time. That is not the nature of the accommodation found in evangelicalism today. Rather, it is sociological accommodation, acceptance of the social trends. In this respect, many evangelicals are far ahead of their more liberal counterparts. In terms of both understanding the characteristics of the two baby-boom generations and the generation in between, and of gearing ministry to suit those characteristics, it is evangelicals who have taken the lead. This, of course, has contributed to their growing faster than less conservative groups. It may also be a sign that they have now succeeded in beating the modernists at their own game.

With respect to those aspects of society which are blatantly in conflict with the ethical teachings of the Bible, the change in evangelicalism's position has been rather small. There are, however, clear indications of shifts in attitude, especially among the young evangelicals.[10] At the same time, one finds strikingly little challenging of any of the other characteristics of the current society. There is more of a tendency to ask how the message and the various resources of the church can pick up on those characteristics. In this respect, evangelicals have not been conservatives recently. Instead of reluctantly adopting the characteristics of society long after others have done so, one now finds evangelicals at the very forefront. Old mainline churches, on the contrary, are now the ones which appear rather stodgy and traditional. There is relatively little vigor within them. The music of the respective groups, for instance, typifies this contrast. It is evangelicals, not liberals, who are involved in gospel rock and Christian rap.

One facet of the accommodation to society is the movement toward horizontal rather than vertical expression of the Christian faith. To an increasing degree, the Christian faith as practiced within evangelicalism is concerned with the relationships between humans. Compare the amount of attention given, on the one hand, to sharing one's feelings with others, small-group discussions, and the like, and, on the other hand, to proclamation, prayer, and similar vertically oriented activities. Consider also the movement known as relational theology, where one's relationship to other persons is more definitive of the Christian posture and activity than is "Thus saith the Lord." The emphasis is upon genuineness. We are to be true to ourselves. That is, we must not attempt to imitate anyone else, not even Jesus. Further, we must not attempt to change others, since this would indicate that they are unacceptable as they are. We must affirm others by listening to them and loving them as

10. James Davison Hunter, *Evangelicalism: The Coming Generation* (Chicago: University of Chicago Press, 1987), p. 62.

they want to be loved, not as we think they ought to be loved. We certainly are not to prescribe to them what they ought to be or become.[11]

Note that the horizontal dimension takes quite a different form in current evangelicalism from what it had in early modernism. There one finds an emphasis upon working to resolve class conflict and remove social inequities. Here the focus is more on the individual. The relationships in view are narrower in scope. A large number of instructional classes in the church are concerned with family relationships, with parenting and with managing conflict within the home. Another evidence is the popularity of certain kinds of radio and television programs and of certain types of books. One way in which to gauge the direction of evangelicalism is to observe what titles are prominently displayed in Christian bookstores. There has been a notable decline in books on the devotional life and on personal holiness; what sells are the sex manuals (which Martin Marty has referred to as "fundies in their undies") and volumes on family dysfunction.[12]

2. A related characteristic of current evangelicalism is its emphasis upon temporal needs. Early fundamentalism was in many ways very otherworldly. "This world is not my home, I'm just a passing thru; My treasures are laid up somewhere beyond the blue," said the words of a popular gospel song. In fact, in those days some Christians were chastised for being "so heavenly minded that they were no earthly good." That no longer seems to be a problem. The needs which earlier generations sought to meet were eternal, spiritual, otherworldly in nature. *Peace with God* was one of Billy Graham's most popular books. A. W. Tozer and others wrote of holiness and how to attain (or obtain) it. Now, however, people are primarily concerned with the needs of the here and now. They want to know how to deal with loneliness, singleness, divorce, bereavement, loss of employment. Self-esteem is the major thrust of much of Robert Schuller's preaching and writing.[13] Compare his "Hour of Power" with Charles E. Fuller's "Old-fashioned Revival Hour" of an earlier generation.

Note as well the emphasis upon physical healing in many streams of evangelicalism, and particularly in the charismatic movement and the third wave. Here is a temporal good which seems to take on a very high value. In fact, there seems to be an insistence that physical healing is God's will for virtually every malady and ailment. Where healing fails to occur, there is a lack of power, an absence of signs and wonders. The gospel of health, wealth, and happiness is an even broader application

11. Bruce Larson, *Ask Me to Dance* (Waco: Word, 1972), pp. 55–69.
12. There do seem, however, to be some recent decline in the psychological self-help volumes and increase in fiction (Nickolay, "Christian Best-Sellers," pp. 3, 5, 7).
13. Robert H. Schuller, *Self-Esteem: The New Reformation* (Waco: Word, 1982).

of this mentality: God will prosper his children in these specific ways. This particular teaching suffered something of a setback when a few of its best-known proponents, notably Jim Bakker, were embroiled in scandal. While these persons were caricatures, exaggerations, they did preach and represent what many evangelicals take for granted—that God invariably showers his children with temporal blessings.

3. The emphasis on temporal needs calls to mind another way in which the current evangelicalism parallels the old modernism. That is the trend toward anthropocentrism. This has, to be sure, taken a considerably different twist in the evangelical version. The old modernism thought of God as being so immanent that there was difficulty in distinguishing between him and the highest human values and ideals. The distinction between God's working and the ordinary processes of history went unrecognized. Perhaps the most extreme example occurred in the 1930s, when the German Christians endorsed Adolf Hitler as God's way of working in his world, as God's good gift to the world.[14] Others saw socialism as God's work to accomplish his ends.

In the case of contemporary evangelicalism, however, the emphasis is again on the individual rather than the social group. Here it is instructive to observe the interest in popular psychology.[15] Whereas a generation ago evangelicals were inclined to pray or to confess their sin, today they turn to psychological counseling to solve their problems. Although not always articulated as such, this constitutes a de facto treatment of psychology as God's means of working. In many cases, however, the Christian counselor's procedure is little different from that which a secular counselor might utilize in the same situation.

There is another aspect to this anthropocentrism. Human values are very highly regarded. Thus, one increasingly hears objections to encroachment by the church and the Christian message and mores upon the freedom of the individual. There is a corresponding tendency to regard human desires as something that God must honor. Expressions of resentment and bitterness against God for human suffering and sorrow assume that his role is to guarantee our happiness, as we define it. He is expected to answer the prayers of the individual. Some prayers, especially if offered by someone with the gift of healing or a similar ability, virtually command God to act.

4. The adoption of certain of the values of society is another point of similarity to the older modernists. In particular, we have in mind the adoption of the material goals of the American dream. The upward economic and social mobility among evangelicals has become incorpo-

14. Karl Barth, *The Church and the Political Problem of Our Day* (New York: Scribner, 1939).
15. Nickolay, "Christian Best-Sellers," p. 3.

rated into their value system. The "good life" often is understood as doing well rather than as doing good.

5. Of special interest is the emulation of society's obsession with success. The philosophy of the megachurch seems to be that big is beautiful. The disregard for the ministry of small neighboring churches, the well-polished image of the pastor as a corporate executive and superstar, the quality and breadth of the programing all contribute to the "winner" syndrome.[16]

6. The adoption of technology by modern evangelicalism is also of interest. Increasingly, the methodology of the social sciences is utilized in ministry. For example, the outreach programs of the church borrow from the research methods developed by secular organizations. Before a new congregation is established, demographic studies ascertain the target group and the best location for the church building. Samplings are taken to arrive at a name which will have maximum appeal (and minimal repulsion). Then a list of the telephone numbers of the residents of the area is compiled, and a massive campaign of calling is begun. Those contacted are asked if they would be interested in the formation of a new congregation. Those who indicate interest are then placed on a mailing list so they can be kept informed of the plans and invited to the first service.[17]

What is of particular interest about this process is the reliability of the results. Ten percent of those contacted by telephone will agree to be placed on the mailing list, and 10 percent of that group, or 1 percent of the original number, will actually appear at the first worship service. One wonders, however, why, if this is God's doing, there is such a uniform set of results. The predictability here is not greatly unlike what is found in the marketing of soap, automobiles, and breakfast cereal.

7. Finally, we must note the de-emphasis of sin. We observed earlier that classic fundamentalism made much of sin, but that modernism did not. On this particular point contemporary evangelicalism shows more of the characteristics of modernism than of fundamentalism. It is not that alternative definitions of sin are given; for example, that sin is merely a mark of incomplete evolution. Rather, the topic simply is not discussed much within certain streams of evangelicalism. One searches in vain in their popular contemporary choruses for references to sin, repentance, remorse, and confession.[18] Nor, for that matter, is there much

16. "Baby Boomers Flock to Full-Service Megachurches," *USA Today*, 6 Aug. 1991, pp. D1, D4.

17. C. Peter Wagner, *Church Planting for a Greater Harvest* (Ventura, Calif.: Regal, 1990), pp. 107–9.

18. E.g., in the 195 contemporary songs in *Maranatha: Praise!* there are only 10 references to "sin," "guilt," and "wicked," and no expressions of confession or repentance.

preaching on such subjects. They are not positive topics, and current evangelicalism, if it is anything, is positive in its thrust. Drawing upon the insights of popular psychology, it aims to build positive self-images and self-esteem. Consequently, suggestions that one not only does wrong things, but may actually be a bad person (in God's sight), tend to be muted. James Davison Hunter speaks of the "civility of evangelicalism," its desire not to be abrasive or offensive to anyone.[19] To some extent, evangelicalism has substituted etiquette for ethics, and for theology as well.

It is ironic that some evangelicals today are loudly decrying godless secular humanism, which they believe is being taught in the public schools. For these same evangelicals rely upon natural means and have adopted earthly values. They emphasize the welfare and happiness of humans—to the relative neglect of concern for the glory of God. Here, certainly, are elements of secularism and of humanism. Perhaps, while not succumbing to the godlessness of modern culture, current evangelicalism has adopted its other salient features.

A Mediating Position

We have seen certain respects in which current evangelicalism resembles classic fundamentalism, and other characteristics which it has in common with the modernism of the early twentieth century. Are these valid comparisons or only superficial resemblances? My readers must answer that question for themselves.

It is the judgment of many that fundamentalism and modernism represented extremes. A preferable form of Christianity would be located somewhere between them. There are two ways to arrive at a mediating position. On the one hand, we might temper the two extremes, striving in every aspect of our faith to find the midpoint between them. This would be like a child all of whose features fall halfway between those of her two parents. On the other hand, we might draw some of the aspects of our faith directly from one group and the rest from the other. This would be like a child some of whose features are replicas of one parent while the rest mirror the other. One thinks here of the beauty queen, devoid of athletic ability, who married a champion athlete, who was anything but handsome. Perhaps, as often is the case, their opposite qualities had attracted them to one another. One day as they talked about their first child, who was to be born in a few months, the husband said, "Won't it be great? A child with your looks and my athletic ability!" Quickly his beautiful wife replied, "But what if our baby has your looks and my athletic ability?"

19. Hunter, *Evangelicalism*, pp. 183–84.

A movement which combines the best features of fundamentalism and modernism would be very desirable indeed. But what about a movement that combines the worst of each? And what do we have in evangelicalism, the best or the worst? In certain respects, it appears that modern evangelicalism has retained some of the less desirable features of the old fundamentalism, and adopted some of the poorer qualities of the modernism which fundamentalism opposed. It has retained anti-intellectualism and an indifference to great social and ethical issues. It perpetuates much of the emotionalism and superficiality of fundamentalism. It is moving toward adopting academic shortcuts and simplistic worship and music. It has returned to the evangelistic strategy of drawing the unconverted to the church building instead of going out to where they are. Yet it has also adopted the tendency of modernism to accommodate to current social trends and to accept secular values as its own. It minimizes the biblical teaching on sin. It is increasingly anthropocentric and horizontally oriented. Evangelicalism, then, incorporates some of the undesirable features of both extremes.

The Future of Evangelicalism

George Santayana's famous statement is worth considering here: "Those who cannot remember the past are condemned to repeat it." I have written elsewhere that history is theology's only laboratory, or at least the only one it can afford to use.[20] We can infer the future of evangelicalism by observing the outcome of earlier religious and theological developments which its salient features resemble or parallel. For example, the rejection of established institutions of ministerial preparation is nothing new. In many cases it stems more from independence and pride in one's own way of doing things than from a sense that the established approach is wrong. Anyone possessing a familiarity with the history of evangelicalism in the nineteenth and twentieth century knows that the attempts of large local churches to train their own staff either were eventually abandoned or resulted in a seminary or even a college. Tennessee Temple, Criswell College, Northwestern College of Minnesota, and Mid-American Baptist Seminary are among the many examples. A negative consideration is the possibility that if evangelicalism continues along this course, it will, like the anti-intellectualism of fundamentalism, alienate its best and most talented young people. Similarly, the decline in vitality that followed modernism's accommodation to the general culture does not augur well for the continued growth of evangelicalism.

20. Millard J. Erickson, "The Church and Stable Motion," *Christianity Today* 18.1 (12 Oct. 1973): 7.

Yet the future of evangelicalism is within the control of its adherents. They can mold a movement that combines the best, rather than the worst, features of both fundamentalism and modernism. Such a combination would be indeed a powerful force within contemporary society. Several goals must be steadfastly kept in mind if this is to be the case. There must be a strong determination to retain the doctrinal and ethical essentials of the faith. The antithesis between the things of God and the things of the world must be maintained. We must emphasize evangelism in its full-orbed form and promote a healthy intellectualism not divorced from the realities of life and ministry. This will show itself both in a well-prepared clergy and in a carefully presented case for the Christian faith.

We must also apply our Christian faith to social issues and problems. Finally, we must make an effort to understand contemporary society; only then will we be able to present the Christian message in a fashion which makes sense and is relevant to people living in the world of today. If we pursue all of these goals with diligence, future evangelicalism will be an effective movement capable of doing its Master's will.

Scripture Index

Subject Index

Subject Index

Pentecostalism, 153
Performance standards in ministry, 178
Perrin, Norman, 92–93
Perseverance, 114, 119
Personalities: in current evangelicalism, 200; in fundamentalism, 193
Philippian jailor, 113
Pinnock, Clark, 35, 133–52
Piper, John, 114–15
Plea for Evangelical Demonstration (Henry), 199
Pluralism, 131–32
Policeman, God as, 162
Political problem of Christology, 89–90, 104–5
Politics, evangelicals and, 27–29, 32
Pollution, reduction of, 72, 77
Poor: concern for the, 15; oppression of the, 64, 79
Positive mentality, 42
Possessions, material, 63–64
Postmillennialism, 145
Postmodernism, 89
Postmortem: chance, 35; evangelism, 138–41
Power encounters, 155
Power evangelism, 154, 156–58. *See also* Signs and wonders movement
Power of Jesus entrusted to all Christians, 156, 171
Practical and ethical solutions, 71–72
Pragmatism of current evangelicalism, 197
"Preacher's kids," 182
Preexistence of Christ, 100–101
Presbyterian Church in the U.S.A., 16, 22
Preservation of the creation, 72–74
Princeton Theological Seminary, 22
Principialism, 70–71
Process Christology, 101
Process metaphysics, 88
Programs in seminaries, specialized, 181
Prohibition, 15, 22, 192
"Prophets" and the sayings of Jesus, 92
Psychology, popular, 203, 205
Publishing, evangelicalism and, 27

Quality of life, 64, 76
Quebedeaux, Richard, 32–33, 34, 35, 37, 46

Rahner, Karl, 131
Ramm, Bernard, 35, 87
Randall, John Herman, Jr., 38

Rationalism, 159
Rauschenbusch, Walter, 18
Raw materials, 75
Reagan, Ronald, 27
REALITY vs. reality, 158
Recycling, 76
Redating the New Testament (Robinson), 90
Redefinition of terms, 37–38, 46–47
Regeneration, 86; in the "lordship salvation" view, 121–22; permanence of, 111
Relational theology, 39, 201
Reliability of the biblical sources, 90–95
Religions: miracles of other, 168; parallels to Jesus in other, 104
Religious vocations, lack of interest in, 181–83
Renewable resources, 75
Repentance: and conversion, 119–20; dispensability of, to salvation, 110, 113; necessity of, for salvation, 45, 115–16
Reproduction, purpose of human, 64–65
Resources of creation, conservation of the, 74–76
Resurrection, 104
Retirement of ministers, 177
Rich man and Lazarus, 146
Riesenfeld, Harald, 91
Riesner, Rainer, 91
Rights of nonhuman creation, 79–80
Ritschl, Albrecht, 194
Robertson, Pat, 32
Robinson, John A. T., 90–91, 94
Rogers, Adrian, 149
Roman Catholic Church, 131, 176
Ryrie, Charles, 109

Salvation: assurance of, 113, 118–19, 121; basic element of, 120–22; from conformity, 78; difficulty of, 118; and discipleship, 111–12, 115, 119; evangelicalism's view of, 86; exclusiveness of, 35; extent of, 129–52; and fellowship with God, distinction between, 113–14; indefectibility of, 114; nature of, 119; requisites for, 125; broadened understanding of, 78
Sanders, John, 135, 136, 149n, 150
Satan, 170; kingdom of, 155–56
Saviorhood and lordship of Christ, 110–11, 117
Sayings of Jesus, authenticity of, 92–93
"Scandinavian School," 91

217